LATE MEDIEVAL ENGLAND

(1377–1485)

LATE MEDIEVAL ENGLAND (1377–1485)

A BIBLIOGRAPHY OF HISTORICAL SCHOLARSHIP

1975–1989

———————

JOEL T. ROSENTHAL

———————

Medieval Institute Publications
WESTERN MICHIGAN UNIVERSITY
Kalamazoo, Michigan, USA—1994

Library of Congress Cataloging-in-Publication Data

Rosenthal, Joel Thomas, 1934-
   Late medieval England (1377-1485) : a bibliography of historical
scholarship, 1975-1989 / Joel T. Rosenthal.
      p.   cm.
   Includes index.
   ISBN 1-879288-16-8 (casebound)
   1. Great Britain--History--Lancaster and York, 1399-1485-
-Bibliography. 2. Great Britain--History--Richard II, 1377-1399-
-Bibliography. 3. England--Civilization--1066-1485--Bibliography.
I. Title.
Z2017.R68 1994
[DA245]
016.94204--dc20   94-6595
                                                        CIP

Cover design by Linda K. Judy

Printed in the United States of America

CONTENTS

INTRODUCTION

The bibliographer's first inclination is to say that no one else is as aware of the shortcomings of the volume being offered. A moment's reflection, however, suffices to suggest that those who use the volume will, quite soon, be even more aware of its shortcomings. The consolation must be that scholarship is built, at least in some part, on foundations of collegiality and of fallibility; imperfect scholars offer their works to an imperfect world.

The motivating force behind this compilation is a recognition of time passing and of a flood of scholarly production. When DeLloyd Guth published his bibliography of scholarship on late medieval England (in 1976) he went, in the proverbial nutshell, from the beginnings of modern scholarly time through material published in 1974. His volume, invaluable far beyond its size (and price), has more than served us since its publication; supplemented by Edgar Graves's reworking of Charles Gross's older guide to the historical literature on medieval England, we have been able to lay our hands, quickly, on a vast corpus of scholarly work.

The years pass. After Guth completed his bibliographic "handbook" he reflected (in *The British Studies Monitor*) on late medieval English history as a growth industry. He was as accurate a prophet as a bibliographer; the high waters he anticipated have run steadily if not wildly through the fifteen years I have surveyed. When I began this project my aim was to make it "comprehensive," which is a seemingly-modest way of saying it covers *everything*. Clearly, such a goal has proved impossible. Annual and serial publications run well behind announced schedules (particularly with the dwindling resources available in Thatcher-Major England); no set of libraries ever has all the items one seeks; each dip into new publications provides still further references and allusions, often of increasing inaccessibility. Further searching also means a further delay in being able to offer this research tool to those who will put it to use. And—as the shortcomings are not all at the door of budgets and resources—I have undoubtedly missed many items through oversight and carelessness.

The two basic guidelines for a bibliography relate to the principles of inclusion (or exclusion) and of arrangement and organization. Though History, in its academic or disciplinary sense, is the center of the circle around which entries have been included, I have tried to incorporate pertinent materials from outside or beyond parochial definitions. An open admissions policy seems a wise guideline.

The two main areas of deliberate, conscious omission (or of strict limitation) are Literature (literary history and literary criticism)—except where such scholarship seemed to be of direct interest for historical inquiry—and Celtic Britain. While current literary scholarship is well served by its own run of bibliographies, produced in both the British Isles and in the United States, scholarship on Celtic Britain awaits the love and labor of one who knows it thoroughly and whose bravery perhaps outruns his or her common sense.

In addition to the areas I have deliberately slighted, I must also admit to an incapacity for learning enough about music to make the jump from personal pleasure to academic counsel. Accordingly, I have limited the music entries (in the Fine Arts section) to items found in a few major journals and a few monographs. I apologize to those who work on late medieval music, as well as to those who come seeking guidance I cannot, in all decency, offer. Another major body of work but touched in passing is archaeology. Since I have been constrained by chronological boundaries—even if they are self-imposed—and since most major site reports span larger periods, only a fraction of the corpus of impressive and serious work now at hand for towns and cities (and rural sites, and particular buildings and monuments) appears below. Where such scholarship can be pinpointed for the England of 1377–1485, I have been more than pleased to guide the reader. Local history has suffered a comparable fate; the very strengths of current work cut against my old-fashioned desire to stick within the announced timespan. Furthermore, I have not covered unpublished dissertations, valuable as these are.

Organization is arbitrary, and there is no real escape from this; neither is total consistency to be expected. Full-length biographical studies have been included (for the most part) in General Works; diplomatic and military history in Political History; medicine, science, and technology in Intellectual History (rather than with the fine arts). The section on Social and Economic History combines family history and women's history with such odd companions as numismatics. Work on the mystics (which includes Margery Kempe) could be seen as intellectual history, but I have put it into the section on Religious History. When the internal organization between and within the various sections seems confusing or inconsistent, there is always the index; would that the British penchant for initials were more honored in the breach than in the observance. In the last analysis, one does not usually read a bibliography with high expectations regarding continuity or plot.

Acknowledgments are many; librarians and library staff are oft-sung heroes of scholarly production, and they fully deserve any praise that comes their way. The Melville Library of The State University of New York at Stony Brook and the Institute of Historical Research of the University of London have been my two main resources. I have also used the libraries of The University of Chicago, Columbia University, Cambridge University, The Library of Congress, The American Numismatic Society, the New York Public Library, and New York University. Peter and Carol Hammond offered the facilities of the library of The Richard III Society, in London, plus personal hospitality and encouragement. Many others have urged me onwards and have assured me they would at least send their students to such a volume. DeLloyd Guth generously encouraged me to push ahead with this, rather than to wait until he had time to make it a joint enterprise (as I originally suggested). At a later stage words of encouragement from Candace Porath and Thomas H. Seiler of Medieval Institute Publications, Western Michigan University, were of critical value, and if this volume's value is enhanced by accuracy and consistency, Candy Porath gets much of the credit. Particular thanks to Alan Stahl, Barrie Dobson, Ralph Griffiths, Compton Reeves, George Beech, Ralph Turner, and Caroline Barron. Naomi Rosenthal has helped me with the word processor and taught me that you can throw away the Brazil nuts. A number of Stony Brook administrators and colleagues were kind enough to procure funds for research travel, in return for various services rendered: thanks to Egon Neuberger, Andy Policanno, and Ted Goldfarb. One of the pleasures in compiling a bibliography—as some compensation for the hours of drudgery—is that it has entailed many trips to London without the need to do all that much serious thinking.

ABBREVIATIONS

ABR	*American Benedictine Review*
AgHR	*Agricultural History Review*
AJ	*Antiquaries Journal*
AJLH	*American Journal of Legal History*
Ancient Monuments	*Transactions of the Ancient Monument Society*
Arch Ael	*Archaeologia Aeliana*
Arch Cant	*Archaeologia Cantiana* (Kent Archaeological Society)
Arch J	*Archaeological Journal*
B & G AS	*Transactions of the Bristol and Gloucestershire Archaeological Society*
BIHR	*Bulletin of the Institute of Historical Research*
BJRL (and) *BJRUL*	*Bulletin of the John Rylands (University) Library*
BLJ	*British Library Journal*
BNJ	*British Numismatic Journal*
BSM	*British Studies Monitor*
Cambridge Bibliographical Society	*Transactions of the Cambridge Bibliographical Society*
Chaucer Rev	*Chaucer Review*
CHR	*Catholic Historical Review*
Cumberland & Westmorland	*Transactions of the Cumberland and Westmorland Antiquarian and Archaeological Society*
D & C N&Q	*Devon and Cornwall Notes & Queries*

Derbyshire	*Derbyshire Archaeological Journal*
Devonshire	*Transactions of the Devonshire Association*
Downside	*Downside Review*
EcHR	*Economic History Review*
EETS	Early English Text Society
EHR	*English Historical Review*
ELN	*English Language Notes*
EMH	*Early Music History*
Essex	*Transactions of the Essex Archaeological Society*
Guildhall	*Guildhall Studies in London History*
HLQ	*Huntington Library Quarterly*
HMSO	Her Majesty's Stationery Office
HR	*Historical Research: The Bulletin of the Institute of Historical Research*
JBAA	*Journal of the British Archaeological Association*
JBS	*Journal of British Studies*
J Eccl H	*Journal of Ecclesiastical History*
JHG	*Journal of Historical Geography*
JIH	*Journal of Interdisciplinary History*
JLH	*Journal of Legal History*
JMH	*Journal of Medieval History*
JMRS	*Journal of Medieval and Renaissance Studies*
JPHS	*Journal of the Printing Historical Society*
JRH	*Journal of Religious History*
JSA	*Journal of the Society of Archivists*
L & HR	*Law and History Review*
Lancashire & Cheshire	*Transactions of the Historic Society of Lancashire and Cheshire*
Leicestershire	*Transactions of the Leicestershire Archaeological and Historical Society*

Lincolnshire	*Lincolnshire History and Archaeology*
London & Middlesex	*Transactions of the London and Middlesex Archaeological Society*
LQR	*Law Quarterly Review*
Med Arch	*Medieval Archaeology*
Med Pros	*Medieval Prosopography*
Midland	*Midland History*
MS	*Medieval Studies* (and) *Mediaeval Studies*
Norfolk	*Norfolk Archaeology*
Northern	*Northern History*
Nottingham	*Nottingham Mediaeval Studies*
Num Chr	*Numismatic Chronicle*
Oxon	*Oxoniensia*
PBA	*Proceedings of the British Academy*
PRO	Public Record Office
Reading	*Reading Medieval Studies*
Somerset	*Proceedings of the Somerset Archaeological and Natural History Society*
Southern	*Southern History*
Suffolk	*Proceedings of the Suffolk Institute of Archaeology*
TRHS	*Transactions of the Royal Historical Society*
UHY	*Urban History Yearbook*
VA	*Vernacular Architecture*
WHR	*Welsh History Review*
Wiltshire	*Wiltshire Archaeological and Natural History Society Magazine*
Worcestershire	*Transactions of the Worcestershire Archaeological Society*
YAJ	*Yorkshire Archaeological Journal*

I. EDITED VOLUMES AND VOLUMES OF COLLECTED PAPERS

1. Alexander, J. J. G., and Paul Binski, eds. *Age of Chivalry: Art in Plantagenet England, 1200–1400*. Royal Academy of Arts. London, 1987.
    [Catalogue of an exhibition, Nov. 1987–Mar. 1988. Also listed in Fine Arts and Crafts (item 1777); many of the individual contributions are listed separately below: items 707, 1807, 1852, 1866, 1869, 1880, 1899.]

2. Alexander, J. J. G., and Margaret T. Gibson, eds. *Medieval Learning and Literature: Essays Presented to Richard William Hunt*. Oxford, 1976.
    [Items 1620, 1723.]

3. Allmand, C. T., ed. *War, Literature, and Politics in the Late Middle Ages*. Liverpool, 1976; New York, 1976.
    [A *Festschrift* in honor of G. W. Coopland; items 321, 619, 645.]

4. Armstrong, C. A. J. *England, France, and Burgundy in the Fifteenth Century*. History Ser., vol. 16. London, 1983.
    [Collected papers from 1976 and before; the following are relevant here: "The Piety of Cicely,

Duchess of York: A Study of Late Medieval Culture" (1942); "The Inauguration Ceremonies of the Yorkist Kings and Their Title to the Throne" (1948); "Some Examples of the Distribution and Speed of News at the Time of the Wars of the Roses" (1948); "Politics and the Battle of St. Albans" (1960); and item 645, first published in item 3 above.]

5. Arnold, Morris S., Thomas A. Green, Sally A. Scully, and Stephen S. White, eds. *On the Laws and Customs of England: Essays in Honor of Samuel E. Thorne.* Chapel Hill, N.C., 1981.
    [In the series University of North Carolina Studies in Legal History. Items 695, 732.]

6. Aston, Margaret. *Lollards and Reformers: Images and Literacy in Late Medieval Religion.* History Ser., 22. London, 1984.
    [Ten papers published 1960–82 including "Lollardy and Sedition" (1960); "Lollards and the Reformation: Survival or Revival" (1964); "John Wyclif's Reformation Reputation" (1965); "Richard II and the Wars of the Roses" (1971); and items 1258, 1259, 1260, 1262, 1263.]

7. Aston, T. H., Peter R. Coss, Christopher Dyer, and Joan Thirsk, eds. *Social Relations and Ideas: Essays in Honour of R. H. Hilton.* Cambridge and New York, 1983.
    [Past and Present Publications. Introduction by Edward Miller, pp. ix–xiii, and a Hilton bibliog-

raphy to 1982, pp. 319–22; items 813, 853, 946, 979.]

8. Aston, T. H., and C. H. E. Philpin, eds. *The Brenner Debate: Agrarian Class Structure and Economic Development in Pre-Industrial Europe.* Cambridge and New York, 1985.
    [Past and Present Publications. Articles from 1976–85; items 1175, 1176, 1188, 1190, 1213, 1235; see also items 867, 1230.]

9. Baker, J. H. *The Legal Profession and the Common Law: Historical Essays.* History Ser., vol. 48. London and Ronceverte, W.Va., 1986.
    [Twenty-three papers, 1969–85, plus three published for the first time; items 649, 650, 651, 652, 653, 655, 657.]

10. Barley, M. W., ed. *The Plans and Topography of Medieval Towns in England and Wales.* Council for British Archaeology Research Report No. 14 (1976). London, 1976.
    [Contributors, D. M. Palliser et al. Items 1000, 1022, 1075, 1116, 1124.]

11. Barron, Caroline M., and Christopher Harper-Bill, eds. *The Church in Pre-Reformation Society: Essays in Honour of F. R. H. Du Boulay.* Woodbridge and Dover, N.H., 1985.
    [An appreciation by C. H. Lawrence, pp. 1–2; introduction, pp. 3–7; a Du Boulay bibliography,

pp. 228–31; items 885, 893, 1003, 1086, 1208, 1310, 1369, 1430, 1493.]

12. Beresford, M. W. *Time and Place: Collected Essays.* History Ser., 31. London, 1984.
[Collected papers; only "Lay Subsidies and Poll Taxes" (*Amateur Historian* 3–4 [1957–58]) covers material later than 1377 (examining the subsidies and taxes of 1377, 1379, and 1381).]

13. Bird, Joanna, Hugh Chapman, and John Clark, eds. *Collectanea Londiniensia: Studies in London Archaeology and History Presented to Ralph Merrifield.* Special Paper No. 2. London and Middlesex Archaeological Society, 1978.
[Item 1505.]

14. Bulst, Neithard, and Jean-Philippe Genet, eds. *Medieval Lives and the Historian: Studies in Medieval Prosopography.* Kalamazoo, Mich., 1986.
[Papers from a Bielefeld Conference, December 1982; items 1613, 1622, 1718.]

15. Buxton, John, and Penry Williams, eds. *New College, Oxford, 1379–1979.* Oxford, 1979.
[Published by the Warden and Fellows of New College in Commemoration of the Sixth Centenary; items 1668, 1753, 1841.]

16. Cantor, Leonard, ed. *The English Medieval Landscape.* London, 1982; Philadelphia, 1982.

[In the Croom Helm Historical Geography Series and the University of Pennsylvania Press's Middle Ages series. The introduction discusses the role and value of historical geography, pp. 17–24; items 836, 837, 1008, 1244, 1256.]

17.   Clough, Cecil H., ed. *Profession, Vocation, and Culture in Later Medieval England: Essays Dedicated to the Memory of A. R. Myers.* Liverpool, 1982.
[The introduction (pp. 1–6) is a tribute to Myers; bibliography, pp. 245–48; items 643, 733, 798, 908, 1082, 1319, 1715.]

18.   Coleman, D. C., and A. H. John, eds. *Trade, Government, and Economy in Pre-Industrial England: Essays Presented to F. J. Fisher.* London, 1976.
[Items 340, 678, 847.]

19.   Crossley, D. W., ed. *Medieval Industry.* Council for British Archaeology Research Report No. 40 (1981). London, 1981.

20.   Custance, Roger, ed. *Winchester College: Sixth-Centenary Essays.* Oxford and New York, 1982.
[Items 1076, 1693, 1694, 1725, 1838.]

21.   Davies, R. G., and J. H. Denton, eds. *The English Parliament in the Middle Ages.* Manchester, 1981; Philadelphia, 1981.
[In The Middle Ages series (Univ. of Pennsylvania). A volume in honor of John Smith Roskell; for a Roskell bibliography, 1937–79, see pp. 201–05; items 342, 533.]

22. Davis, R. H. C., and J. M. Wallace-Hadrill, eds., with the assistance of R. J. A. I. Catto and M. H. Keen. *The Writing of History in the Middle Ages: Essays Presented to Richard William Southern.* Oxford and New York, 1981.
[Items 265, 1684.]

23. Dobson, Barrie, ed. *The Church, Politics, and Patronage in the Fifteenth Century.* Gloucester, 1984; New York, 1984.
[From a colloquium at York, September 1982; introduction, pp. 9–22; items 394, 954, 1261, 1373, 1409, 1444, 1510, 1526.]

24. Edwards, A. S. G., ed. *Middle English Prose: A Critical Guide to Major Authors and Genres.* New Brunswick, N.J., 1984.
[With bibliographies and lengthy discussions of current scholarship; items 1270, 1374, 1398, 1459, 1538, 1571, 1579, 1618, 1696, 1769.]

25. *La "France anglaise" au moyen âge. Colloque des historiens médiévistes français et brittaniques.* Actes du 111ᵉ Congrès national des sociétés savantes, Poitiers, 1986. Section d'histoire médiévale et de philologie, t. 1. Paris, 1988.
[Items 326, 364, 395, 736.]

26. Fryde, E. B. *Studies in Medieval Trade and Finance.* History Ser., vol. 13. London, 1983.
[Sixteen papers published since 1951, two since 1975; relevant: "Parliament and the Peasants'

Revolt of 1381" (1970); "Anglo-Italian Commerce in the Fifteenth Century: Some Evidence about Profits and the Balance of Trade" (1972); "Italian Maritime Trade with Medieval England (c. 1270– c. 1530)" (1974); also items 863, 864.]

27. Glasscoe, Marion, ed. *The Medieval Mystical Tradition in England: Papers Read at Dartington Hall, July 1982.* Exeter, 1982.
[In the University of Exeter Medieval English Texts and Studies series. A 1982 conference; items 1278, 1433, 1434, 1492.]

28. ———, ed. *The Medieval Mystical Tradition in England: Papers Read at Dartington Hall, July 1987.* Cambridge and Wolfeboro, N.H., 1987.
[Exeter Symposium IV. Items 1385, 1417, 1476.]

29. Gray, Douglas, and E. G. Stanley, eds. *Middle English Studies: Presented to Norman Davis in Honour of His Seventieth Birthday.* Oxford and New York, 1983.
[Items 1397, 1549, 1740.]

30. Griffiths, Jeremy, and Derek Pearsall, eds. *Book Production and Publishing in Britain, 1375–1475.* Cambridge and New York, 1989.
[In the series Cambridge Studies in Publishing and Printing History. Pearsall's introduction, pp. 1–10, and a collection of papers offering full treatment of the transition from script books to printed ones; items 1326, 1344, 1403, 1572, 1597, 1658, 1700, 1770.]

31. Griffiths, Ralph A., ed. *Patronage, the Crown and the Provinces in Later Medieval England.* Gloucester, 1981; Atlantic Highlands, N.J., 1981.

    [Papers from a Swansea colloquium, July 1979; items 349, 357, 482, 584, 891, 1061, 1328.]

32. Griffiths, Ralph A., and James Sherborne, eds. *Kings and Nobles in the Later Middle Ages: A Tribute to Charles Ross.* Gloucester, 1986; New York, 1986.

    [A Ross bibliography, compiled by Anne Crawford, pp. 304–07; items 329, 371, 374, 430, 462, 484, 500, 555, 564, 639, 1044, 1329.]

33. Guy, J. A., and H. G. Beale, eds. *Law and Social Change in British History: Papers Presented to the Bristol Legal History Conference, 14–17 July 1981.* Studies in History, no. 40. Royal Historical Society, 1984.

    [Items 567, 807.]

34. Hamilton, J. S., and Patricia J. Bradley, eds. *Documenting the Past: Essays in Medieval History Presented to George Peddy Cuttino.* Wolfeboro, N.H., 1989.

    [A Cuttino bibliography, pp. 225–35; items 339, 558, 604, 1736.]

35. Hammond, P. W., ed. *Richard III: Loyalty, Lordship and Law.* Richard III and Yorkist History Trust. London, 1986.

    [From a 1983 symposium, with editor's introduction; items 359, 375, 437, 485, 518, 576, 608, 720.]

36. Harriss, G. L., ed. *Henry V: The Practice of Kingship*. Oxford and New York, 1985.
   [Eight university lectures, 1982–83; introduction (pp. 1–29) and conclusion (pp. 201–10) by Harriss; items 325, 347, 445, 446, 447, 491, 777, 1296.]

37. Harte, N. B., and K. G. Ponting, eds. *Cloth and Clothing in Medieval Europe: Essays in Memory of Professor E. M. Carus-Wilson*. Pasold Studies in Textile History, 2. London and Edington, 1983.

38. Hartung, A. E., ed. *A Manual of the Writings in Middle English, 1050–1500, by Members of the Middle English Group of the Modern Language Association of America*. 8 vols. Connecticut Academy of Arts and Sciences. New Haven, 1967–89.
   [Long sections on genres, with extensive bibliographies; items 140, 159, 163, 192. Volumes 3 (1972)–8 (1989) are edited by Hartung.]

39. Harvey, P. D. A., ed. *The Peasant Land Market in Medieval England*. Oxford, 1984; New York, 1984.
   [Useful editor's introduction on "standard holdings," on chronological developments and change (pp. 1–28), and a conclusion (pp. 328–56). Reviewed by Edmund King, *EHR* 101 (1986), 424–26. Items 1200, 1220, 1224.]

40. Hay, Denys. *Renaissance Essays*. London and Ronceverte, W.Va., 1988.
   [In Hambledon's History Series. Collected papers; published before 1975 and relevant are: "Booty

in Border Warfare" (1954); "History and Historians in France and England during the Fifteenth Century" (1962); "The Early Renaissance in England" (1965); "The Church in England in the Later Middle Ages" (1969); also item 1659.]

41. Heffernan, Thomas J., ed. *The Popular Literature of Medieval England.* Tennessee Studies in Literature, vol. 28. Knoxville, 1985.
[Items 1508, 1629, 1671.]

42. Helmholz, R. H. *Canon Law and the Law of England.* London and Ronceverte, W.Va., 1987.
[A reprinting of eighteen papers, 1969–83; "Abjuration *sub pena nubendi* in the Church Courts of Medieval England" (1972); also items 710, 711, 712, 713, 714, 715, 716, 717, 719, 721.]

43. Highfield, J. R. L., and Robin Jeffs, eds. *The Crown and Local Communities in England and France in the Fifteenth Century.* Gloucester and Atlantic Highlands, N.J., 1981.
[A Sheffield colloquium, September 1976, with editors' introduction, pp. 10–18; items 393, 622, 1001.]

44. Hilton, R. H., ed. *Peasants, Knights, and Heretics: Studies in Medieval English Social History.* Cambridge and New York, 1976.
[Past and Present Publications. Relevant articles from *Past and Present* are: Margaret Aston, "Lollardy and Sedition, 1381–1431" (1960);

Christopher Dyer, "A Redistribution of Incomes in Fifteenth-Century England?" (1968); Barbara J. Harris, "Landlords and Tenants in England in the Later Middle Ages: The Buckingham Estates" (1969); J. C. Holt, "The Origins and Audience of the Ballads of Robin Hood" (1960); Maurice Keen, "Robin Hood—Peasant or Gentleman?" (1961).]

45. Hilton, Rodney. *Class Conflict and the Crisis of Feudalism: Essays in Medieval Social History*. History Ser., vol. 28. London and Ronceverte, W.Va., 1985.
[Twenty-three of Hilton's papers, nine published since 1975; items 894, 895, 896, 897, 899, 1212.]

46. Hilton, R. H., and T. H. Aston, eds. *The English Rising of 1381*. Cambridge and New York, 1987, 1984.
[Past and Present Publications. From a 1981 conference, with additional contributions from R. B. Dobson and Alan Harding; Hilton's introduction, pp. 1–8. Reviewed by C. M. Barron, *EcHR*, 2nd ser., 29 (1986), 461–63. Items 616, 701, 855, 860, 1021, 1032.]

47. Hinton, David A., ed. *25 Years of Medieval Archaeology*. Department of Prehistory and Archaeology, University of Sheffield. Sheffield, 1983.
[Item 250.]

48. Hudson, Anne. *Lollards and Their Books*. London and Ronceverte, W.Va., 1985.
[Sixteen papers from 1971–83; relevant: "The Expurgation of a Lollard Sermon Cycle" (1971);

"A Lollard Quaternion" (1971); "A Lollard Compilation and the Dissemination of Wycliffite Thought" (1972); "A Lollard Mass" (1972); "Some Aspects of Lollard Book Production" (1972); "Contributions to a History of Wycliffite Writings" (1973); "The Examination of Lollards" (1973); "A Lollard Compilation in England and Bohemia" (1974); also items 1391, 1392, 1394, 1397.]

49.   Hudson, Anne, and Michael Wilks, eds. *From Ockham to Wyclif.* Studies in Church History, Subsidia, 5. Ecclesiastical History Society, 1987.
[Items 1264, 1297, 1332, 1336, 1371, 1376, 1427, 1437, 1453, 1483, 1494, 1530, 1540, 1543, 1632, 1698, 1730.]

50.   Hunnisett, R. F., and J. B. Post, gen. eds. *Medieval Legal Records: Edited in Memory of C. A. F. Meekings.* HMSO, 1978.
[Items 659, 679, 708, 764, 797.]

51.   IJsewijn, Jozef, and Jacques Paquet, eds. *The Universities in the Late Middle Ages.* Mediaevalia Lovaniensia, ser. 1, studia 6. Louvain, 1978.
[Also, Publications de l'Institut d'études médiévales de l'Université catholique de Louvain, 2nd ser., vol. 2. Items 1675, 1691.]

52.   Ives, E. W., R. J. Knecht, and J. J. Scarisbrick, eds. *Wealth and Power in Tudor England: Essays Presented*

to S. T. Bindoff. London and Atlantic Highlands, N.J., 1978.
[Items 620, 731.]

53.   Ives, E. W., and A. H. Manchester, eds. *Law, Litigants, and the Legal Profession: Papers Presented to the Fourth British Legal History Conference at the University of Birmingham, 10–13 July 1979.* Studies in History, no. 36. Royal Historical Society, 1983.
[Items 699, 748, 766, 774.]

54.   Jones, Michael, ed. *Gentry and Lesser Nobility in Late Medieval Europe.* Gloucester, 1986; New York, 1986.
[A Nottingham colloquium, September 1984; items 852, 930, 1187.]

55.   Jones, Michael, and Malcolm Vale, eds. *England and Her Neighbours, 1066–1453: Essays in Honour of Pierre Chaplais.* London and Ronceverte, W.Va., 1989.
[Items 418, 492, 683, 1448, 1638.]

56.   Kenny, Anthony, ed. *Wyclif in His Times.* Oxford and New York, 1986.
[Oxford lectures to mark the six-hundredth anniversary (1984) of Wyclif's death; items 1400, 1401, 1414, 1415, 1419, 1422, 1426, 1674.]

57.   Lander, J. R. *Crown and Nobility, 1450–1509.* London, 1976; Montreal, 1976.
[Ten papers, 1956–73, printed in their original versions with an introduction (pp. 1–56) that brings them up to date; important papers on

Edward IV, forfeiture and attainder, the Wydevilles and Nevilles, the council, Henry VII and
the peerage, Clarence, Henry VI's second protectorate, and useful appendices on the peers,
attainder, and military involvement. See also
item 272.]

58.   Lewis, P. S. *Essays in Later Medieval French History*.
London and Ronceverte, W.Va., 1985.
[Fifteen papers, since 1958; relevant are "Sir
John Fastolf's Lawsuit over Titchwell, 1448–55"
(1958); "The English Kill Their Kings" (1964);
"War, Propaganda, and Historiography in Fif-
teenth-Century France and England" (1965);
also item 507.]

59.   Liddell, W. H., and R. G. E. Wood, eds. *Essex and the
Great Revolt of 1381: Lectures Celebrating the Six-
Hundredth Anniversary*. Essex Record Office Publica-
tions, no. 84. Chelmsford, 1982.
[Items 370, 381, 560, 640, 1043.]

60.   McFarlane, K. B. *England in the Fifteenth Century:
Collected Essays*. Introduction by G. L. Harriss. Lon-
don, 1981.
[Twelve papers, 1944–65, valuable introduction.
Relevant papers include the 1964 Raleigh Lec-
ture on the Wars of the Roses, plus work on Car-
dinal Beaufort, Sir John Fastolf, and William of
Worcester. A major collection of seminal work.]

61. Medcalf, Stephen, ed. *The Later Middle Ages.* London, 1981; New York, 1981.
    [In the Context of English Literature series. Items 1737, 1752, 1801.]

62. Myers, A. R. *Crown, Household, and Parliament in Fifteenth Century England.* Edited by Cecil H. Clough. History Ser., vol. 46. London and Ronceverte, W.Va., 1985.
    [Introduction by R. B. Dobson, pp. ix–xix (an appreciation and discussion of Myers's work); twelve of Myers's papers, 1937–78, including no. 4 (pp. 87–92), from the *BIHR* (1978): see item 532.]

63. Newman, Francis X., ed. *Social Unrest in the Late Middle Ages: Papers of the Fifteenth Annual Conference of the Center for Medieval and Early Renaissance Studies, University Center at Binghamton.* Medieval & Renaissance Texts & Studies, 39. Binghamton, N.Y., 1986.
    [Papers of a conference, October 1981; items 880, 949, 962, 1727, 1825.]

64. Nichols, John A., and Lillian Thomas Shank, eds. *Medieval Religious Women,* 1: *Distant Echoes*; 2: *Peace Weavers.* 2 vols. Cistercian Studies Ser., nos. 71, 72. Kalamazoo, Mich., 1984, 1987.
    [Items 1281, 1312, 1458, 1545.]

65.   Orme, Nicholas. *Education and Society in Medieval and Renaissance England*. London and Ronceverte, W.Va., 1989.

[Sixteen papers, two printed for the first time, and the rest from 1978–87; items 534, 937, 1460, 1462, 1712, 1713, 1714, 1715, 1717, 1720, 1721.]

66.   Ormrod, W. M., ed. *England in the Fourteenth Century: Proceedings of the 1985 Harlaxton Symposium*. Woodbridge and Dover, N.H., 1986.

[Items 414, 1445, 1742, 1764, 1901.]

67.   *The Peasants' Revolt in Hertfordshire: The Rising and Its Background: A Symposium*. Stevenage Old Town, Herts., 1981.

[Items 1010, 1143, 1172, 1251.]

68.   Plucknett, T. F. T. *Studies in English Legal History*. History Ser., 14. London, 1983.

[Twenty papers, 1924–61; relevant are "The Case of the Miscreant Cardinal" (1924); "Chaucer's Escapade" (1948); "State Trials under Richard II" (1952); "Impeachment and Attainder" (1953).]

69.   Pollard, Tony, ed. *Property and Politics: Essays in Later Medieval English History*. Gloucester, 1984; New York, 1984.

[Papers from a Reading symposium, 1983; items 514, 590, 599, 646, 810, 1333, 1685.]

70.   Raftis, J. A., ed. *Pathways to Medieval Peasants*. Pontifical Institute of Mediaeval Studies, Papers in Mediaeval Studies, 2. Toronto, 1981.
[Items 675, 1218.]

71.   Riden, Philip, ed. *The Medieval Town in Britain: Papers from the First Gregynog Seminar in Local History, December 1978*. University College, Department of Extra-Mural Studies, Cardiff Papers in Local History, 1. Cardiff, 1980.
[Items 1009, 1023, 1272.]

72.   Rosenthal, Joel, and Colin Richmond, eds. *People, Politics, and Community in the Later Middle Ages*. Gloucester, 1987; New York, 1987.
[Papers from two conferences in 1985; items 330, 405, 582, 763, 794, 824, 1104, 1372, 1450, 1609.]

73.   Roskell, J. S. *Parliament and Politics in Late Medieval England*. 3 vols. History Ser., 7, 8, 20. London, 1981–83.
[Volume 1, eight papers (1950–68), mainly on constitutional aspects of Parliament; vols. 2 and 3 contain thirty-three of Roskell's studies of Commons' Speakers. In vol. 3, the studies of John Tiptoft (pp. 107–50), Thomas Chaucer (pp. 151–91), and John Tyrell (pp. 277–315) are published for the first time.]

74.   Ross, Charles, ed. *Patronage, Pedigree, and Power in Later Medieval England*. Gloucester, 1979; Totowa, N.J., 1979.

[From a Bristol symposium, 1978; items 322, 354, 363, 372, 426, 453, 551, 566.]

75.   Rowe, J. G., ed. *Aspects of Late Medieval Government and Society: Essays Presented to J. R. Lander*. Toronto and Buffalo, 1986.

    [Items 431, 563, 680, 705.]

76.   Sargent, Michael G., ed. *De Cella in seculum: Religious and Secular Life and Devotion in Late Medieval England: An Interdisciplinary Conference in Celebration of the Eighth Centenary of the Consecration of St. Hugh of Avalon, Bishop of Lincoln, 20–22 July 1986*. Cambridge and Wolfeboro, N.H., 1989.

    [Items 1283, 1389, 1406, 1615.]

77.   Scattergood, V. J., and J. W. Sherborne, eds. *English Court Culture in the Later Middle Ages*. London, 1983; New York, 1983.

    [The Colston Symposium, University of Bristol, 1981; items 911, 937, 1614, 1651, 1748, 1750, 1776, 1803, 1905.]

78.   Simpson, A. W. B. *Legal Theory and Legal History: Essays on the Common Law*. London and Ronceverte, W.Va., 1987.

    [Four papers are relevant: "The Circulation of Yearbooks in Fifteenth-Century England" (1957); "The Early Constitution of the Inns of Court" (1970); "The Source and Function of the Later Year Books" (1971); "The Early Constitution of Gray's Inn" (1975).]

79.   Skelton, R. A., and P. D. A. Harvey, eds. *Local Maps and Plans from Medieval England.* Oxford and New York, 1986.
>[Limited edition (500). Introduction by Harvey; all known local maps to c. 1500 are published, with texts, transcriptions, legends, and bibliography; a lavish project that grew from a 1967 conference on the history of cartography; items 1007, 1026, 1028, 1036, 1049, 1050, 1051, 1052, 1053, 1066, 1067, 1074, 1087, 1090, 1115, 1128, 1134, 1135, 1164, 1171, 1231, 1232, 1245, 1246, 1247, 1248, 1366.]

80.   Smith, Richard M., ed. *Land, Kinship, and Life-Cycle.* Cambridge Studies in Population, Economy, and Society in Past Time, 1. Cambridge and New York, 1984.
>[Valuable collection of essays on the boundaries of legal, social, and manorial history; items 1174, 1197, 1198, 1241.]

81.   Taylor, Jane H. M., ed. *Dies Illa: Death in the Middle Ages: Proceedings of the 1983 Manchester Colloquium.* Vinaver Studies in French, 1. Liverpool, 1984.
>[Item 1844.]

82.   Thomson, John A. F., ed. *Towns and Townspeople in the Fifteenth Century.* Gloucester and Wolfboro, N.H., 1988.
>[A Glasgow colloquium, September 1986, with introduction (pp. ix–xiii); items 871, 1064, 1085, 1119, 1142, 1147, 1521.]

83.   Thrupp, Sylvia L. *Society and History: Essays.* Edited by Raymond Grew and Nicholas H. Steneck. Ann Arbor, 1977.

[Twenty-three of Thrupp's papers, 1940–73 (one newly published); introduction by Philippe Wolff, M. M. Postan, Eric R. Wolf, and Thomas C. Cochran, and a bibliographical note, pp. 347–49.]

84.   Williams, Daniel, ed. *England in the Fifteenth Century: Proceedings of the 1986 Harlaxton Symposium.* Woodbridge and Wolfeboro, N.H., 1987.

[Items 190, 538, 600, 956, 974, 1291, 1365, 1619, 1754, 1755, 1781, 1798, 1821, 1849, 1867, 1872, 1873, 1882, 1898.]

II. BIBLIOGRAPHIES, CATALOGUES, GUIDES, HANDBOOKS, HISTORIOGRAPHY, AND REFERENCE STUDIES

85. *Agricultural History Review.*
     [Each volume carries an "annual list and brief reviews of articles on agrarian history" compiled by Raine Morgan.]

86. Alford, John A., and Dennis P. Seniff. *Literature and Law in the Middle Ages: A Bibliography of Scholarship.* Garland Reference Library of the Humanities, vol. 378. New York, 1984.

87. Aston, Margaret. "Huizinga's Harvest: England and *The Waning of the Middle Ages.*" *Medievalia et Humanistica,* n.s. 9 (1979), 1–24.
     [A defense of Huizinga's value and continuing relevance.]

88. Awdry, George. *The Richard III Society: The First Fifty Years: A Personal Account.* Upminster, 1977.
     [To commemorate fifty years of the Society.]

89. (Bacon, Nicholas, Sir.) *Papers of Sir Nicholas Bacon in the University of Chicago Library.* PRO, Special Ser., vol. 25. List & Index Society, 1989.

[Most categories of documents have some material 1377–1485, especially those covering the court rolls, manorial records, charters, and deeds.]

90. Baker, J. H., comp. *English Legal Manuscripts in the United States of America: A Descriptive List*, Pt. 1: *Medieval and Renaissance Period (to 1558)*. Selden Society, 1985.
[A list of 205 unpublished legal MSS in twenty-seven locations, plus a description of their contents.]

91. ———. *A Centenary Guide to the Publications of the Selden Society*. 3 pts. London, 1987.
[A volume-by-volume discussion of contents.]

92. Beresford, Maurice. "English Medieval Boroughs: A Hand List: Revision, 1973–81." *UHY* (1981), 59–61.
[Updates the volume he published as "a hand-list" in 1973.]

93. Berkhout, Carl T., and Jeffrey B. Russell. *Medieval Heresies: A Bibliography, 1960–1979*. Pontifical Institute of Mediaeval Studies, Subsidia Mediaevalia, 11. Toronto, 1981.

94. Blake, N. F. *William Caxton: A Bibliographical Guide*. Garland Reference Library of the Humanities, vol. 524. New York, 1985.

95.   Boyce, Gray Cowan, comp. and ed. *Literature of Medieval History, 1930–1975: A Supplement to Louis John Paetow's A Guide to the Study of Medieval History.* Foreword by Paul Meyvaert. 5 vols. Medieval Academy of America. Millwood, N.Y., 1981.

[Paetow's *Guide*, 1917 (rev. ed., New York, 1959). Published with an index volume; general medieval coverage, of limited value for late medieval England.]

96.   Campbell, Louise, and Francis Steer, comps. *A Catalogue of Manuscripts in the College of Arms*, 1: *Collections.* Index and biographical notes by Robert Yorke, foreword by Anthony Wagner. College of Arms. London, 1988.

[Very little material before 1485.]

97.   Candido, Joseph, and Charles R. Forker, comps. *Henry V: An Annotated Bibliography.* Garland Shakespeare Bibliographies, no. 4, Reference Library of the Humanities, vol. 281. New York, 1983.

[Pages 461–532 cover the play's sources and its historical and intellectual background. Also see items 128, 148, 164.]

98.   Cannon, John, with R. H. C. Davis, William Doyle, and Jack P. Greene, eds. *The Blackwell Dictionary of Historians.* Oxford, 1988; New York, 1988.

[Biographical entries, with bibliography, covering leading contemporary practitioners, including many medievalists.]

99.   Chaloner, W. H., and R. C. Richardson, comps. *Bibliography of British Economic and Social History*. Rev. ed. Manchester, 1984.
[*British Economic and Social History: A Bibliographical Guide* (Manchester and Totowa, N.J., 1976). Late medieval England is covered, pp. 22–37.]

100.   Chibnall, Marjorie. "Eleanora M. Carus-Wilson." *PBA* 68 (1982), 503–20.
[Worthy tribute to a great scholar.]

101.   Condon, Margaret M., and Elizabeth M. Hallam. "Government Printing of the Public Records in the Eighteenth Century." *JSA* 7/6 (1984), 348–88.
[Especially good on Rymer and the Rolls of Parliament.]

102.   Cooper, J. P. "K. B. McFarlane, 1903–66." In Cooper's collected papers, *Land, Men, and Beliefs: Studies in Early-Modern History*. Edited, with introduction by G. E. Aylmer and J. S. Morrill. History Ser., vol. 24. London, 1983. Pp. 243–50.
[The admiration of a former student, first published in *Oxford Magazine*, May 1967.]

103.   Creaton, Heather J., comp. *Writings on British History*. University of London, Institute of Historical Research. London.
[Volume titles provide the dates, followed by subtitle *A Bibliography of Books and Articles on the History of Great Britain from about 450 A.D. to*

1949, Published during the Years 19 . . . Inclusive with an Appendix Containing a Select List of Publications in These Years on British History since 1939. Volumes covering 1958–59 (1977), 1962–64 (1979), 1965–66 (1981), 1967–68 (1982), 1969–70 (1984), 1971–72 (1985), and 1973–74 (1986). See items 150, 157, 172, 173; publication ceased. For continuation see item 108.]

104. Crosby, Everett U., C. Julian Bishko, and Robert L. Kellogg. *Medieval Studies: A Bibliographical Guide.* Garland Reference Library of the Humanities, vol. 427. New York, 1983.
[Many general and topical chapters, plus medieval England, pp. 148–65.]

105. Duls, Louisa DeSaussure. *Richard II in the Early Chronicles.* Studies in English Literature, vol. 79. The Hague and Paris, 1975.
[Mainly literary; only limited references to historical scholarship on Richard.]

106. *Economic History Review.*
[Each November issue contains an "annual list of publications" for the previous year; since 1981 the February issue also carries a review of periodical literature, compiled by Ian Blanchard.]

107. Ellis, Roger H., comp. *Catalogue of Seals in the Public Record Office.* Plates from photographs by J. D. Millen:

a.) *Personal Seals.* 2 vols. HMSO, 1978–81.
[By Owners.]

b.) *Monastic Seals.* HMSO, 1986.
[Reviewed by Brigitte Bedos-Rezak, *Speculum* 58 (1983), 793–95, and 64 (1989), 158–62.]

108. Elton, Geoffrey R., et al., eds. *Annual Bibliography of British and Irish History.* Published for the Royal Historical Society, London, since 1977 (for 1976 publications).
["England, 1066–1500" has been covered by David M. Palliser since 1985; Barbara English and J. J. N. Palmer have edited the volume since 1988.]

109. *English Historical Review.*
[The annual July issue contains "Notices of Periodical and Occasional Publications," mainly of the previous calendar year.]

110. Fairfield, Leslie P. *John Bale, Mythmaker for the English Reformation.* West Lafayette, Ind., 1976.

111. Frankforter, A. Daniel. "The Episcopal Registers of Medieval England: An Inventory." *BSM* 6/2 (1976), 3–22.

112. Fryde, E. B., D. E. Greenway, S. Porter, and I. Roy, eds. *Handbook of British Chronology.* Guides and Handbooks, no. 2. 3rd ed. Royal Historical Society, 1986.
[Builds on the 1939 volume edited by F. M. Powicke, assisted by Charles Johnson and W. J.

Harte, and the second edition, prepared by
Powicke and Fryde in 1961.]

113. Gilbert, V. F., and Darshan S. Tatla, comps. *Women's
Studies: A Bibliography of Dissertations 1870–1982.*
Oxford, 1985; New York, 1985.
[Blackwell Reference series.]

114. Gillingham, John. "Croyland Chronicle Communications: Memories of a Yorkist Civil Servant." *Ricardian*
7/99 (December 1987), 523–24.
[Item 287, on the Chronicle and chronicler.]

115. Gransden, Antonia. "Propaganda in English Medieval
Historiography." *JMH* 1 (1975), 363–82.
[With attention to the fifteenth century, cover-
ing both Lancastrian and Yorkists efforts.]

116. ———. "Antiquarian Studies in Fifteenth-Century
England." *AJ* 60 (1980), 75–97.
[An active field: Rous, William Worcester,
Thomas Elmham, and some lesser lights.]

117. ———. *Historical Writing in England II: c. 1307 to the
Early 16th Century.* London, 1982; Ithaca, N.Y., 1982.
[The major and comprehensive treatment. Re-
viewed at length and favorably by V. H. H.
Green, *History and Theory* 23 (1984), 105–16.]

118. Graves, Edgar B., ed. *A Bibliography of English History to 1485: Based on The Sources and Literature of*

English History from the Earliest Times to about 1485 by Charles Gross. Oxford and New York, 1975.
[Sponsored by the Royal Historical Society, the American Historical Association, and the Mediaeval Academy of America. In the footsteps of Gross's volume of 1900, a major contribution, with useful comments and fully detailed analyses of collected volumes.]

119. Gray, Irvine Egerton. *Antiquaries of Gloucestershire and Bristol.* Bristol and Gloucestershire Archaeological Society, Records Section, 1981.
[Covers William of Worcestre, pp. 31–33, and Robert Ricard (fl. 1466–1508), pp. 34–35.]

120. Green, Richard Firth. "The Short Version of *The Arrival of Edward IV.*" *Speculum* 56 (1981), 324–36.
[A College of Arms MS, in response to J. A. F. Thomson, *Speculum* 46 (1971), 84–93.]

121. Guth, DeLloyd J. *Late-Medieval England, 1377–1485.* Cambridge and New York, 1976.
[Conference on British Studies Bibliographical Handbooks. The volume with which one begins the search for references and citations, and the progenitor of the present volume.]

122. ———. "Fifteenth-Century England: Recent Scholarship and Future Directions." *BSM* 7/2 (Spring 1977), 3–50.
[Useful discussion and some addenda to the 1976 bibliography above.]

123.   Hanawalt, Barbara A. "Golden Ages for the History of
       Medieval English Women." In *Women in Medieval His-
       tory & Historiography*.   Edited by Susan Mosher
       Stuard. Philadelphia, 1988. Pp. 1–24.
       [Middle Ages series. Survey of women scholars
       and women's history.]

124.   Hanham, Alison. *Richard III and His Early Histor-
       ians, 1483–1535*. Oxford, 1975.
       [Detailed examination of early accounts: Man-
       cini, the Croyland Continuation, More, etc.]

125.   ———. "Croyland Chronicle Communications: Richard
       Lavender, Continuator." *Ricardian* 7/99 (December
       1987), 516–19.
       [Item 287, for the Chronicle.]

126.   Hanna, Ralph, III. *The Index of Middle English Prose,
       Handlist 1: A Handlist of Manuscripts Containing
       Middle English Prose in the Henry E. Huntington
       Library*. Cambridge and Totowa, N.J., 1984.
       [Though mainly literary, covers the Hastings pa-
       pers. See also item 189.]

127.   Harvey, John. *English Mediaeval Architects: A Bio-
       graphical Dictionary down to 1550: Including Master
       Masons, Carpenters, Carvers, Building Contractors,
       and Others Responsible for Design*. Rev. ed. Glouces-
       ter, 1984.
       [First published in London, 1954. Reviewed by
       C. J. Law, *Med Pros* 7/2 (Autumn 1986), 63–67.]

128. Hinchcliffe, Judith, comp. *King Henry VI, Parts 1, 2, and 3: An Annotated Bibliography.* Garland Shakespeare Bibliographies, no. 5, Reference Library of the Humanities, vol. 422. New York, 1984.
[As noted in item 97; pp. 229–49 on the play's sources, pp. 263–69 for bibliography.]

129. Historical Association. *Annual Bulletin of Historical Literature.* London.
[Issued annually (if often a bit late); the compilers of the "Later Middle Ages, British History (1200–1500)" since 1975 have been Christopher T. Allmand, Colin Platt, and S. H. Rigby. Running comments on publications.]

130. Horn, Joyce M. *History Theses, 1971–80: Historical Research for Higher Degrees in the Universities of the United Kingdom.* University of London, Institute of Historical Research. London, 1984.
[Work listed by fields and by chronology.]

131. Hudson, Anne. "Middle English." In *Editing Medieval Texts: English, French and Latin Written in England: Papers Given at the Twelfth Annual Conference on Editorial Problems, University of Toronto, 5–6 November 1976.* Edited by A. G. Rigg. New York, 1977. Pp. 34–57.
[Also New York, 1988.]

132. Institute of Historical Research (University of London). *Historical Research for Higher Degrees in the United Kingdom.* London, 1986–.

[Annual guide; *Part I: Theses Completed*; *Part II: Theses in Progress*. The latter is always much larger than the former. A continuation of the older *Historical Research for University Degrees in the United Kingdom, Part I: Theses Completed*, 19 vols. (London, 1967–84), and *Part II: Theses in Progress*, 19 vols. (1967–85).]

133. *International Bibliography of Historical Science*. From volume 43/44 (1974–75) to 1979, published at Paris; since 1979, in Munich, New York, London, and Paris. [Rather hard to use.]

134. *International Directory of Medievalists/Répertoire International des Médiévistes*. 6th ed. 2 vols. CNRS, Institut de recherche et d'histoire des textes. Paris, London, Munich, and New York, 1987. [Good bibliographies of the work of active scholars. N.B., bibliographies were discontinued in the 7th edition (FIDEM, 1990).]

135. *International Medieval Bibliography*. Leeds, annually. [First organized and compiled by Peter Sawyer and Robert S. Hoyt in 1968; tries for total coverage of journals, *Festschriften*, conference proceedings, and collections of essays (not of monographs); issued in two parts per year; vol. 23 (1990) covers 1989. Edited at times by Sawyer, R. J. Walsh, Catherine Coutts, Catherine Cubitt, and currently by Simon Forde.]

136. Jacobs, P. M., comp. *History Theses, 1901–70: Historical Research for Higher Degrees in the Universities of the United Kingdom.* University of London, Institute of Historical Research. London, 1976.

137. James, M. R. *A Descriptive Catalogue of the Latin Manuscripts in the John Rylands University Library.* Introduction and additional notes by Frank Taylor. Munich, 1980.
    [Reprint of the two-volume catalogue (1921), plus the material by Taylor.]

138. Kaufman, Peter I. "Polydore Vergil's Fifteenth Century." *Historian* 47 (1984–85), 512–23.
    [His grand themes and how he tailored events to fit the predetermined explanatory mold.]

139. Kelly, Henry A. "Croyland Chronicle Communications: The Croyland Chronicle Tragedies." *Ricardian* 7/99 (December 1987), 498–515.
    [Item 287 for the Chronicle.]

140. Kennedy, Edward D. "XII: Chronicles and Other Historical Writing." In vol. 8 (1989) of item 38. Pp. 2629–2720.
    [Bibliography, pp. 2781–2947. The bibliographies are not conveniently arranged but are very comprehensive.]

141. Kincaid, Arthur N. "George Buck Senior and George Buck Junior: A Literary-Historical Mystery Story." *Ricardian* 4/60 (March 1978), 2–8.

142. Kuehl, Warren F. *Dissertations in History, 1970–June 1980: An Index to Dissertations Completed in History Departments of United States & Canadian Universities.* Santa Barbara, Denver, and Oxford, 1985.
[Medieval Britain, pp. 13–17.]

143. Lagorio, Valerie Marie, and Ritamary Bradley. *The Fourteenth-Century English Mystics: A Comprehensive Annotated Bibliography.* Garland Reference Library of the Humanities, vol. 190. New York, 1981.
[Some eight hundred items, with coverage of Julian of Norwich and Margery Kempe.]

144. Leyser, Karl. "Kenneth Bruce McFarlane." *PBA* 62 (1970), 487–506.
[The obituary tribute to the master of fifteenth-century historical studies.]

145. Life, Page West. *Sir Thomas Malory and the* Morte Darthur: *A Survey of Scholarship and Annotated Bibliography.* Bibliographical Society of the University of Virginia, 1980.
[Mostly on literary topics.]

146. Loyn, H. R., gen. ed. *The Middle Ages: A Concise Encyclopaedia.* London and New York, 1989.
[One volume, with incisive illustrations and bibliographies for most of the short entries.]

147. *Medieval Archaeology.*
[The annual volume covers "news and notes" and a survey of work done on ten types of sites and buildings, by counties and regions.]

148.   Moore, James A., comp. *Richard III: An Annotated Bibliography.* Garland Shakespeare Bibliographies, no. 11, Reference Library of the Humanities, vol. 425. New York, 1986.
[Similar to items 97, 128, 164 and mostly concerned with the play; but see pp. 489–527 (covering 1975–83) for "sources and background." Informative and useful.]

149.   Mullins, E. L. C. *Texts and Calendars II: An Analytical Guide to Serial Publications, 1957–1982.* Guides and Handbooks, no. 12. Royal Historical Society, 1983.
[Updates the volume of 1958, reprinted with corrections in 1978.]

150.   Munro, D. J., ed. *Writings on British History, 1949–1951.* University of London, Institute of Historical Research. London, 1975.

151.   Murph, Roxane C. *Richard III: The Making of a Legend.* Metuchen, N.J., 1977.
[Covers historians, plus historical fiction and popular materials.]

152.   *Numismatic Literature.*
[An annual; an international abstract and bibliography of numismatics, with a section on Great Britain and Ireland.]

153.   O'Regan, Mary, and Arthur Cockerill. *A Gazetteer of Yorkshire in the 15th Century.* Wakefield, 1985.

[Published by the Yorkshire Branch of The Richard III Society as a guide to what is still to be seen of fifteenth-century monuments.]

154. Owen, Dorothy M., and Robin L. Storey. "The Canterbury and York Society." *BSM* 6/1 (1975), 28–37.
[Reprinted in *Archives* 23 (1986), 170–75.]

155. Palmer, J. J. N. "The Authorship, Date, and Historical Value of the French Chronicles on the Lancastrian Revolution." *BJRUL* 61 (1978–79), 145–81, 398–421.
[Low marks for the *Chronique de la Traison et Mort de Richard II.*]

156. Parkes, M. B., comp. *The Medieval Manuscripts of Keble College, Oxford: A Descriptive Catalogue with Summary Descriptions of the Greek and Oriental Manuscripts.* London, 1979.
[Hardly any fifteenth-century material.]

157. Philpin, C. H. E., and H. J. Creaton, comps. *Writings on British History, 1960–1961.* University of London, Institute of Historical Research. London, 1978.

158. Potter, Jeremy. *Good King Richard? An Account of Richard III and His Reputation, 1483–1983.* London, 1983.
[From Tudor lies to the current attempts to champion the king; bibliography also covers historical fiction.]

159.   Raymo, Robert R. "Works of Religious and Philosophical Instruction." In vol. 7 (1986) of item 38. Pp. 2255–2378.

[Covers manuals of instruction; bibliography, pp. 2467–2582.]

160.   Reel, Jerome V., Jr. *Index to Biographies of Englishmen, 1000–1485, Found in Dissertations and Theses.* Westport, Conn., 1975.

[Covers U.S. and British dissertations 1930–70.]

161.   Rhodes, Dennis E. *A Catalogue of Incunabula in All the Libraries of Oxford University outside the Bodleian.* Oxford and New York, 1982.

[Twenty-seven repositories and collections, by author, with a basic description and the publication data.]

162.   Richmond, Colin F. "Review Article: After McFarlane." *History* 68 (1983), 46–60.

[Reviews works of John Gillingham, Anthony Goodman, R. A. Griffiths, M. A. Hicks, J. R. Lander, K. B. McFarlane, and C. D. Ross.]

163.   Robbins, Rossell Hope. "Poems Dealing with Contemporary Conditions." In vol. 5 (1975) of item 38. Pp. 1385–1536.

[Bibliography, pp. 1631–1725; valuable and thorough guide to literature as a source for social and political history.]

164. Roberts, Josephine A., comp. *Richard II: An Annotated Bibliography*. 2 vols. Garland Shakespeare Bibliographies, no. 14, Reference Library of the Humanities, vol. 833. New York, 1988.
   [Similar to item 97; vol. 2, sources and historical background, pp. 120–43; bibliography, pp. 585–94.]

165. Robinson, P. R. *Catalogue of Dated and Datable Manuscripts c. 737–1600 in Cambridge Libraries*. 2 vols. Cambridge and Wolfeboro, N.H., 1988.
   [Volume 1: *The Text*, catalogue with descriptions; vol. 2: *The Plates*. Some 165 items between 1377 and 1485.]

166. Rosenthal, Joel T. "English Medieval Education Since 1970: So Near and Yet So Far." *History of Education Quarterly* (Winter 1982), 499–511.

167. ———. "Bibliography of English Scholarship: 1970–82: Part II—1307–1509." *Med Pros* 4/2 (Autumn 1983), 47–61.

168. Sawyer, Michael E, comp. and annotat. *A Bibliographical Index of Five English Mystics: Richard Rolle, Julian of Norwich, the Author of The Cloud of Unknowing, Walter Hilton, Margery Kempe*. Clifford E. Barbour Library, Pittsburgh Theological Seminary, Bibliographia Tripotamopolitana, no. 10. Pittsburgh, 1978.

169.   Serjeant, W. R., and R. K. Serjeant, eds., comp. M. E.
         Grimwade. *Index of the Probate Records of the Court of
         the Archdeacon of Suffolk, 1444–1700*. 2 vols. British
         Record Society, Index Library, 90–91. Keele, 1979–80.
         [Volume 1, A–K; vol. 2, L–Z. Only a few from be-
         fore 1500.]

170.   ————. *Index of the Probate Records of the Court of the
         Archdeacon of Sudbury, 1354–1700*. 2 vols. British
         Record Society, Index Library, 95–96. Keele, 1984.
         [Suffolk Record Office, Bury St. Edmunds
         Branch. Volume 1, A–K; vol. 2, L–Z.]

171.   Serpell, M. F. "Sir John Fenn, His Friends, and the
         Paston Letters." *AJ* 673 (1983), 95–121.
         [Biography of Fenn (1739–94) and how he came
         to publish the Paston Letters.]

172.   Sims, J. M., comp. *Writings on British History, 1952–
         1954*. University of London, Institute of Historical
         Research. London, 1975.

173.   Sims, J. M., and P. M. Jacobs, comps. *Writings on
         British History, 1955–1957*. University of London,
         Institute of Historical Research. London, 1977.

174.   Smith, David Michael. *Guide to Bishops' Registers of
         England and Wales: A Survey from the Middle Ages to
         the Abolition of the Episcopacy in 1646*. Guides and
         Handbooks, no. 11. Royal Historical Society, 1981.

[Diocese by diocese, as a guide to MSS and published materials. Preface is useful introduction to the topic.]

175. Smurthwaite, David. *The Ordnance Survey Complete Guide to the Battlefields of Britain.* Exeter, 1984.
[Published in New York as *Battlefields of Britain: The Complete Illustrated Guide* (1984).]

176. Spufford, Peter, with the assistance of Wendy Wilkinson and Sarah Tolley. *Handbook of Medieval Exchange.* Guides and Handbooks, no. 13. Royal Historical Society, 1986.
[Good introduction to banking and currency; volume treats exchange rates of all of Europe at various dates. England is covered, pp. 198–210.]

177. Stow, George B., Jr. "Some New Manuscripts of the *Vita Ricardi Secundi*, 1377–1402." *Manuscripta* 19 (1975), 107–15.
[Seven are generally used, but eight others are noted here, with an assessment of their value; for an edition of the text see item 305.]

178. Strayer, Joseph R., ed.-in-chief. *Dictionary of the Middle Ages.* 13 vols. New York, 1982–89.
[Twelve volumes plus an index volume; longish signed articles with bibliographies.]

179. Taylor, John. *English Historical Literature in the Fourteenth Century.* Oxford and New York, 1987.

[A *vade mecum*, building on Gransden; appendix 5 covers chroniclers' accounts of the peasants' rebellion. Reviewed by George B. Stow, Jr., *Speculum* 64 (1989), 771–75.]

180. Theilmann, John M. "Stubbs, Shakespeare, and Recent Historians of Richard II." *Albion* 8 (1976), 107–24.
[A survey of how the king has fared at our hands.]

181. Thomson, R. M., ed. *The Archives of the Abbey of Bury St. Edmunds.* Suffolk Records Society, vol. 21 (1982); Suffolk Charters, vol. 21, Suffolk Records Society (1980).
[Extensive fifteenth-century reorganization of the richest monastic collection extant in England.]

182. ———. *Catalogue of the Manuscripts of Lincoln Cathedral Chapter Library.* Woodbridge and Wolfeboro, N.H., 1989.
[On behalf of the Dean and Chapter of Lincoln. Only a smattering of fifteenth-century materials.]

183. *Urban History Yearbook.*
[Contains an annual summary of archaeology, periodical literature, research projects, and a current bibliography.]

184. Visser-Fuchs, Livia. "Croyland Chronicle Communications: A Commentary on the Continuation." *Ricardian* 7/99 (December 1987), 520–22.

[Item 287 for the Chronicle and its modern commentators.]

185. Voigts, Linda E. "Editing Middle English Texts: Needs and Issues." In *Editing Texts in the History of Science and Medicine: Papers Given at the Seventeenth Annual Conference on Editorial Problems, University of Toronto, 6–7 November 1981.* Edited by Trevor H. Levere. New York, 1982. Pp. 39–68.
[Instructive survey of extant materials, 1350–1500, with elaborate notes and references.]

186. Watson, Andrew G. *Catalogue of Dated and Datable Manuscripts, c. 700–1600, in the Department of Manuscripts, the British Library.* 2 vols. London, 1979.
[Volume 1: *The Text*; 2: *The Plates*.]

187. ———, ed. *Medieval Libraries of Great Britain: A List of Surviving Books, Edited by N. R. Ker: Supplement to the Second Edition.* Guides and Handbooks, no. 15. Royal Historical Society, 1987.
[Ker's 2nd edition (1964) is Guides and Handbooks no. 3; by repositories, donors, and scribes (as explained, ibid).]

188. Watson, Charles A. *The Writing of History in Britain: A Bibliography of Post–1945 Writings about British Historians and Biographers.* Garland Reference Library of Social Science, vol. 91. New York, 1982.
[The Middle Ages are covered, pp. 1–109.]

189. Watson, Kim. *Henry E. Huntington Library: Hastings Manuscripts.* Special Ser., vol. 22. List & Index Society, 1987.
[Accounts and financial papers are "too numerous to list"; also covers personal papers and manorial records. See item 126.]

190. Williams, Daniel. "The Crowland Chronicle, 616–1500." In item 84. Pp. 371–90.
[The case for Piers Curtis as author; see also item 287.]

191. Yeager, R. F. "A Bibliography of John Gower Materials through 1975." *Mediaevalia* 3 (1977), 261–306.
[With a section on "political philosophy and social criticism."]

192. Zacher, Christian K. "Travel and Geographical Writings." In vol. 7 (1986) of item 38. Pp. 2235–54.
[Includes work on Margery Kempe, William Wey, and maps; bibliography, pp. 2449–66.]

193. Zupko, Ronald Edward. *A Dictionary of Weights and Measures for the British Isles: The Middle Ages to the Twentieth Century.* Memoirs of the American Philosophical Society, vol. 168 (1985).

III. General Studies (Including Full-Length Bibliographies and Editions of Primary Sources)

194. Aers, David. "Rewriting the Middle Ages: Some Suggestions." *JMRS* 18 (1988), 221–40.
     [The market economy, reflected in literature.]

195. Allmand, C. T. *Lancastrian Normandy, 1415–1450: The History of a Medieval Occupation.* Oxford, 1983; New York, 1983.
     [Reprinted with corrections, 1986. A tale of conquest, settlement, and assimilation.]

196. ———. *The Hundred Years War: England and France at War, c. 1300–c. 1450.* Cambridge and New York, 1988.
     [In the Cambridge Medieval Textbooks series. Good general treatment.]

197. Armstrong, C. A. J., ed. and trans. *The Usurpation of Richard III: Dominicus Mancinus ad Angelum Catonem de occupatione Regni Anglie per Riccardum Tercium Libellus.* Gloucester, 1984.
     [Reprint of the 2nd edition (Oxford, 1969). Important source for the critical events of 1483, if not to be taken at Mancini's face value.]

198.   Astill, Grenville, and Annie Grant, eds. *The Country-side of Medieval England.* Illustrations by Brian Williams. Oxford, 1988; New York, 1988.
        [Valuable survey, concerned with resources and ecology; useful essays by Astill, Christopher Dyer, Grant, James Greig, John Langdon, Richard Smith, and Paul Stamper.]

199.   Barber, Richard, ed. *The Pastons: A Family in the Wars of the Roses.* Penguin version, Harmondsworth and New York, 1984; Folio Society, 1981.
        [Barber also did the Introduction and made the selections.]

200.   Barker, Juliet R. V. *The Tournament in England, 1100–1400.* Woodbridge and Wolfeboro, N.H., 1986.
        [General treatment, mostly before 1377.]

201.   Bean, J. M. W. *From Lord to Patron: Lordship in Late Medieval England.* Manchester, 1989; Philadelphia, 1989.
        [In the Middle Ages series. A study of indentured retinues and the growth of state (royal) control over such matters.]

202.   Bennett, Michael. *The Battle of Bosworth.* Gloucester, 1985; New York, 1985.
        [Best recent book on events before and during, and the significance of, the battle.]

203.   ———. *Lambert Simnel and the Battle of Stoke.* Gloucester, 1987; New York, 1987.

[A sequel to his Bosworth volume, running into early Tudor times.]

204. Bolton, J. L. *The Medieval English Economy, 1150–1500*. London, 1980; Totowa, N.J., 1980.
[Valuable *vade mecum* for current and complex scholarship.]

205. Bossy, John. *Christianity in the West, 1400–1700*. Oxford, 1985; New York, 1985.
[Erudite essay on spirituality and on the teaching and reception of sacramental religion.]

206. Boulton, D'Arcy Jonathan Dacre. *The Knights of the Crown: The Monarchical Orders of Knighthood in Later Medieval Europe, 1325–1520*. Woodbridge and Dover, N.H., 1987; New York, 1987.
[Covers the Order of the Garter from 1344 onwards, pp. 96–166.]

207. Bourassin, Emmanuel. *La France anglaise, 1414–1453. Chronique d'une occupation*. Paris, 1981.

208. Brown, A. L. *The Governance of Late Medieval England, 1272–1461*. The Governance of England, 3. Stanford, 1989.
[Mainly concerned with administrative history and the king's government.]

209. Buck, George, Sir. *The History of King Richard the Third (1619)*. Edited with introduction and notes by Arthur Noel Kincaid. Gloucester, 1982.

[Well-annotated reprint with corrections (1979), the 1619 edition, with a long introduction on historiography.]

210. Childs, Edmund. *William Caxton: A Portrait in a Background.* New York, 1979, 1976; London, 1976. [Popular presentation, with useful illustrations on early printing.]

211. Clanchy, M. T. *England and Its Rulers, 1066–1272: Foreign Lordship and National Identity.* London, 1983; Oxford, 1983; Totowa, N.J., 1983. [Fontana History of England series.]

212. Coleman, D. C. *The Economy of England, 1450–1750.* London and New York, 1977. [Good short survey of problems and current views.]

213. Collins, Marie. *Caxton, The Description of Britain: A Modern Rendering.* London, 1988; New York, 1988. [The 1480 volume, retold (in current English) and well illustrated. Picture research, Deborah Pownall. Paperback version (1989), *Caxton: The Description of Britain: A Modern Rendering by Marie Collins.*]

214. Cook, David R. *Lancastrians and Yorkists: The Wars of the Roses.* London and New York, 1984. [In the Seminar Studies in History series. Short narrative with a few documents.]

215.   Coward, Barry. *The Stanleys, Lords Stanley, and Earls of Derby, 1385–1672: The Origins, Wealth, and Power of a Landowning Family.* Remains Historical and Literary Connected with the Palatine Counties of Lancaster and Chester, 3rd ser., vol. 30. Chetham Society, 1983.
        [A narrative; pp. 1–19 run to 1504.]

216.   Cross, Claire. *Church and People, 1450–1660: The Triumph of the Laity in the English Church.* London, 1987, 1983, 1976; Hassocks, 1976; Atlantic Highlands, N.J., 1976.
        [In the Fontana Library of English History. Revised bibliography, 1987. The fifteenth century mainly treated as background for the Reformation.]

217.   Davies, R. R. *Lordship and Society in the March of Wales, 1282–1400.* Oxford, 1978.

218.   Davis, Norman, ed. *Paston Letters and Papers of the Fifteenth Century.* Vol. 2. Oxford, 1976.
        [Volume 1 was published in 1971. Davis's edition is now the standard scholarly edition, replacing James Gairdner's volumes. Kenneth G. Madison, *Speculum* 54 (1979), 361–64, critically reviews and compares Davis with Gairdner as editors. The long-promised third volume will presumably not see the light of day.]

219.   ———, ed. and intro. *The Paston Letters.* Oxford and New York, 1983.

[A selection in The World's Classics series and Oxford Paperbacks. Reprint of the London 1963 edition, but new introduction and list of dates.]

220. Deacon, Richard. *A Biography of William Caxton: The First English Editor, Printer, Merchant, and Translator*. London, 1976.

[Popular and reasonable retelling of the tale.]

221. Dickinson, J. C. *The Later Middle Ages: From the Norman Conquest to the Eve of the Reformation*. London, 1979; New York, 1979.

[*An Ecclesiastical History of England*, vol. 2. Emphasis on the constitutional history of the church.]

222. Dobson, R. B., ed. *The Peasants' Revolt of 1381*. 2nd ed. London, 1983; New York, 1983.

[History in Depth series. Replaces the 1st edition (1970). The basic collection of documents, in translation, with invaluable comments; the one book to use when teaching about 1381, if one must make such a choice.]

223. Dockray, Keith. *Richard III: A Reader in History*. Gloucester, 1988.

[Short narrative with selections from primary sources and modern scholarship.]

224. ———, intro. *Three Chronicles of the Reign of Edward IV*. Gloucester, 1988; Gloucester and Wolfeboro, N.H., 1988.

[Reprint, with new introduction. Three nine-teenth-century editions: that of John Bruce, of the *Historie of the Arrivall of Edward IV*; that of J. O. Halliwell, of Warkworth's *Chronicle*; that of John Gough Nichols, of the *Chronicle of the Rebellion in Lincolnshire, 1470.*]

225. Edwards, Rhoda. *The Itinerary of King Richard III, 1483-1485.* Richard III Society, 1983.
[Maps and detailed itinerary, 7 April 1483 to 22 August 1485, with sources cited for each move.]

226. Ellis, Steven. " 'Not Mere English': The British Perspective, 1400–1650." *History Today* 38 (December 1988), 41–48.
[The new interpretation: a less Anglocentric view of the islands' history.]

227. Falkus, Gila. *The Life and Times of Edward IV.* Introduction by Antonia Fraser. London, 1981.
[Coffee-table book with illustrations.]

228. Fryde, E. B. *The Great Revolt of 1381.* Historical Association, General Ser., 100. London, 1981.
[Revolt in the context of a long tale of regional uprisings: tenure, tax, and foreign policy implications.]

229. Gardner, John. *The Life and Times of Chaucer.* New York, 1977.
[Pleasant volume by a major contemporary writer.]

230.   Gillingham, John. *The Wars of the Roses: Peace and Conflict in Fifteenth-Century England.* London, 1981; Baton Rouge, La., 1981.
[The familiar story told with verve and fresh insights; strong on both military descriptions and the effects of war on society.]

231.   Given-Wilson, Chris. *The Royal Household and the King's Affinity: Service, Politics, and Finance in England, 1360–1413.* London, 1987; New Haven, 1986.
[Valuable survey, linking politics and administrative developments, with an eye on the personnel and prosopography of royal service.]

232.   ———. *The English Nobility in the Late Middle Ages: The Fourteenth-Century Political Community.* London and New York, 1987.

233.   Given-Wilson, Chris, and Alice Curteis. *The Royal Bastards of Medieval England.* London and New York, 1988; London and Boston, 1984.
[Late medieval kings tried but fell short of their Plantagenet ancestors.]

234.   Goller, Karl H. "War and Peace in Middle English Romances and Chaucer." In *War and Peace in the Middle Ages.* Edited by Brian Patrick McGuire. Copenhagen, 1987. Pp. 118–45.

235.   Goodman, Anthony. *The Wars of the Roses: Military Activity and English Society, 1452–97.* London and Boston, 1981; New York, 1981.

[Political and military narrative, with chapters on effects of war on society.]

236. ———. *The New Monarchy: England 1471-1534*. Oxford, 1988; Oxford and New York, 1988.
[Historical Association Studies. Short discussion of the "new monarchy" controversy with good bibliographic foundation for students.]

237. Griffiths, Ralph A. *The Reign of King Henry VI: The Exercise of Royal Authority, 1422-1461*. London, 1981; Berkeley, 1981.
[The major study of the reign: vast, well-informed. Reviewed by Michael Altschul, " 'Less Than I Was Born To': Two Studies of King Henry VI," *Medievalia et Humanistica*, n.s. 11 (1982), 291-97 (covering Bertram Wolffe's study as well: item 319). Reviewed by R. B. Dobson, *J Eccl H* 34 (1983), 130-34; A. J. Pollard, "The Last of the Lancastrians," *History of Parliament* 2 (1983), 203-08.]

238. ———. "The Later Middle Ages (1290-1485)." In *The Oxford Illustrated History of Britain*. Edited by Kenneth O. Morgan. Oxford and New York, 1984. Pp. 166-222.

239. ———. "Monarch and Nation, 1216-1509." In *The Oxford Illustrated History of the British Monarchy*. Edited by John Cannon and Ralph Griffiths. Oxford and New York, 1988. Pp. 176-298.

[Also Oxford, 1988. Reprinted with corrections, 1989.]

240. Griffiths, Ralph A., and Roger S. Thomas. *The Making of the Tudor Dynasty.* Gloucester, 1987, 1985; New York, 1985.
[Careful tracing of the family background and an assessment of its Welsh roots and traditions.]

241. Hall, Louis Brewer. *The Perilous Vision of John Wyclif.* Chicago, 1983.
[Popular biography but rather bland.]

242. Hallam, Elizabeth, ed. *The Chronicles of the Wars of the Roses.* Preface by Hugh Trevor-Roper. London, 1988; Markham, Ont., 1988; New York, 1988.
[Lavish volume, with narrative and longish excerpts from sources. Note: the New York title is *The Wars of the Roses.*]

243. Halsted, Caroline A. *Richard III: As Duke of Gloucester and King of England.* 2 vols. Gloucestershire, 1980, 1977.
[Reprint of her perceptive 1844 study. There is also a 1980 (Gloucester) Facsimile Edition of the 1844 edition.]

244. Hammond, P. W., intro. and notes. Walpole, Horace. *Historic Doubts on the Life and Reign of King Richard the Third: Including the Supplement, Reply, Short Observations, and Postscript.* Wolfeboro, N.H., 1989, 1987; Gloucester, 1987.
[Original publication, Dublin, 1768.]

245.   [No entry.]

246.   Hammond, P. W., and Anne F. Sutton. *Richard III: The Road to Bosworth Field.* London, 1985.
[Sympathetic biography with long source-quotes and good illustrations.]

247.   Hampton, W. E. *Memorials of the Wars of the Roses: A Biographical Guide.* Richard III Society, 1979.
[By counties, burial sites, brasses, monuments, and arms of the illustrious participants, with brief biographies.]

248.   Hands, Rachel. *English Hawking and Hunting in the Boke of St. Albans: A Facsimile Edition of Sigs. a2–f8 of the Boke of St. Albans (1486).* London, 1975.
[Oxford English Monographs. A partial facsimile of Caxton's 1486 edition of Juliana Berners's "how to do it" volume.]

249.   Harriss, G. L. *Cardinal Beaufort: A Study of Lancastrian Ascendency and Decline.* Oxford, 1988; Oxford and New York, 1988.
[Major political biography and study of Lancastrian government.]

250.   Harvey, P. D. A. "English Archaeology after the Conquest: A Historian's View." In item 47. Pp. 74–82.
[A comparison of the data of the written and the unwritten records.]

251.   Haswell, Jock. *The Ardent Queen: Margaret of Anjou and the Lancastrian Heritage.* London, 1976.

252.   Hector, L. C., and Barbara F. Harvey, eds. and trans.
        The Westminster Chronicle, 1381–1394. Oxford and
        New York, 1982.
        [Oxford Medieval Texts. Major political source,
        now accessible and well introduced.]

253.   Hicks, M. A. *False, Fleeting, Perjur'd Clarence:
        George, Duke of Clarence, 1449–78.* Gloucester, 1980.
        [A serious treatment, at long last.]

254.   Hieatt, Constance B., ed. *An Ordinance of Pottage: An
        Edition of the Fifteenth Century Culinary Recipes in
        Yale University's MS. Beinecke 163.* London, 1988.
        [Based on item 255, adapted here for the modern
        kitchen.]

255.   Hieatt, Constance B., and Sharon Butler, eds. *Curye
        on Inglysch: English Culinary Manuscripts of the Four-
        teenth Century (Including the Forme of Cury).* EETS,
        1985.
        [Middle English texts of *Diuersa Cibaria, Diuer-
        sa Servisa, Utilis Coquinario, The Forme of
        Cury,* and *Goud Kokery.*]

256.   Hindley, Geoffrey. *England in the Age of Caxton.* New
        York, 1979; London, 1970.
        [Reasonable life-and-times volume.]

257.   Horrox, Rosemary, ed. *Richard III and the North.*
        Centre for Regional and Local History, Department of
        Adult and Continuing Education, University of Hull,
        Studies in Regional and Local History, no. 6. Hull,
        1986.

[Contains papers by Michael A. Hicks, Horrox, Michael Jones, David M. Palliser, and Pamela Tudor-Craig.]

258. Horrox, Rosemary, and P. W. Hammond, eds. *British Library Harleian Manuscript 433*. 4 vols. Richard III Society, 1979–83.
[Volume 1: *Register of Grants for the Reigns of Edward V and Richard III*; 2: *Second Register of Richard III*; 3: *Second Register of Edward V and Miscellaneous Material*; 4 (by Horrox), the index; a vast miscellany of material on the Yorkist court and government.]

259. Jarman, Rosemary Hawley. *Crispin's Day: The Glory of Agincourt*. London, 1979; Boston, 1979.
[Illustrated and reasonable popular account.]

260. Jenkins, Elizabeth. *The Princes in the Tower*. London, 1978; New York, 1978.
[The intent is to judge Richard evenly and fairly.]

261. Jones, Terry. *Chaucer's Knight: The Portrait of a Medieval Mercenary*. London, 1985, 1982, 1980; New York, 1985; Baton Rouge, La., 1980.
[Methuen Paperback series (1985). The literary creation set into a social and military context.]

262. Kaeuper, Richard W. *War, Justice, and Public Order: England and France in the Later Middle Ages*. Oxford and New York, 1988.
[Valuable contribution to comparative studies of government.]

263. Keegan, John. "Agincourt." In his *The Face of Battle*. New York, 1976. Pp. 79–116.

[Also London, 1986, 1976; Harmondsworth, 1983, 1978; New York, 1977; later, *The Face of Battle: A Study of Agincourt, Waterloo, and the Somme* (London, 1988); (rev. ed.) *The Illustrated Face of Battle* (same subtitle) (New York, 1989). Brilliant military history.]

264. Keen, Maurice H. "Chivalrous Culture in Fourteenth-Century England." *Historical Studies* 10 (1976), 1–24.

265. ———. "Chivalry, Heralds, and History." In item 22. Pp. 393–414.

266. ———. *Chivalry*. 2nd printing, with corrections. New Haven, 1984.

[Important book with an interest in the fifteenth century and the "real-life" meaning of chivalry.]

267. ———. "War, Peace, and Chivalry." As item 234. Pp. 94–117.

268. King, Edmund. *England, 1175–1425*. London, 1979; New York, 1979.

[In the Development of English Society series. Uneven as a survey, but valuable essays with numerous original and critical ideas.]

269. Krochalis, Jeanne, and Edward Peters, eds. and trans. *The World of Piers Plowman*. Philadelphia, 1975.

[In The Middle Ages series. A collection of readings, in translation, on a wide range of topics.]

270. Labarge, Margaret Wade. *Henry V: The Cautious Conqueror*. London, 1975.
[American title, *King Henry V* (New York, 1976). Serious biography aimed at the general audience.]

271. ———. *Gascony, England's First Colony, 1204–1453*. London, 1980.
[Useful political history that also covers the commercial links.]

272. Lander, J. R. *Politics and Power in England, 1450–1509*. London, 1976.
[A separate paperback publication of the new introduction (ch. 1) Lander wrote when his articles were assembled for *Crown and Nobility* in 1976: item 57.]

273. ———. *Conflict and Stability in Fifteenth-Century England*. 3rd ed. London, 1979, 1977.
[Hutchinson University Library series. An important overview, first published in 1969, 2nd edition 1974.]

274. ———. *Government and Community: England, 1450–1509*. London, 1980; Cambridge, Mass., 1980.
[Volume 1 of The New History of England series; not as innovative as other Lander volumes listed here.]

275. Macfarlane, Alan. *The Origins of English Individualism: The Family, Property and Social Transition.* New York, 1979; Oxford, 1978.
[Reprinted with corrections, Oxford, 1979. An odd and unconvincing essay on peasants as capitalists. Critically reviewed by Stephen D. White and Richard T. Vann, "The Invention of English Individualism: Alan Macfarlane and the Modernization of Pre-Modern England," *Social History* 8 (1983), 345–63.]

276. McLean, Teresa. *The English at Play, in the Middle Ages.* Windsor Forest, Berks., 1983.
[Old-fashioned social history, but numerous odds and ends of useful information.]

277. Mescal, John. *Henry VI.* Catholic Truth Society, 1980.
[Published to rehabilitate Henry and his reputation.]

278. Mézières, Philippe de. *Letter to King Richard II: A Plea Made in 1395 for Peace between England and France.* Introduced and translated by G. W. Coopland. New York, 1976; Liverpool, 1975.
[Original text and English version, *Epistre au Roi Richart.* An "off-beat" source; medieval doves tried their best.]

279. Morgan, Philip. *War and Society in Medieval Cheshire, 1277–1403.* Remains, Historical and Literary, Connected with the Palatine Counties of Lancaster and Chester, 3rd ser., vol. 34. Chetham Society, 1987.
[From the mid-fourteenth century, pp. 149–227.]

280. Moriarty, Catherine, ed. *The Voice of the Middle Ages: In Personal Letters 1100–1500*. Oxford, 1989; New York, 1989.
[A little thin on the historical aspects of the material.]

281. Norman, A. V. B., and Don Pottinger. *English Weapons & Warfare, 449–1660*. New York, 1985; London and Melbourne, 1979; Englewood Cliffs, N.J., 1979.
[First published in 1966 as *Warrior to Soldier, 449 to 1660: A Brief Introduction to the History of English Warfare* (London) and as *A History of War and Weapons, 449 to 1660: English Warfare from the Anglo-Saxons to Cromwell* (New York). See pp. 77–144 for a general treatment of the topic in the fourteenth and fifteenth centuries.]

282. Petre, James, ed. *Richard III: Crown and People*. Richard III Society, 1985.
[Selected articles from *The Ricardian*, March 1975 through December 1981: sixty-five articles, many of high quality but too many, and mostly too short, to itemize here.]

283. Platt, Colin. *Medieval England: A Social History and Archaeology from the Conquest to A.D. 1600. . . .* London, 1978; New York, 1978.
[Title varies with place of publication: New York, *to 1600 A.D.*]

284. ———. *Medieval Britain from the Air*. London, 1984.
[Chapters 4 ("Hearth and Home") and 5 ("The

Late Medieval Church") are relevant and useful
surveys.]

285. Pollard, A. J. *The Wars of the Roses.* Basingstoke,
1988; New York, 1988.
[British History in Perspective series. Concise
and well-informed brief treatment.]

286. Price, Mary. *The Peasants' Revolt.* London, 1980.
[Then and There Series for young readers; a
good short introduction to everyone's heritage.]

287. Pronay, Nicholas, and John Cox., eds. *The Crowland
Chronicle Continuations, 1459–1486.* Richard III and
Yorkist History Trust. London, 1986; Gloucester,
1986.
[Latin and English, with useful introduction. Re-
viewed with approval by A. J. Pollard, "Review
Article: Memoirs of a Yorkist Civil Servant,"
Ricardian 7/96 (March 1987), 380–85; much dis-
cussion, for which see items 114, 125, 139, 184,
190, 343, 495.]

288. Rawcliffe, Carole. *The Staffords: Earls of Stafford and
Dukes of Buckingham, 1394–1521.* Cambridge Studies
in Medieval Life and Thought, 3rd ser., vol. 11. Cambridge and New York, 1978.
[Detailed family history: important study of
lands, politics, and bastard feudalism.]

289. Rees, David. *The Son of Prophecy: Henry Tudor's
Road to Bosworth.* London, 1985.

[The story from 1400 onwards, from a Welsh perspective.]

290. Reeves, A. C. *Lancastrian Englishmen*. Washington, D.C., 1981.
[Careful biographical studies of William Booth, John Cornewaille, Henry, Lord Fitzhugh, Adam Moleyns, and John Pelham.]

291. Rosenthal, Joel T. *Nobles and the Noble Life, 1295–1500*. Historical Problems: Studies and Documents, 25. London, 1976; New York, 1976.
[An essay on the aristocracy, plus documents on the aristocracy (in translation).]

292. Ross, Charles. *The Wars of the Roses: A Concise History*. London, 1976.
[Balanced short account, with handsome illustrations.]

293. ———. *Richard III*. London, 1981; Berkeley, 1981.
[In the English Monarchs series. Favorable assessment but not a whitewash: the definitive study. (For a review of Ross's *Edward IV* [1974] see Bryce Lyon, "Review Article: Edward IV," *JBS* 16 [1976], 178–86: "best yet written on Edward IV.") On *Richard III* see *Ricardian* 6/77 (June 1982), 41–47, for a discussion by Lorraine Attreed, Robert Hairsine, Isolde Wigram, James Petre, and William Hampton.]

294. Rowley, Trevor. *The High Middle Ages, 1200–1550*. London, 1988; London and New York, 1986.

[In The Making of Britain, 1066–1939, series. Useful general survey with some attention to social and economic developments.]

295. Royal Commission on Historical Monuments. [These volumes, published by HMSO, London, continue to appear, covering regions as well as specific sites and monuments.]

296. St. Aubyn, Giles. *The Year of Three Kings, 1483.* London, 1983; New York, 1983. [Anniversaries are good for the historian business.]

297. Senior, Michael. *The Life and Times of Richard II.* Introduction by Antonia Fraser. London, 1981.

298. Seward, Desmond. *The Hundred Years War.* New York, 1984, 1982, 1978; London, 1978. [Paperback series is Atheneum, 281. Sometime subtitle, *The English in France, 1337–1453.*]

299. ———. *Richard III, England's Black Legend.* New York, 1984; London, 1983; London and New York, 1983. [The Tudor legends of the king, plus modern scholarly views.]

300. ———. *Henry V: The Scourge of God.* New York, 1988. [Popular biography with some scholarly foundation.]

301.　　Simon, Linda. *Of Virtue Rare: Margaret Beaufort, Matriarch of the House of Tudor.* Boston, 1982.
[Readable.]

302.　　Smith, George, ed. *The Coronation of Elizabeth Wydeville, Queen Consort of Edward IV, on May 26th, 1465: A Contemporary Account Set Forth from a XV Century Manuscript.* Cliftonville, Kent, 1975.
[Useful facsimile reprint of the 1935 London first edition; makes contemporary accounts available.]

303.　　Snyder, William H., ed. and researcher. *The Crown and the Tower: The Legend of Richard III: A Condensation of Caroline Amelia Halsted's Important Biography of 1884, Richard III as Duke of Gloucester and King of England, with the Views of Other Authors and Additional Commentary.* Richard III Society, 1981.
[Not arranged to facilitate an easy distinction between Snyder and Halsted.]

304.　　Steane, John. *The Archaeology of Medieval England and Wales.* London, 1985; Athens, Ga., 1985.
[In the Croom Helm Studies in Archaeology series. By social units: government, housing, industry, and crafts, etc.]

305.　　Stow, George B., Jr., ed. and intro. *Historia Vitae et Regni Ricardi Secundi.* Haney Foundation Ser., University of Pennsylvania, 21. Philadelphia, 1977.
[Valuable source, now (finally) available in useful format and edition. See items 177, 601.]

306.　Talbot, Hugh. *The English Achilles: An Account of the Life and Campaigns of John Talbot, 1st Earl of Shrewsbury (1383–1453)*. Introduction by C. V. Wedgwood. London, 1981.
[Old-fashioned, detailed narrative, with useful scholarly apparatus.]

307.　Taylor, Frank, and John S. Roskell, trans., intro., and notes. *Gesta Henrici Quinti [:] The Deeds of Henry the Fifth*. Oxford, 1975.
[Oxford Medieval Texts. Contemporary source, on the road to hagiography, c. 1416–17; handy edition with valuable appendices on the king and the source's sources.]

308.　Thomas, Arthur H., and Isobel D. Thornley, eds. *The Great Chronicle of London*. Gloucester, 1983.
[A reprint (in reduced format) of the 1938 edition.]

309.　Thompson, M. W. *The Decline of the Castle*. Cambridge and New York, 1987.
[Serious treatment: changing warfare, the domestic house and courtyard, and finally the age of destruction and nostalgia.]

310.　Thomson, John A. F. *The Transformation of Medieval England, 1370–1529*. London and New York, 1983.
[Foundations of Modern Britain series. A useful survey of changes that were often less radical than we are led to believe.]

311.   Tuck, Anthony. *Crown and Nobility, 1272-1461: Political Conflict in Late Medieval England.* Oxford, 1986; Totowa, N.J., 1986; London, 1985.
[The Fontana History of England series. Synthesis of recent work, emphasizing political and constitutional history.]

312.   Tyerman, Christopher. *England and the Crusades, 1095-1588.* Chicago, 1988.
[Important treatment of a neglected topic, though mainly looking at the thirteenth century.]

313.   Vale, Malcolm. *War and Chivalry: Warfare and Aristocratic Culture in England, France, and Burgundy at the End of the Middle Ages.* London, 1981; Athens, Ga., 1981.

314.   *Victoria County History.* Oxford University Press, for the Institute of Historical Research, University of London. Oxford, 1900–.
[Work on this vast project continues: twelve counties are actively moving towards the publication of further volumes.]

315.   Virgoe, Roger, ed. *Private Life in the Fifteenth Century: Illustrated Letters of the Paston Family.* London and New York, 1989; New York, 1989.
[Handsome edition with thoughtful comments; selected letters, in translation, against the background of political events and social life of the day.]

316. Webber, Ronald. *The Peasants' Revolt: The Uprising in Kent, Essex, East Anglia, and London in 1381 during the Reign of King Richard II.* Lavenham, 1980.
[Short narrative.]

317. Weightman, Christine. *Margaret of York, Duchess of Burgundy, 1446–1503.* Gloucester, 1989; New York, 1989.
[The first modern scholarly study of this woman of political and cultural eminence.]

318. Williamson, Audrey. *The Mystery of the Princes: An Investigation into a Supposed Murder.* Dursley, Eng., 1978; Totowa, N.J., 1978.

319. Wolffe, Bertram. *Henry VI.* London, 1983, 1981, 1980.
[English Monarchs series. A good try at a biography, not likely to be replaced for this particular purpose. For reviews see item 237.]

320. Wood, Charles T. *Joan of Arc and Richard III: Sex, Saints, and Government in the Middle Ages.* New York, 1988.
[Includes papers previously published, in revised form, on Edward V and Richard III: items 637, 638, 639.]

IV. POLITICAL HISTORY
(INCLUDING DIPLOMATIC AND MILITARY)

321. Alban, J. R., and Christopher T. Allmand. "Spies and Spying in the Fourteenth Century." In item 3. Pp. 73–101.
[Efforts to spy and to control and neutralize the other side's spies.]

322. Allan, Alison. "Yorkist Propaganda: Pedigree, Prophecy, and the 'British History' in the Reign of Edward IV." In item 74. Pp. 171–92.
[Efforts to push propaganda, though for a limited audience.]

323. ———. "Royal Propaganda and the Proclamations of Edward IV." *BIHR* 59 (1986), 146–54.
[Edward's style and how the government's views and policies were publicized.]

324. Allmand, Christopher T. "The Aftermath of War in Fifteenth Century France." *History* 61 (1976), 344–57.
[How hard it was to restore law and order.]

325. ———. "Henry V: The Soldier and the War in France." In item 36. Pp. 117–35.

[A great soldier leading his troops and his nation.]

326. ——. "France-Angleterre à la fin de la guerre de cent ans et le 'Boke of Noblesse' de William Worcester." In item 25. Pp. 103–11.

327. Allmand, C. T., and C. A. J. Armstrong, eds. *English Suits before the Parlement of Paris, 1420–1436.* Camden Fourth ser., vol. 26. Royal Historical Society, 1982.
[The texts of thirty-one suits, some of English peer vs. English peer, with biographical materials and glossary.]

328. Anglo, Sydney. "How to Win at Tournaments: The Technique of Chivalric Combat." *AJ* 63 (1988), 248–64.
[Books and manuals gave instructions to improve skills and techniques.]

329. Antonovics, A. V. "Henry VII, King of England, 'By the Grace of Charles VIII of France'." In item 32. Pp. 169–84.
[French help when it was needed.]

330. Arthurson, Ian. "The Rising of 1497: A Revolt of the Peasantry?" In item 72. Pp. 1–18.
[How Henry VII dealt with widespread discontent.]

331. Attreed, Lorraine C. "An Indenture between Richard, Duke of Gloucester and the Scrope Family of Masham and Upsall." *Speculum* 58 (1983), 1018–25.
[The indenture is from 1476.]

332. Baldwin, David. "King Richard's Grave in Leicester." *Leicestershire* 60 (1986), 21–24.
[Almost no physical certainty about the site in the Franciscan church.]

333. Ballard, M., and C. S. L. Davies. "Etienne Fryon: Burgundian Agent, English Royal Secretary, and 'Principal Counsellor' to Perkin Warbeck." *HR* 62 (1989), 245–59.
[The tangled skeins as woven by Margaret of Burgundy.]

334. Barron, C. M. "The Art of Kingship: Richard II, 1377–1399." *History Today* 35 (June 1985), 30–37.
[Richard's shortcomings were but replaced by Henry IV's own weaknesses.]

335. Bean, J. M. W. "The Financial Position of Richard, Duke of York." In *War and Government in the Middle Ages: Essays in Honour of J. O. Prestwich.* Edited by John Gillingham and J. C. Holt. Cambridge, 1984; Totowa, N.J., 1984. Pp. 182–98.

336. Bennett, Michael J. " 'Good Lords' and 'King-Makers': The Stanleys of Latham in English Politics, 1385–1485." *History Today* 31 (July 1981), 12–17.
[Not an attractive family.]

337.   ———. "Memoirs of a Yeoman in the Service of the
House of York, 1452–61." *Ricardian* 8/106 (September
1989), 259–64.
[Hugh Wiot by name, and a puzzle to identify;
with a transcription of a petition he presented
on his own behalf.]

338.   Bornstein, Diane. "Military Manuals in Fifteenth-
Century England." *MS* 37 (1975), 469–77.
[Vegetius's influence on Lord Berkeley, the
Knyghthod and Bataile, and William of Worces-
ter.]

339.   Bradley, Patricia J. "Henry V's Scottish Policy: A
Study in Realpolitik." In item 34. Pp. 177–95.
[The formulation of the ideas and practices of a
border policy.]

340.   Bridbury, Anthony R. "The Hundred Years War: Costs
and Profits." In item 18. Pp. 80–95.
[Using resources and spreading costs; dissenting
from the views of M. M. Postan (1942 and 1964)
and K. B. McFarlane (1962).]

341.   Brooke, Christopher N. L., and V. Ostenberg. "The
Birth of Margaret of Anjou." *HR* 61 (1988), 357–58.
[She was a year younger, being born in 1430;
the question arises from a look at her endowment of Queens' College, Cambridge.]

342.   Brown, Alfred L. "Parliament, c. 1377–1422." In item
21. Pp. 109–40.

[Useful summary of what we accept about structure and function of the institution.]

343. Burr, K. E. "The Second Continuation of the Croyland Chronicle." *Ricardian* 3/51 (December 1975), 21–27.
[See item 287 for the Chronicle.]

344. Carpenter, Christine. "Sir Thomas Malory and Fifteenth-Century Local Politics." *BIHR* 53 (1980), 31–43.
[The local background of his criminal activities.]

345. ———. "The Beauchamp Affinity: A Study of Bastard Feudalism at Work." *EHR* 95 (1986), 514–32.
[A complex web explicated and analyzed, 1401–39.]

346. ———. "The Duke of Clarence and the Midlands: A Study in the Interplay of Local and National Politics." *Midland* 11 (1986), 23–48.
[His special touch helped keep the factions at odds with each other.]

347. Catto, Jeremy. "The King's Servants." In item 36. Pp. 75–95.
[Who served Henry V, and how and why they were bound to such loyal service.]

348. Cherry, Martin. "The Courtenay Earls of Devon: The Formation and Disintegration of a Late Medieval Aristocratic Family." *Southern* 1 (1979), 71–97.
[Detailed family and local study.]

349.   ———. "The Struggle for Power in Mid-Fifteenth
Century Devonshire." In item 31. Pp. 123–44.
[The anatomy and physiology of the Courtenay-
Bonville feud.]

350.   ———. "The Liveried Personnel of Edward Courtenay,
Earl of Devon, 1384–85." *D & C N&Q* 35/5 (Spring
1984), 189–93; 35/6 (Autumn 1984), 219–25; 35/7
(Spring 1985), 255–63; 35/8 (Autumn 1985), 302–10.
[Biographical and prosopographical informa-
tion.]

351.   Clark, Linda, and Carole Rawcliffe. "The History of
Parliament, 1386–1422: A Progress Report." *Med Pros*
4/2 (Autumn 1983), 9–41.
[A status report on the major biographical project, now nearing publication.]

352.   Clayton, Dorothy J. "Peace Bonds and the Mainte-
nance of Law and Order in Late Medieval England:
The Example of Cheshire." *BIHR* 58 (1985), 133–48.
[Cheshire functioned without justices of the
peace; mainprizes and bonds were fairly effective.]

353.   Coleman, C. H. D. "The Execution of Hastings: A Neglected Source." *BIHR* 53 (1980), 244–47.
[Argues for 13 June 1483: a running controversy
with A. Hanham and J. A. F. Thomson: items
440, 612, 632, 636.]

354. Condon, Margaret M. "Ruling Elites in the Reign of Henry VII." In item 74. Pp. 109–42.
[The turnover at the dynastic change and the importance of the early Tudor council.]

355. Coss, Peter R. "Bastard Feudalism Revisited." *Past and Present* 125 (1989), 27–64.
[Historiography and some pre-fifteenth-century examples.]

356. Crawford, Anne. "John Howard, Duke of Norfolk: A Possible Murderer of the Princes." *Ricardian* 5/70 (September 1980), 230–34.
[He is exonerated: lack of motive and opportunity.]

357. ———. "The King's Burden? The Consequences of Royal Marriage in Fifteenth Century England." In item 31. Pp. 33–56.
[Much-needed survey of the queens and royal marriages.]

358. ———. "The Mowbray Inheritance." *Ricardian* 5/73 (June 1981), 334–40.
[A tale of royal interference.]

359. ———. "The Private Life of John Howard: A Study of a Yorkist Lord, His Family and Household." In item 35. Pp. 6–24.
[Mainly covers the 1460s and 1470s; appendix lists household members.]

360. ———. "Victims of Attainder: The Howard and de Vere Women in the Late Fifteenth Century." *Reading* 15 (1989), 59–74.
[Women victimized for their families' political blunders.]

361. Crew, Brian. "Lydgate's 1445 Pageant for Margaret of Anjou." *ELN* 18 (1980–81), 170–74.
[Merging the decorative arts and political propaganda.]

362. Crook, David. "The Confessions of a Spy, 1380." *HR* 62 (1989), 346–50.
[Geoffrey Brun and possible treachery on the south coast amidst seemingly serious threats of invasion.]

363. Curry, Anne. "The First English Standing Army? Military Organisation in Lancastrian Normandy, 1420–1450." In item 74. Pp. 193–214.
[Patronage and feudal ties hampered professionalization.]

364. ———. "Le service féodale en Normandie pendant l'occupation anglaise (1417–1450)." In item 25. Pp. 233–57.

365. ———. "Sex and the Soldier in Lancastrian Normandy, 1415–50." *Reading* 14 (1988), 17–45.
[Efforts to control the boys: the rules about soldiers' behavior, how realistic they were, and re-

lated social issues about a medieval army in the field.]

366.   Cutler, S. H. "A Report to Sir John Fastolf on the Trial of Jean, Duke of Alençon." *EHR* 96 (1981), 808–17.
[College of Arms, Arundel MS. 48, fols. 222^r–224^r.]

367.   Dahmus, Joseph W. "Thomas Arundel and the Baronial Party under Henry IV." *Albion* 16 (1984), 131–49.
[Doubts the strength of a baronial party, doubts that Arundel was its obvious leader; disagrees with K. B. McFarlane.]

368.   Danbury, Elizabeth. "England and French Artistic Propaganda during the Period of the Hundred Years War: Some Evidence from Royal Charters." In *Power, Culture, and Religion in France c. 1350–c. 1550.* Edited by C. T. Allmand. Woodbridge and Wolfeboro, N.H., 1989. Pp. 75–97.
[Also Woodbridge, 1989. Propaganda as found in illuminated initial letters of royal charters in both realms: neglected evidence now explicated.]

369.   Davies, Richard G. "Richard II and the Church in the Years of 'Tyranny'." *JMH* 1 (1975), 329–62.
[The king was often co-operative; spiritual considerations were often a factor.]

370.   Dobson, R. B. "Remembering the Peasants' Revolt, 1381–1981." In item 59. Pp. 1–20.

[The myth of defeated peasants was often used by conservatives to build a "sterile" image; some suggestions for further work.]

371. ———. "Richard III and the Church of York." In item 32. Pp. 130–54.
[Ambitious plans and strong local feelings.]

372. Dockray, Keith R. "Japan and England in the Fifteenth Century: The Onin War and the Wars of the Roses." In item 74. Pp. 143–70.
[Feudalism compared in two societies.]

373. ———. "The Yorkshire Rebellion of 1469." *Ricardian* 6/83 (December 1983), 146–57.
[A series of puzzles revolving around loyalty and factionalism.]

374. ———. "The Political Legacy of Richard III in Northern England." In item 32. Pp. 205–27.
[The mixed fate of his men under Henry VII's rule.]

375. ———. "Richard III and the Yorkshire Gentry, c. 1471–1485." In item 35. Pp. 38–57.
[Richard's successful efforts to win over these families—a key to his policies and government.]

376. Drewett, Richard, and Mark Redhead. *The Trial of Richard III.* Wolfeboro, N.H., 1989; Gloucester, 1985, 1984.

[From a London Weekend Television production, 21 February 1984; the trial for the murder of the princes was conducted with A. J. Pollard, Jeffrey Richards, Jean Ross, and David Starkey prosecuting, Jeremy Potter, Anne Sutton, and C. Veronica Wedgwood defending. Serious fun.]

377.   Driver, J. T. "Worcestershire Knights of the Shire, Part 3: Biographies, F–W." *Worcestershire*, 3rd ser., 5 (1976), 7–22.

[Part 2 (A–E) appeared in ibid. 4 (1974), 19–33; pt. 1, the analysis, ibid., n.s. 40 (1963), 42–64.]

378.   ———. "Richard Quatremains: A Fifteenth Century Squire and Knight of the Shire for Oxfordshire." *Oxon* 51 (1986), 87–103.

[A tale of service and of useful friends (first on behalf of the Lancastrians, then for Richard of York).]

379.   Dunham, William H., Jr. " 'The Books of the Parliament' and 'The Old Record,' 1396–1604." *Speculum* 51 (1976), 694–712.

[Looks at the MSS underlying the work of Camden, Dugdale, and Dethick.]

380.   Dunham, William H., Jr., and Charles T. Wood. "The Right to Rule in England: Depositions and the Kingdom's Authority, 1327–1485." *American Historical Review* 81 (1975), 738–61.

[A Whiggish assessment of Parliament's role and power in the many crises; exception taken in a rejoinder by J. W. McKenna, item 521.]

381. Dyer, Christopher. "Causes of the Revolt in Rural Essex." In item 59. Pp. 21–36.
[A region of nobles and smallholding peasants; some prosopography of identifiable rebels.]

382. ———. "The Rising of 1381 in Suffolk." *Suffolk* 36 (1988), 277–87.

383. Elliott, Bernard. *William, First Lord Hastings (c. 1430–1483)*. Leicester Research Department of the Chamberlain: Music and Books. Leicester, 1984.
[A pamphlet. Biography and local ties.]

384. Ellis, Steve. "Crown, Community, and Government in the English Territories." *History* 71 (1986), 187–204.

385. English, Barbara. *Richard III and the North of England*. Department of Adult and Continuing Education, University of Hull, Primary Sources for Regional and Local History, no. 1. Hull, 1986.
[Facsimiles and transcripts of twenty-two documents; useful teaching device, although some facsimiles are unclear and hard to read. See also item 390.]

386. Ferris, Sumner. "Chaucer at Lincoln (1387): The *Prioress's Tale* as a Political Poem." *Chaucer Rev* 15 (1980–81), 295–321.

[The poem was presented to build support for the king and to win over the duke of Buckingham.]

387.   Ford, C. J. "Piracy or Policy: The Crisis in the Channel, 1400–1403." *TRHS*, 5th ser., 29 (1979), 63–78.
[French initiative and the drift towards the renewal of hostilities.]

388.   Foss, P. J. *The Battle of Bosworth: Where Was It Fought?* Stoke Golding, 1985.

389.   ———. "The Battle of Bosworth: Towards a Reassessment." *Midland* 13 (1988), 21–33.
[To correct topographical uncertainty and confusion.]

390.   Freedman, Rita, and Eileen White, comps. and intro. *Richard III and the City of York*. 2 vols. York City Archives. York, 1983.
[Facsimilies and transcriptions of eight documents, with explanatory pamphlet; similar to item 385.]

391.   Friedrichs, Rhoda L. "Ralph, Lord Cromwell, and the Politics of Fifteenth-Century England." *Nottingham* 32 (1988), 207–27.
[National and local politics woven together.]

392.   Genet, Jean-Philippe. "Droit et histoire en Angleterre: la 'préhistoire' de la révolution historique." *Annales de Bretagne et des Pays de l'Ouest* 87 (1980), 319–66.

393.   ———. "Political Theory and Local Communities in Later Medieval France and England." In item 43. Pp. 19–32.
[Survey of what English treatises on political theory we have: not a very rich harvest.]

394.   ———. "Ecclesiastics and Political Theory in Late Medieval England: The End of a Monopoly." In item 23. Pp. 23–44.
[Survey of English contributions.]

395.   ———. "L'influence française sur la littérature politique anglaise au temps de la France anglaise." In item 25. Pp. 75–90.

396.   Gillespie, James L. "Richard II's Cheshire Archers." *Lancashire & Cheshire* 125 (1974–75), 1–39.
[Who they were, and why, and how effective.]

397.   ———. "Thomas Mortimer and Thomas Molineux: Radcot Bridge and the Appeal of 1397." *Albion* 7 (1975), 161–73.
[An old feud and murder from 1387, still unsettled.]

398.   ———. "Medieval English Multiple Biography: Richard II's Cheshire Archers." *Historian* 40 (1978), 675–85.

399.   ———. "Richard II's Yeomen of the Chamber." *Albion* 10 (1978), 319–29.

[Many were useful servants and yet innocuous enough to weather the changes of 1399.]

400. ———. "Richard II's Archers of the Crown." *JBS* 18 (1979), 14–29.
[How they were organized and paid: not intended as a praetorian guard.]

401. ———. "Sir John Fortescue's Concept of Royal Will." *Nottingham* 23 (1979), 47–65.
[The limited power of Parliament to constrain.]

402. ———. "The Forest and the Trees: Prosopographical Studies and Richard II." *Med Pros* 1/1 (Spring 1980), 9–14.

403. ———. "Richard, Duke of York, as King's Lieutenant in Ireland: The White Rose A-Blooming." *Ricardian* 5/69 (June 1980), 194–201.

404. ———. "Ladies of the Fraternity of St. George and of the Society of the Garter." *Albion* 17 (1985), 259–78.
[Their not-insignificant role.]

405. ———. "Cheshiremen at Blore Heath: A Swan Dive." In item 72. Pp. 77–89.
[Reality may have been less bloody than the local myth maintains.]

406. ———. "Richard II's Knights: Chivalry and Patronage." *JMH* 13 (1987), 143–59.

[Richard believed in chivalry, though practice
may have tarnished the ideal.]

407. ———. "Dover Castle: Key to Richard II's Kingdom?"
Arch Cant 105 (1988), 179–95.
[Examines the appointment of Burley as keeper
in 1385, in terms of domestic politics and French
relations.]

408. Given-Wilson, Chris. "Richard II and His Grand-
father's Will." *EHR* 93 (1978), 320–37.
[How slowly the clauses were carried out; two
ancient petitions are published.]

409. ———. "Purveyance for the Royal Household, 1362–
1413." *BIHR* 56 (1983), 145–63.

410. ———. "The King and the Gentry in Fourteenth
Century England." *TRHS*, 5th ser., 37 (1987), 87–102.
[Royal use of county gentry in local and royal
government.]

411. Goodman, Anthony. "The Military Subcontracts of Sir
Hugh Hastings, 1380." *EHR* 95 (1980), 114–20.
[How a retinue was raised and used; the delega-
tion of power and authority.]

412. ———. "Henry VII and Christian Renewal." In *Religion and Humanism: Papers Read at the Eighteenth
Summer Meeting and the Nineteenth Winter Meeting of
the Ecclesiastical History Society.* Edited by Keith

Robbins. Studies in Church History, 17. Ecclesiastical History Society, 1981. Pp. 115–25.
[To vindicate Henry from his Machiavellian reputation.]

413.   ————. "Responses to Requests in Yorkshire for Military Service under Henry V." *Northern* 17 (1981), 240–52.
[Analysis of a report, c. 1416–20.]

414.   ————. "John of Gaunt." In item 66. Pp. 67–87.
[Biographical, with emphasis on policies and contemporary repute: a progress report, towards his full-length biographical study.]

415.   ————. "John of Gaunt, Portugal's Kingmaker." *History Today* 36 (June 1986), 16–21.

416.   ————. "The Anglo-Scottish Marches in the Fifteenth Century: A Frontier Society?" In *Scotland and England, 1286–1815*. Edited by Roger A. Mason. Edinburgh and Atlantic Highlands, N.J., 1987. Pp. 18–33.
[Movements for disjunction vs. the bonds of common culture.]

417.   ————. "John of Gaunt: Paradigm of the Late Fourteenth-Century Crisis." *TRHS*, 5th ser., 37 (1987), 133–48.

418.   ————. "England and Iberia in the Middle Ages." In item 55. Pp. 73–96.

[Diplomatic, social, and political contact and interaction.]

419. Goodman, Anthony, and D. A. L. Morgan. "The Yorkist Claim to the Throne of Castile." *JMH* 11 (1985), 61–69.
[A minor issue, but kept alive until a final settlement in 1466–67.]

420. Green, Richard F. "An Epitaph for Richard, Duke of York." *Studies in Bibliography* 41 (1988), 218–24.
[Written for the 1476 reburial; from BL MS. Harley 48, fol. 81ᵛ.]

421. Griffiths, Ralph A. "Duke Richard of York's Intentions in 1450 and the Origins of the Wars of the Roses." *JMH* 1 (1975), 187–209.
[York's bill of grievances and first steps towards open opposition; documents published from Beverley town archives.]

422. ———. "Richard, Duke of York and the Royal Household in Wales, 1449–50." *WHR* 8 (1976–77), 14–25.
[The presence of the royal affinity helped assure Lancastrian loyalty.]

423. ———. "William Wawe and His Gang, 1427." *Transactions of the Hampshire Field Club and Archaeological Society* 33 (1977), 89–93.
[Local thuggery and the building of an affinity.]

424.   ———. "The Winchester Sessions of the 1449 Parliament: A Further Comment." *HLQ* 42 (1978–79), 181–91.
[Huntington MS. 202; attendance and a précis of business.]

425.   ———. "Un espion breton à Londres, 1425–29." *Annales de Bretagne et de l'Ouest* 86 (1979), 399–403.
[The death of Ivo Caret.]

426.   ———. "The Sense of Dynasty in the Reign of Henry VI." In item 74. Pp. 13–36.
[Identification and definition, largely as seen through the eyes of the aristocracy.]

427.   ———. "The Hazards of Civil War: The Mountford Family and the 'Wars of the Roses'." *Midland* 5 (1979–80), 1–19.
[With some documents on the local twists and turns of treason.]

428.   ———. *"This Royal Throne of Kings, This Scept'red Isle": The English Realm and Nation in the Later Middle Ages.* Swansea, 1983.
[Inaugural Lecture, 1 November 1983, University College of Swansea.]

429.   ———. "The King's Council and the First Protectorate of the Duke of York, 1453–54." *EHR* 99 (1984), 67–82.
[Harvard Houghton Library MS. Eng. 751: minutes of three council meetings between November 1453 and April 1454.]

430. ———. "The Crown and the Royal Family in Later Medieval England." In item 32. Pp. 15–26.

431. ———. "The English Realm and Dominions and the King's Subjects in the Later Middle Ages." In item 75. Pp. 83–105.
[The idea of a "multi-national" realm was put together.]

432. ———. "Henry Tudor: The Training of a King." *HLQ* 49 (1986), 197–218.

433. Haines, Roy M. " 'Our Master Mariner, Our Sovereign Lord': A Contemporary Preacher's View of King Henry V." *MS* 38 (1976), 85–96.
[A sermon from Bodley MS. 649; Bodley MS. 649, no. 25.]

434. Hammond, P. W. *The Bones of the Princes in Westminster Abbey*. Richard III Society, Upminster, 1976.

435. ———. "The Illegitimate Children of Richard III." *Ricardian* 5/66 (September 1979), 92–96.

436. ———. "The Funeral of Richard Neville, Earl of Salisbury." *Ricardian* 6/87 (December 1984), 410–16.
[Transcription of the account.]

437. Hammond, Peter W., and W. J. White. "The Sons of Edward IV: A Reexamination of the Evidence on Their Deaths and on the Bones in Westminster Abbey." In item 35. Pp. 104–47.

[Thorough study of narrative and forensic
materials; no conclusive evidence to link Tower
bones with the princes.]

438.   Hampton, W. E. "John Hoton of Hunwick and Tudhoe,
Co. Durham, Esquire for the Body to Richard III."
Ricardian 7/88 (March 1985), 2–17.

439.   ———. "Sir Robert Brakenbury of Selaby, Co. Durham." *Ricardian* 7/90 (September 1985), 97–114.
[Loyal service and upward mobility.]

440.   Hanham, Alison. "Hastings Redivivus." *EHR* 90
(1975), 821–27.
[An argument with Bertram Wolffe on the date
of Hastings's death; see *EHR* (1972), 233–48,
and ibid. (1974), 835–44; also items 353, 612,
632.]

441.   Hansen, Harriet M. "The Peasants' Revolt of 1381 and
the Chronicles." *JMH* 6 (1980), 393–415.
[Compares eight accounts of the London scene
and suggests some possible links between MSS.]

442.   Hare, J. N. "The Wiltshire Risings of 1450: Political
and Economic Discontent in Mid-Fifteenth-Century
England." *Southern* 4 (1982), 13–31.
[Local vs. national quarrels, plus local economic
difficulties.]

443.   Harris, O. D. "The Transmission of News—Tudor
Landing." *Ricardian* 4/55 (December 1976), 5–12.

[Where Henry landed and how the news was carried across the realm.]

444.　　——. "... 'Even Here, in Bosworth Field': A Disputed Site of Battle." *Ricardian* 7/92 (March 1986), 194–207.

445.　　Harriss, G. L. "Financial Policy." In item 36. Pp. 159–79.
[Vast sums raised in the context of good governance. These papers by Harriss are major contributions to the volume and to K. B. McFarlane's picture of Henry V as the great late medieval English king.]

446.　　——. "The King and His Magnates." In item 36. Pp. 31–51.

447.　　——. "The Management of Parliament." In item 36. Pp. 137–58.
[This and item 446, sympathetic but perceptive studies, argue that Henry almost always got what he wanted.]

448.　　Hepburn, Frederick. "Some Posthumous Representations of Richard III." *Ricardian* 6/82 (September 1983), 210–19.

449.　　Hickman, Robert M. "Richard III, King or Knave." *Numismatist* 89 (1976), 2405–23.
[Standard historical account to accompany discussion of coinage and minting.]

450.   Hicks, M. A. "The Neville Earldom of Salisbury."
        Wiltshire 72 (1977–78), 141–47.
        [The political and legal paths to the acquisition,
        control, and use of the earldom.]

451.   ———. "The Case of Sir Thomas Cook, 1468." *EHR*
        93 (1978), 81–96.
        [A Lancastrian circle and treason in Yorkist
        times.]

452.   ———. "Dynastic Change and Northern Society: The
        Career of the Fourth Earl of Northumberland, 1470–
        89." *Northern* 14 (1978), 78–107.
        [Political tangles and the earl's relations with
        Henry VII.]

453.   ———. "The Changing Role of the Wydevilles in York-
        ist Politics to 1483." In item 74. Pp. 60–86.
        [Edward's major political error, lucidly expli-
        cated.]

454.   ———. "Descent, Partition, and Extinction: The 'War-
        wick Inheritance'." *BIHR* 52 (1979), 116–28.
        [The resources that provided a power base for
        Gloucester and others.]

455.   ———. "The Beauchamp Trust, 1439–87." *BIHR* 54
        (1981), 135–49.
        [Trusts and enfeoffments of use governed the
        transmission, inheritance, and effective control
        of the estates.]

456. ———. "The Middling Brother: 'False, Fleeting, Perjur'd Clarence'." *Ricardian* 5/72 (March 1981), 302–10. [Previews his full treatment. Also see Wigram, item 633; then Hicks, "Clarence's Calumniator Corrected," *Ricardian* 5/74 (September 1981), 399–401, and "False, Fleeting, Perjur'd Clarence: A Further Exchange," ibid. 6/78 (March 1982), 20–21.]

457. ———. "Restraint, Mediation, and Private Justice: George, Duke of Clarence, as 'Good Lord'." *JLH* 4/2 (1983), 56–71. [A positive assessment of Clarence as a political patron and a force in favor of mediation and arbitration.]

458. ———. "The Warwick Inheritance—Springboard to the Throne." *Ricardian* 6/81 (June 1983), 174–81.

459. ———. "Attainder, Resumption, and Coercion, 1461–1529." *Parliamentary History* 3 (1984), 15–31. [Crises, forfeitures, and royal opportunities: a clear and useful statement.]

460. ———. "Edward IV, the Duke of Somerset, and Lancastrian Loyalism in the North." *Northern* 20 (1984), 23–37. [Why Edward IV was so lenient, at first, after the battle of Towton.]

461. ———. "Counting the Cost of War: The Moleyns Ransom and the Hungerford Land Sales, 1453–87." *Southern* 8 (1986), 11–35.

[Elaborates K. B. McFarlane's views about losses as well as profits; appendix on alienations of land.]

462. ———. "Piety and Lineage in the Wars of the Roses: The Hungerford Experience." In item 32. Pp. 90–108.
[A family's religious history and spiritual life.]

463. ———. *Richard III as Duke of Gloucester: A Study in Character*. University of York, Borthwick Papers, no. 70. Heslington, York, 1986.
[An effort to capture Richard's perspective and the motives for his ambitions and the search for his own niche. Reviewed by A. J. Pollard, "Richard III and the North," *Northern* 23 (1987), 235–37.]

464. ———. "What Might've Been: George Neville, Duke of Bedford, 1465–83: His Identity and Significance." *Ricardian* 7/95 (December 1986), 321–26.

465. ———. "The Yorkshire Rebellion of 1489 Reconsidered." *Northern* 22 (1986), 39–62.
[Detailed examination of a "loyal rebellion."]

466. ———. "The Last Days of Elizabeth, Countess of Oxford." *EHR* 103 (1988), 76–95.
[A deposition (from the PRO) traces the loss of property and the tale of Richard III's coercion.]

467. Hillier, Kenneth. "The Rebellion of 1483: A Study of Sources and Opinions." Pts. 1 and 2. *Ricardian* 6/78 (September 1982), 81–86; 6/80 (March 1983), 146–54.

468.   Hodges, Geoffrey. "The Civil War of 1459 to 1461 in
the Welsh Marches": pt. 1: "The Route of Ludford
Bridge, 12–13 October 1459"; pt. 2: "The Campaign
and Battle of Mortimer's Cross—St. Blaise's Day, 3
February 1461." *Ricardian* 6/84 (March 1984), 186–93;
6/85 (June 1984), 330–45.

469.   ———. *Ludford Bridge and Mortimer's Cross: The
Wars of the Roses in Herefordshire and the Welsh
Marches and the Accession of Edward IV.* Drawings by
John Gibbs. Woonton, Almeley, Herefordshire, 1989.
[A booklet on local events and their significance
in the national context, summing up and extend-
ing his articles in *The Ricardian*].

470.   Holland, P. "The Lincolnshire Rebellion of March
1470." *EHR* 103 (1988), 849–69.
[The roles of Clarence and Warwick re-examined, with Edward IV working behind the
scenes.]

471.   Holmes, George. *The Good Parliament.* Oxford, 1975.
[Late Edward III (1376), but it sets the table for
Ricardian politics.]

472.   Horrox, Rosemary. "Review Article: Recent Work on
Richard III—A Survey." *History* 72 (1987), 279–83.
[Useful guide to the plethora of anniversary-ori-
ented publications.]

473.   ———. *Richard III: A Study of Service.* Cambridge
Studies in Medieval Life and Thought, 4th ser., 11.
Cambridge, 1989; Cambridge and New York, 1989.

[Major study of Ricardian government, patronage, and service from the North to Westminster.]

474.   Housley, Norman. "The Bishop of Norwich's Crusade, May 1383." *History Today* 33 (May 1983), 15–20.
[Bishop Despenser's foolish expedition to the Low Countries.]

475.   Hughes, Mark H. "John Damard, Knight (d. 1392)." *D & C N&Q* 35 (1985), 310–12.
[Courtenay arms depicted in stained glass seen as a sign of political allegiance.]

476.   James, Susan E. "Sir Thomas Parr (1407–61)." *Cumberland & Westmorland* 81 (1981), 15–25.
[Office holding, disputes, and a move into Yorkist circles by the great-grandfather of Henry VIII's queen.]

477.   Jesson, Brian A. "The Battle of Bosworth." *Ricardian* 3/51 (December 1975), 15–20.

478.   Johnson, P. A. *Duke Richard of York, 1411–1460.* Oxford and New York, 1988.
[Oxford Historical Monographs. By necessity, a public life rather than a biography.]

479.   Johnston, Dorothy. "The Interim Years: Richard II and Ireland, 1395–1399." In *England and Ireland in the Later Middle Ages: Essays in Honour of Jocelyn Otway-Ruthven.* Edited by James Lydon. Dublin and Totowa, N.J., 1981. Pp. 175–95.

[Richard's Irish gains of 1395 gradually trickled away.]

480. ———. "The Draft Indenture of Thomas, Duke of Gloucester as Lieutenant of Ireland, 1391." *JSA* 7/3 (1983), 173–82.
[From British Library Cotton MS. Titus B xi, with two illustrations.]

481. ———. "Richard II's Departure from Ireland, July 1399." *EHR* 98 (1983), 785–805.
[The sources and reasons for his failure to return home with adequate military support.]

482. Jones, Michael K. "John Beaufort, Duke of Somerset and the French Expedition of 1443." In item 31. Pp. 79–102.
[Some light on a complicated and tangled tale.]

483. ———. "Edward IV and the Beaufort Family: Conciliation in Early Yorkist Politics." *Ricardian* 6/83 (December 1983), 258–63.

484. ———. "Henry VII, Lady Margaret Beaufort, and the Orléans Ransom." In item 32. Pp. 254–73.
[It took 102 years to collect, but Beaufort-Tudor greed eventually carried the day.]

485. ———. "Richard III and Lady Margaret Beaufort: A Reassessment." In item 35. Pp. 25–37.
[Tougher times were at hand for this difficult lady.]

486. ———. "Sir William Stanley of Holt: Politics and
Family Allegiance in the Late Fifteenth Century."
WHR 14 (1988), 1–22.
[Career and estates of a younger son; the family
stuck together.]

487. ———. "Somerset, York, and the Wars of the Roses."
EHR 104 (1989), 285–307.
[The split of the early 1450s traced to failures in
Normandy and to lack of personal sympathy and
trust.]

488. Jones, Michael K., and Malcolm Underwood. "Lady
Margaret Beaufort." *History Today* 35 (August 1985),
23–30.

489. Jones, William R. "Purveyance for War and the Community of the Realm in Late Medieval England."
Albion 7 (1975), 300–16.
[Growth of an unpopular institution and the
bureaucratic ideology behind it.]

490. ———. "The English Church and Royal Propaganda
during the Hundred Years War." *JBS* 19 (1979),
18–30.
[The use of *pro rege* prayers as arguments for
dynastic publicity.]

491. Keen, Maurice. "Diplomacy." In item 36. Pp. 181–99.
[Compares the treaties of Bretigny (1360) and
Troyes (1420).]

492. ———. "The End of the Hundred Years War: Lancastrian France and Lancastrian Normandy." In item 55. Pp. 297–311.
[Public response to defeat and the growth of national identity.]

493. Kekewich, Margaret. "The Attainder of the Yorkists in 1459: Two Contemporary Accounts." *BIHR* 55 (1982), 25–34.
[Two lively versions: *Somnium Vigilantis* and Whethamstede's *Registrum*.]

494. Kelly, Henry A. "English Kings and the Fear of Sorcery." *MS* 39 (1977), 206–38.
[Delightful "off-beat" material with attention to the duchess of Gloucester and the fall of Clarence.]

495. ———. "The Last Chroniclers of Croyland." *Ricardian* 7/91 (December 1985), 142–77.
[Various candidates discussed; see item 287.]

496. Kenyon, J. R. "Early Artillery Fortifications in England and Wales: A Preliminary Survey and Reappraisal." *Arch J* 138 (1981), 205–40.
[Much late-medieval material, with an emphasis on defensive characteristics of contemporary artillery.]

497. Kirby, John L. "Henry V and the City of London." *History Today* (April 1976), 223–31.

[How the king publicized and popularized his policies.]

498. Knapp, Juanita L. "The Lincolnshire Rebellion and Its Part in the Downfall of the Earl of Warwick." *Ricardian* 4/62 (September 1978), 23–32.
[Events of March 1470 in some detail.]

499. Lander, J. R. "The Crown and Aristocracy in England, 1450–1509." *Albion* 8 (1976), 203–18.
[Sees the aristocracy as largely withdrawn, passive, and compliant.]

500. ———. "Family, 'Friends,' and Politics in Fifteenth-Century England." In item 32. Pp. 27–40.
[Largely devoted to the Nevilles and the Percies.]

501. ———. *The Limitations of English Monarchy in the Later Middle Ages.* Toronto and Buffalo, 1989.
[The Joanne Goodman Lectures (1986). On royal power and constitutionalism.]

502. Leland, John L. "Knights of the Shire in the Parliament of 1386: A Preliminary Study of Factional Affiliations." *Med Pros* 9/1 (Spring 1988), 89–103.

503. ———. "Percy Pardons." *Med Pros* 10/2 (Autumn 1989), 81–96.
[The Percy faction: how wide an avenue upwards did it prove to be?]

504. Leslau, Jack. "Did the Sons of Edward IV Outlive Henry VII?" *Ricardian* 4/62 (September 1978), 2–14.
[Codes and secret messages in Holbein paintings.]

505. Lester, G. A. "The Fifteenth-Century English Heralds and Their Fees: A Case of Forgery?" *JSA* 7/8 (1985), 526–29.
[Material copied from John Paston's "Grete boke."]

506. Lewis, Norman B. "The Feudal Summons of 1385." *EHR* 100 (1985), 729–43.
[Regarding Lewis's 1958 view that the call was based on a desire for prestige; see J. J. N. Palmer, commenting on Lewis's views, ibid., pp. 743–46.]

507. Lewis, P. S. "France and England: The Growth of the Nation State." In *Britain and France, Ten Centuries.* Edited by Douglas Johnson, François Crouzet, and François Bédarida. Folkestone, Kent, 1980. Pp. 32–36, 366–67. Reprinted in item 58. Pp. 235–40.
[French title, *De Guillaume le Conquérant au Marche commun.*]

508. Lewis, William G. "The Exact Date of the Battle of Banbury." *BIHR* 55 (1982), 194–96.
[24 July rather than 26 July, as the Welsh sources would indicate.]

509. Lloyd, Terence H. "A Reconsideration of Two Anglo-Hanseatic Treaties of the Fifteenth Century." *EHR* 102 (1987), 916–33.

[Re-examines M. M. Postan's views on treaties of
1437 and 1474.]

510. Lowe, David E. "The Council of the Prince of Wales
and the Decline of the Herbert Family during the
Second Reign of Edward IV (1471–83)." *Bulletin of the
Board of Celtic Studies/Bwletin y Bwrdd Gwybodau
Celtaidd* 27/2 (1977), 278–97.

511. Maddicott, John R. "The County Community and the
Making of Public Opinion in Fourteenth-Century England." *TRHS*, 5th ser., 28 (1978), 27–43.
[Many examples offered to support the argument
for a widespread political consciousness.]

512. Madison, Kenneth G. "The Seating of the Barons in
Parliament, December 1461." *MS* 37 (1975), 494–503.
[Harley MS. 158, fol. 124^b, published and discussed: was seating a key to rank and prece-
dence?]

513. Mahoney, Dhira B. "Malory's Great Guns." *Viator* 20
(1989), 291–310.
[His "threw engynnes" meant siege engines, not
(necessarily) canons.]

514. Massey, Robert. "The Land Settlement in Lancastrian
Normandy." In item 69. Pp. 76–96.
[Designed to cement a permanent English pres-
ence.]

515. Maxfield, David K. "Pardoners and Property: John
Macclesfield, 1351–1422, Builder of Macclesfield

Castle." *Journal of the Chester Archaeological Society* 69 (1988 for 1986), 79–95.

516. McCulloch, D. M., and E. D. Jones. "Lancastrian Politics, the French War, and the Rise of the Popular Element." *Speculum* 58 (1983), 95–138.
[The links between government, foreign policy, and the public.]

517. Macdougall, Norman A. T. "Foreign Relations: England and France." In *Scottish Society in the Fifteenth Century.* Edited by Jennifer M. Brown. London, 1977. Pp. 101–11.
[Also New York, 1977.]

518. ———. "Richard III and James III: Contemporary Monarchs, Parallel Mythologies." In item 35. Pp. 148–71.
[Compares the role of royal personality and style in judging success.]

519. McHardy, Alison K. "John Buckingham and Thomas Beauchamp, Earl of Warwick." *Nottingham* 19 (1975), 48–52.
[How Buckingham's career depended on Warwick's support.]

520. McIntosh, Marjorie K. "Local Change and Community Control in England, 1465–1500." *HLQ* 49 (1986), 219–43.

521. McKenna, John W. "The Myth of Parliamentary Sovereignty in Late-Medieval England." *EHR* 94 (1979), 481–506.
[A critical response to item 380, on the role of Parliament and king-making.]

522. ———. "How God Became an Englishman." In *Tudor Rule and Revolution: Essays for G. R. Elton from His American Friends.* Edited by DeLloyd J. Guth and John W. McKenna. Cambridge and New York, 1982. Pp. 25–43.
[The role of propaganda and the growth of national consciousness.]

523. McNiven, Peter. "The Scottish Policy of the Percies and the Strategy of the Rebellion of 1403." *BJRUL* 62 (1979–80), 498–530.
[Family policy and northern ambitions were among the motivating factors.]

524. ———. "The Men of Cheshire and the Rebellion of 1403." *Lancashire & Cheshire* 129 (1980), 1–29.
[Heavy Cheshire involvement; most survivors quickly made their peace.]

525. ———. "Prince Henry and the English Political Crisis of 1412." *History* 65 (1980), 1–16.
[Both men gained: Henry IV reasserted himself, and Hal was assured of his eventual succession.]

526. ———. "Legitimacy and Consent: Henry IV and the Lancastrian Title, 1399–1406." *MS* 44 (1982), 470–88.

[Dynastic and statutory attempts to assert legitimacy.]

527.   ———. "The Problem of Henry IV's Health, 1405–1413." *EHR* 100 (1985), 747–72.
[No convincing evidence of the nature of Henry's illness or of its effects on governance.]

528.   ———. *Heresy and Politics in the Reign of Henry IV: The Burning of John Badby.* Woodbridge, 1987; Woodbridge and Wolfeboro, N.H., 1987.
[Sets the persecution of Lollards into the context of Henry's search for political consensus; see item 592.]

529.   Milner, John. "Sir Simon Felbrigg, K.G.: The Lancastrian Revolution and Personal Fortune." *Norfolk* 37 (1978), 84–91.
[He fell with Richard II, but he kept local status as he switched sides.]

530.   More, Thomas, Sir. *The History of King Richard III and Selections from the English and Latin Poems.* Edited by Richard S. Sylvester. St. Thomas More Project, Yale University. New Haven, 1976.
[A volume in *The Yale Edition of the Works of St. Thomas More: Selected Works.* Introduction, with text (pp. 3–96) in modernized English.]

531.   Morgan, D. A. L. "The House of Policy: The Political Role of the Late Plantagenet Household, 1422–85." In *The English Court: From the Wars of the Roses to the*

Civil War. Edited by David Starkey et al. London and New York, 1987. Pp. 25–70.
[The mid-fifteenth century as a watershed in household development and functions.]

532. Myers, Alec R. "A Parliamentary Debate of 1449." *BIHR* 51 (1978), 78–83.
[Brief note, and transcript of a College of Arms MS; reprinted in item 62.]

533. ———. "Parliament, 1422–1509." In item 21. Pp. 141–84.

534. Orme, Nicholas. "The Education of Edward V." *BIHR* 57 (1984), 119–30. Reprinted in item 65. No. 10, pp. 177–88.
[Prints a 1435 ordinance for the duke of Norfolk plus two (1473 and 1483) written for Prince Edward.]

535. Osberg, Richard. "The Jesse Tree in the 1432 London Entry of Henry VI: Messianic Kingship and the Rule of Justice." *JMRS* 16 (1986), 213–32.
[Examination of the use of iconography, poetry, and symbolism in public events.]

536. Parkhouse, Carole. "The Career of a Fifteenth Century Lawyer: Miles Metcalfe of Wenslydale." *Ricardian* 8/109 (September 1989), 174–79.
[Tied into Richard's service.]

537. Payling, Simon J. "The Coventry Parliament of 1459: A Privy Seal Writ Concerning the Election of Knights of the Shire." *HR* 60 (1987), 349–52.
[Sheriffs were not told whom to return; the writ is PRO C219/16/5/32.]

538. ———. "The Widening Franchise—Parliamentary Election in Lancastrian Nottinghamshire." In item 84. Pp. 167–85.
[Discussion of statutes and then details for the 1450s and 1460s: small freeholders were important.]

539. ———. "The Ampthill Dispute: A Study in Aristocratic Lawlessness and the Breakdown of Lancastrian Government." *EHR* 104 (1989), 881–907.
[Henry Holland's self-help and how Cromwell, the Percies, and the Nevilles all got caught up: a case study of the ripple effect.]

540. Pedersen, Frederik. "The German Hanse and the Peasants' Revolt of 1381." *BIHR* 57 (1984), 92–98.
[From the perspective of the German merchants in London.]

541. Petre, James. "The Nevilles of Brancepath and Raby, 1425–1499": pt. 1: "1425–1469: Neville vs. Neville"; pt. 2: "1470–1499: Recovery and Collapse." *Ricardian* 5/75 (December 1981), 418–35; 6/76 (March 1982), 2–13.

542.   Philips, M. J. "The Battle of Bosworth: Further Reflection on the Battlefield Site." *Ricardian* 7/96 (March 1987), 350–62.
[Supplemented by Margaret Condon, "Bosworth Field: A Footnote to a Controversy," ibid., pp. 363–65.]

543.   Phillpotts, Christopher. "The French Plan of Battle during the Agincourt Campaign." *EHR* 99 (1984), 59–66.
[The plan had some flaws: BL Cotton MS. Caligula, D v, fols. 43ᵛ–44.]

544.   Pistono, Stephen. "Henry IV and the English Privateers." *EHR* 90 (1975), 322–30.
[English maritime enterprise and self-help messed up diplomatic efforts; Henry lacked the strength to crack down.]

545.   ———. "Flanders and the Hundred Years War: The Quest for the *Treve Marchande*." *BIHR* 49 (1976), 185–97.
[The failure of the peace talks of 1403.]

546.   ———. "Henry IV and Charles VI: The Confirmation of the Twenty-Eight-Year Truce." *JMH* 3 (1977), 353–65.
[A diplomatic minuet that kept both sides short of a declaration of war.]

547.   ———. "Henry IV and T. Lawley, Privateer, 1399–1408." *Devonshire* 111 (1979), 145–63.

[A case study on the themes developed in item 546.]

548. Pollard, A. J. "The Northern Retainers of Richard Neville, Earl of Salisbury." *Northern* 11 (1975), 52–69.
[Information drawn from the Clervaux cartulary.]

549. ———. "The Tyranny of Richard III." *JMH* 3 (1977), 147–65.
[The reliance on northerners helped stoke the myth of tyranny.]

550. ———. "Lord Fitzhugh's Rising in 1470." *BIHR* 52 (1979), 170–75.
[A serious threat; some of the personnel analyzed.]

551. ———. "The Richmondshire Community of Gentry during the Wars of the Roses." In item 74. Pp. 37–59.
[Careful study of local networks and their political commitments.]

552. ———. "North, South, and Richard III." *Ricardian* 5/74 (September 1981), 384–89.
[Many of our sources reflect a southeastern bias.]

553. ———. *John Talbot and the War in France, 1427–1453*. Studies in History, no. 35. Royal Historical Society, 1983.
[Basic scholarly study of the major commander.]

554.   ———. *The Middleham Connection: Richard III and Richmondshire, 1471–1485.* University of York Lecture, June 1983: Old School Arts Workshop. Middleham, 1988, 1983.

555.   ———. "St. Cuthbert and the Hog: Richard III and the County Palatine of Durham, 1471–85." In item 32. Pp. 109–29.
[How a foothold was consolidated: personnel and activities.]

556.   Post, J. B. "The Peace Commissions of 1381." *EHR* 91 (1976), 98–101.
[In the footsteps of the special commissions.]

557.   ———. "The Obsequies of John of Gaunt." *Guildhall* 5 (1981), 1–12.
[The funeral and the executors' discharge of their duties.]

558.   Powicke, Michael R. "War as a Means to Peace: Some Late Medieval Themes." In item 34. Pp. 217–24.
[Interesting views on war and peace as a two-sided coin.]

559.   Pratt, John H. "Was Chaucer's Knight Really a Mercenary?" *Chaucer Rev* 22 (1987–88), 8–27.
[Where Englishmen were fighting, and the arguments for "just war" and professionalism.]

560.   Prescott, A. J. "Essex Rebel Bands in London." In item 59. Pp. 55–66.

[Material drawn from trespass actions shows a fragmented movement.]

561. Prestwich, Michael. "An Estimate by the Commons of Royal Revenue in England under Richard II." *Parliamentary History* 3 (1984), 147–55.
[The Commons had an unrealistic view of the revenue; Durham Dean & Chapter Muniment, Locellus, 20, n. 7.]

562. Pronay, Nicholas, and John Taylor, eds. and trans. "A Colchester Account of the Proceedings of the Parliament of 1485 by the Representatives of the Borough of Colchester, Thomas Christmas and John Vertue" and "A Draft of the Protestation of the Speaker." In Nicholas Pronay and John Taylor, *Parliamentary Texts of the Later Middle Ages.* Oxford and New York, 1980. Pp. 77–193 and 197–201, respectively.
[The second document is probably from 1504.]

563. Pugh, T. B. "Richard Plantagenet (1411–60), Duke of York, as the King's Lieutenant in France and Ireland." In item 75. Pp. 107–41.
[Not much to show for so many opportunities.]

564. ———. "The Southampton Plot of 1415." In item 32. Pp. 62–89.

565. ———. *Henry V and the Southampton Plot of 1415.* Southampton Records Ser., 30. Southampton, 1988; Wolfeboro Falls, N.H., 1988.

[Thorough study of the plot, with scepticism about its reality; appendices treat the confessions and the sources.]

566.   Rawcliffe, Carole. "Baronial Councils in the Later Middle Ages." In item 74. Pp. 87–108.
[That they worked and how well they worked.]

567.   ———. "The Great Lord as Peacekeeper: Arbitration by English Noblemen and Their Councils in the Later Middle Ages." In item 33. Pp. 34–54.
[Many examples and details of their importance and widespread use; appendix on arbitration between John Talbot and Lord Sudeley, 1450.]

568.   ———. "A Tudor Nobleman as Archivist: The Papers of the Third Duke of Buckingham." *JSA* 5/5 (April 1986), 294–300.

569.   ———. "Richard, Duke of York, the King's 'Obeisant liegeman': A New Source for the Protectorates of 1454 and 1455." *HR* 60 (1987), 232–39.
[Two Battle Abbey MSS in the Huntington Library; Cecily to the queen and to York and Edward, earl of March.]

570.   ———. "The Politics of Marriage in Later Medieval England: William, Lord Botreaux, and the Hungerfords." *HLQ* 51 (1988), 161–75.
[An agreement defining a merger: a marriage contract of 1421.]

571. Rawcliffe, Carole, and Susan Flower. "English Noblemen and Their Advisers: Consultation and Collaboration in the Later Middle Ages." *JBS* 25 (1986), 157–77.
[Personnel, range of skills, and other such problems in a concise survey.]

572. Rhodes, Philip. "The Physical Deformity of Richard III." *British Medical Journal* 2, no. 6103 (1977), 1650–52.

573. Richmond, Colin F. "The Nobility and the Wars of the Roses, 1459–61." *Nottingham* 21 (1977), 71–86.
[Who was on which side, when, and on what occasions; useful tabulations where the sources are often vague and reticent.]

574. ———. "Thomas, Lord Morley (d. 1416) and the Manor of Hingham." *Norfolk* 39 (1984), 1–12.
[Lands and income: closer to £400 than the £600 H. L. Gray attributed to him in 1934.]

575. ———. "The Battle of Bosworth." *History Today* 35 (August 1985), 16–22.
[How politics were carried to and enacted upon the battlefield.]

576. ———. "1485 and All That, or What Was Going on at the Battle of Bosworth." In item 35. Pp. 172–206.
[Loyalty of various peers and affinities: Edward IV's measures that may have undermined loyalty to Richard.]

577. ———. "The Death of Edward V." *Northern* 25 (1988),
      278–80.
      [27 June 1483, according to an entry in the
      Anlaby cartulary.]

578. Roberts, David E. *The Battle of Stoke Field, 1487.*
      Newark and Sherwood District Council, 1987.

579. Robertson, Craig A. "Local Government and the King's
      'Affinity' in Fifteenth Century Leicestershire and War-
      wickshire." *Leicestershire* 52 (1976–77), 37–45.
      [Royal partisanship as a strong factor in local
      and gentry political life.]

580. Rose, Susan. "Henry V's *Grace Dieu* and the Mutiny at
      Sea: Some New Evidence." *Mariner's Mirror* 63 (1977),
      3–7.
      [With a note on the ship's dimensions by
      Michael Prynne (pp. 6–7).]

581. Rosenthal, Joel T. "The Lancastrian Peerage, 1399–
      1461." *Studies in Medieval Culture* 8 and 9 (1976),
      181–86.
      [A quantitative overview and some computerized
      tabulations.]

582. ———. "Kings, Continuity, and Ecclesiastical Benefac-
      tion in Fifteenth Century England." In item 72. Pp.
      161–75.

583. Roskell, J. S. *The Impeachment of Michael de la Pole,
      Earl of Suffolk in 1386: In the Context of the Reign of
      Richard II.* Manchester, 1984.

[General treatment and then a detailed analysis of the articles of impeachment.]

584. Ross, Charles. "Rumour, Propaganda and Popular Opinion during the War of the Roses." In item 31. Pp. 15–32.
[Propaganda was important, if not necessarily successful, and public opinion was a force.]

585. Rowling, Marjorie A. "New Evidence on the Disseisin of the Pastons from Their Norfolk Manor of Gresham, 1448–51." *Norfolk* 40 (1989), 302–08.
[They retook the house and manor; two letters in Norman Davis's edition should be redated.]

586. Rowney, Ian. "Arbitration in Gentry Disputes of the Later Middle Ages." *History* 67 (1982), 367–76.
[Valuable procedure, especially when the courts could not or would not act.]

587. ———. "The Curzons of Fifteenth-Century Derbyshire." *Derbyshire* 103 (1983), 107–17.
[Never rich enough for major power, but an active and affluent local family.]

588. ———. "Government and Patronage in the Fifteenth Century: Staffordshire, 1439–59." *Midland* 8 (1983), 49–69.
[The Staffords at the center, but only mixed success.]

589. ———. "The Hastings Affinity in Staffordshire and the Honour of Tutbury." *BIHR* 57 (1984), 35–45.

590.   ————. "Resources and Retaining in Yorkist England: William, Lord Hastings and the Honour of Tutbury." In item 69. Pp. 139–55.
[The difficult steps between landholding and the building of a reliable affinity.]

591.   Sanderlin, S. "Chaucer and Ricardian Politics." *Chaucer Rev* 22 (1987–88), 175–84.
[Chaucer was a "cautious nonpartisan."]

592.   Saul, Nigel. "Politics, Privilege, and Piety in Late Medieval England." *Parliamentary History* 7 (1988), 139–46.
[Review article of Jeffrey H. Denton and John P. Dooley, *Representatives of the Lower Clergy in Parliament, 1295–1340*, Royal Historical Society Studies in History, no. 50 (1987), and P. McNiven, item 528.]

593.   Sayer, Michael. "Norfolk Involvement in Dynastic Conflict, 1469–1471 and 1483–1487." *Norfolk* 36 (1979), 305–26.
[How local families chose sides, and the gradual waning of aristocratic power.]

594.   Sayles, George O. "Richard II in 1381 and 1399." *EHR* 94 (1979), 820–29.
[Some Exchequer documents as evidence for royal activity and energy.]

595.   ————. "The Deposition of Richard II: Three Lancastrian Narratives." *BIHR* 54 (1981), 257–70.

[Two of the accounts published here, giving views independent of the usual chronicle sources.]

596. Sherborne, J. W. "The Cost of English Warfare with France in the Later Fourteenth Century." *BIHR* 50 (1977), 135–50.
[Covers 1361–81: loans, taxes, and parliamentary suspicion.]

597. ———. "Charles VI and Richard II." In *Froissart: Historian*. Edited by J. J. N. Palmer. Woodbridge, 1981; Totowa, N.J., 1981. Pp. 50–63.
[Some gaps and weaknesses in Froissart's view of the two men.]

598. ———. "Perjury and the Lancastrian Revolution of 1399." *WHR* 14 (1988), 217–41.
[The extent to which Henry lied about his ambition after his return from exile.]

599. Smith, Anthony. "Litigation and Politics: Sir John Fastolf's Defence of His English Property." In item 69. Pp. 59–75.
[A rational policy; litigation was not his first resort.]

600. Staniland, Kay. "Royal Entry into the World." In item 84. Pp. 297–313.
[Henry VII's use of pomp and circumstance, especially accompanying royal births.]

601.   Stow, George B., Jr. "Thomas Walsingham, John Malvern, and the *Vita Ricardi Secundi*, 1377–1381: A Reassessment." *MS* 39 (1977), 490–97.
[See item 305.]

602.   ———. "Richard II in Thomas Walsingham's Chronicles." *Speculum* 59 (1984), 68–102.
[Close reading of different versions of the portrait given us by the St. Albans school.]

603.   ———. "Richard II in Jean Froissart's *Chroniques*." *JMH* 11 (1985), 333–45.
[More critical of Richard than we might expect.]

604.   ———. "Chronicles versus Records: The Character of Richard II." In item 34. Pp. 155–76.
[The record sources support the critical views offered in so many of the chronicles.]

605.   Strong, Patrick, and Felicity Strong. "The Last Will and Codicils of Henry V." *EHR* 96 (1981), 79–102.
[Document of June 1421: Eton College Rec. 59 is published, plus three enrolled letters patent.]

606.   Styles, Dorothy, and Christopher T. Allmand. "The Coronation of Henry VI." *History Today* 32 (May 1982), 28–33.

607.   Sutton, Anne. "Richard III's 'tytle and right': A New Discovery." *Ricardian* 4/57 (1977), 2–8.

[A statement of the king's right, from April 1484, found in the records of the Ironmongers' Company.]

608.   ———. " 'A Curious Searcher for our Weal Public': Richard III, Piety, Chivalry, and the Concept of the 'Good Prince'." In item 35. Pp. 58–90.
[Views of princely and public behavior, and Richard's piety and upbringing.]

609.   ———. "Richard Gowle, Supplier of Mercery to Richard III and Anne Neville." *Ricardian* 7/93 (June 1986), 238–45.

610.   Theilmann, John M. "The Miracles of King Henry VI of England." *Historian* 42 (1979–80), 456–71.
[Some statistical analysis and popular piety.]

611.   ———. "A Dramaturgical Perspective on Ricardian Absolutism." *Mediaevalia* 10 (1988 for 1984), 255–77.
[Politics and ritual: a discussion informed by anthropological material.]

612.   Thomson, John A. F. "Richard III and Lord Hastings: A Problematical Case Reviewed." *BIHR* 48 (1975), 22–30.
[The argument about the date of accession and execution: see items 353, 440.]

613.   ———. "John de la Pole, Duke of Suffolk." *Speculum* 54 (1979), 528–42.
[Political and biographical.]

614. Tillotson, J. H. "Peasant Unrest in the England of Richard II: Some Evidence from Royal Records." *Historical Studies* 16 (1974–75), 1–16.

615. Tuck, J. A. "Why Men Fought in the Hundred Years War." *History Today* 33 (April 1983), 35–40.
["Patriotism, propaganda, and profit."]

616. ———. "Nobles, Commons, and the Great Revolt of 1381." In item 46. Pp. 194–212.
[How the upper classes saw the revolt, and significant consequences after 1381.]

617. ———. "War and Society in the Medieval North." *Northern* 21 (1985), 33–52.
[Border warfare was big and important business.]

618. ———. "The Emergence of a Northern Nobility, 1250–1400." *Northern* 22 (1986), 1–17.

619. Vale, M. G. A. "New Techniques and Old Ideals: The Impact of Artillery on War and Chivalry at the End of the Hundred Years War." In item 3. Pp. 57–72.
[Growing importance of canon: ordnance generally remained conservative.]

620. Virgoe, Roger. "The Recovery of the Howards in East Anglia, 1485 to 1529." In item 52. Pp. 1–20.

621. ———. "The Murder of James Andrews: Suffolk Factions in the 1430s." *Suffolk* 34 (1980), 263–68.

[An early chapter in the feud between the dukes
of Suffolk and Norfolk.]

622. ———. "The Crown, Magnates, and Local Government
in Fifteenth Century East Anglia." In item 43. Pp.
72–87.
[Penetrating study of how local society
"worked."]

623. ———. "Sir John Risley (1443–1512), Courtier and
Councillor." *Norfolk* 38 (1982), 140–48.
[Knight of the Body to Henry VII; had served
Edward IV and rose again.]

624. ———. "An Election Dispute of 1483." *HR* 60 (1987),
24–44.
[Common plea role published: case study of a
dispute in which many, at high and middling
levels, got involved.]

625. Walker, J. A. "John Holand, a Fifteenth-Century Admiral." *Mariner's Mirror* 65 (1979), 235–42.
[Biographical; his seals as admiral depicted.]

626. Walker, Simon K. "Lordship and Lawlessness in the
Palatinate of Lancaster, 1370–1400." *JBS* 28 (1989),
325–48.
[John of Gaunt a captive as well as instigator of
bastard feudalism.]

627. Warnicke, Retha M. "Lord Morley's Statements about
Richard III." *Albion* 15 (1983), 173–78.

[He wrote in the 1550s: a semi-independent and hostile source, at best.]

628.   ———. "The Lady Margaret, Countess of Richmond: A Noblewoman of Independent Wealth and Status." *Fifteenth-Century Studies* 9 (1984), 215–48.

629.   ———. "The Physical Deformities of Anne Boleyn and Richard III: Myth *and* Reality." *Pargeron,* n.s. 4 (1986), 135–53.
[Little contemporary evidence in either case.]

630.   Weiss, M. "A Power in the North? The Percies in the Fifteenth Century." *Historical Journal* 19 (1976), 501–09.
[Towards a revision concerning the seriousness of their threat to the king, and how thoroughly Henry VII had to reduce their regional power.]

631.   White, W. J. "The Death and Burial of Henry VI: A Review of the Facts and Theories." Pts. 1 and 2. *Ricardian* 6/78 (September 1982), 70–80; 6/79 (December 1982), 106–17.
[No reason to implicate Richard of Gloucester.]

632.   Wigram, Isolde. "The Death of Hastings." *Ricardian* 3/150 (1975), 27–29.
[Sides with B. Wolffe: items 353, 440, 636.]

633.   ———. "Clarence Still Perjur'd." *Ricardian* 4/73 (June 1981), 352–55.

[Exchange with Hicks, item 456; followed by Wigram's "False, Fleeting, Perjur'd Clarence: A Further Exchange," *Ricardian* 6/78 (March 1982), 17–20.]

634.   Williams, Brian D. "The Foreign Policy of Edward IV, 1475–83, and the Anglo-Breton Marriage Alliance of 1481." *Ricardian* 7/94 (September 1986), 270–80.

635.   Williams, Daniel. " 'A Place Mete for Twoo Battayles to Encountre': The Siting of the Battle of Bosworth, 1485." *Ricardian* 7/90 (September 1985), 86–96.

636.   Wolffe, Bertram P. "Hastings Reinterred." *EHR* 91 (1976), 813–24.
[Why he sticks with 13 June as date of execution; and see items 353, 632.]

637.   Wood, Charles T. "The Deposition of Edward V." *Traditio* 31 (1975), 247–86. Revised and reprinted in item 320. Pp. 152–74.
[Examination of Richard's claim and the role of Parliament.]

638.   ———. "Queens, Queans, and Kingship: An Inquiry into Theories of Royal Legitimacy in Late Medieval England and France." In *Order and Innovation in the Middle Ages: Essays in Honor of Joseph R. Strayer.* Edited by William C. Jordan, Bruce McNab, and Teofilo F. Ruíz. Princeton, 1976. Pp. 385–400, 562–66. Revised and reprinted in item 320. Pp. 12–28.
[Mostly on France, but interesting comparisons.]

639.   ———. "Richard III, William, Lord Hastings, and
Friday the Thirteenth." In item 320. Pp. 155–68.
[An unravelling of the details surrounding the
fall of Hastings.]

640.   Wood, Robert G. E. "Essex Manorial Records and the
Revolt." In item 59. Pp. 67–98.
[Wide destruction of and gaps in manorial records, but a quick return to normalcy; gazetteer
of manors affected.]

641.   Woodward, G. W. O. *King Richard III*. London, 1977.
[First published in 1972. A Pitkin Pride of Britain pictorial guide to Richard's life and times.]

V. CONSTITUTIONAL, ADMINISTRATIVE, AND LEGAL HISTORY

642. Alford, John A. *Piers Plowman: A Glossary of Legal Diction*. Piers Plowman Studies, 5. Cambridge, 1988.
[All legal terms used in the poem defined and discussed.]

643. Allmand, Christopher T. "The Civil Lawyers." In item 17. Pp. 155–80.
[Their education and training, role, and some of their writings.]

644. Archer, Rowena E., and B. E. Ferme. "Testamentary Procedure with Special Reference to the Executrix." *Reading* 15 (1989), 3–34.
[Women's rights and roles.]

645. Armstrong, C. A. J. "Sir John Fastolf and the Law of Arms." In item 3. Pp. 46–56. Reprinted in item 4. Pp. 123–33.
[Policies and practices covering prisoners and the sharing of ransoms.]

646. Arnold, Carol. "The Commissions of the Peace for the West Riding of Yorkshire, 1437–1504." In item 69. Pp. 116–38.

[Who served, and the political implications of the commissions.]

647. Arnold, Morris S., ed. *Year Books of Richard II: 2 Richard II, 1378–1379.* Year Books Ser., vol. 1. Ames Foundation, 1975.

648. ———, ed. *Select Cases of Trespass from the King's Courts, 1307–1399.* 2 vols. Publications of the Selden Society, vols. 100, 103 (1985, 1987).
[Mostly pre-1377, but a useful glimpse at the law.]

649. Baker, J. H. "The Inns of Court in 1388." *LQR* 92 (1976), 184–87. Reprinted in item 9. Pp. 3–6.

650. ———. "The Law Merchant and the Common Law before 1700." *Cambridge Law Review* 38 (1979), 295–322. Reprinted in item 9. Pp. 341–68.

651. ———. "The English Legal Profession, 1450–1550." In *Lawyers in Early Modern Europe and America.* Edited by Wilfrid Prest. London, 1981. Pp. 16–41. Reprinted in item 9. Pp. 75–98.
[Also New York, 1981.]

652. ———. "The Pecunes." *LQR* 98 (1982), 204–09. Reprinted in item 9. Pp. 171–75.
[Galleries at Lincoln's Inn in the 1480s.]

653. ———. "The Inns of Court and Chancery as Voluntary Associations." *Quaderni Fiorentini per la Storia del*

pensiero giuridico Moderno 11/12 (1982–83), 9–38. Reprinted in item 9. Pp. 45–74.

654. ———. "Lawyers Practicing in Chancery, 1474–1486." *JLH* 4 (1983), 54–76.
[Londoners who were pledges in Chancery.]

655. ———. "English Law and the Renaissance." *Cambridge Law Journal* 44 (1985), 46–61. Reprinted in item 9. Pp. 461–77.
[Learned, of course, though mostly concerned with the Tudors and F. W. Maitland.]

656. ———. "The Inns of Court and Legal Doctrine." In *Lawyers and Laymen: Studies in the History of Law Presented to Professor Dafydd Jenkins on His Seventy-Fifth Birthday, Gwyl Ddewi 1986.* Edited by T. M. Charles-Edwards, Morfydd E. Owen, and D. B. Walters. Cardiff, 1986. Pp. 274–86.
[Mainly on fifteenth-century developments and the role of the Inns in legal education.]

657. ———. "Learning Exercises in the Medieval Inns of Court and Chancery." In item 9. Pp. 7–23.
[A discussion of legal education, not previously published.]

658. Baker, J. H., and S. F. C. Milsom, comps. *Sources of English Legal History: Private Law to 1750.* London, 1986; Stoneham, Mass. and London, 1986.
[A source book, with many cases from 1377–1485. Brief summation of cases and decisions.]

659.   Barnes, Patricia M. "The Chancery *corpus cum causa* File, 10–11 Edward IV." In item 50. Pp. 429–76. [A list of Chancery suits and an edition of some documents.]

660.   Beckerman, J. S. "The Forty-Shilling Jurisdictional Limit in Medieval English Personal Actions." In *Legal History Studies, 1972: Papers Presented to the Legal History Conference, Aberystwyth, 18–21 July 1972.* Edited by Dafydd Jenkins. Cardiff, 1975. Pp. 110–17.

661.   Bellamy, John G. *Criminal Law and Society in Late Medieval and Tudor England.* Gloucester, 1984; New York, 1984. [Both the substance of the law and legal procedures are treated.]

662.   ———. *Bastard Feudalism and the Law.* London, 1989; Portland, Ore., 1989. [The title hides its considerable value for social and political history; runs into early Tudor times.]

663.   Bland, D. S. "Learning Exercises and Readers at the Inns of Chancery in the Fifteenth and Sixteenth Centuries." *LQR* 95 (1979), 144–52. [By the time the sources permit a detailed examination the Inns had become a well-organized system for legal education.]

664.   Blatcher, Marjorie. *The Court of King's Bench, 1450– 1550: A Study in Self-Help.* University of London,

Institute of Advanced Legal Studies, Legal Ser., 12. London and Atlantic Highlands, N.J., 1978.
[The court's importance and level of activity revived in these years; an important case study.]

665.   Bolton, W. F. "Middle English in the Law Reports and Records of 11–13 Richard II." *ELN* 24 (1986), 1–8.
[Year Books and plea rolls as a source to study the development of the language.]

666.   Bonfield, L. "The Nature of Customary Law in the Manor Courts of Medieval England." *Comparative Studies in Society and History* 31 (1989), 514–34.

667.   Bonfield, L., and L. R. Poos. "The Development of the Deathbed Transfer in Medieval English Manorial Courts." *Cambridge Law Journal* 47 (1988), 403–27.
[Important implications both for legal and social and for family studies.]

668.   Brand, Paul. "Courtroom and Schoolroom: The Education of Lawyers in England Prior to 1400." *HR* 60 (1987), 147–65.
[Argues for organized education before the Inns flourished in the fifteenth century.]

669.   Braswell, Mary F. "Sin, the Lady, and the Law: The English Noble Woman in the Late Middle Ages." *Medievalia et Humanistica*, n.s. 14 (1986), 81–101.

670.   Brown, Sandra. *The Medieval Courts of the York Minster Peculiar.* University of York, Borthwick Papers, no. 66. York, 1984.

[Six jurisdictional peculiars in Yorkshire, ten in Nottinghamshire.]

671.   Burgess, L. A., ed. *The Southampton Terrier of 1454.* Introduction by L. A. Burgess, P. D. A. Harvey, and A. D. Saunders. Historical Manuscripts Commission, no. 21, in joint publication with Southampton Records Ser., vol. 15. HMSO, 1976.

672.   Burson, Malcolm C. ". . . For the Sake of My Soul: Activities of a Medieval Executor." *Archives* 13, no. 59 (1978), 131–36.
[Tracking down an Exeter case study, c. 1415.]

673.   Carpenter, Christine. "Law, Justice and Landowners in Late Medieval England." *L & HR* 1 (1983), 205–37.
[Uses the Mountford case (Warwickshire) to illustrate the incidence of corruption and social instability.]

674.   Chaplais, Pierre. *English Medieval Diplomatic Practice.* 2 vols. in 3. HMSO, 1975–82.
[Part 1: *Documents and Interpretation*; pt. 2: *Plates.* An elaborate source book with many late medieval documents and illustrative plates.]

675.   Clark, Elaine. "Debt Litigation in a Late Medieval English Village." In item 70. Pp. 247–79.
[Writtle, Essex: an active scene for loans, litigation, and economic stratification.]

676.   ———. "Medieval Labor Law and English Local Courts." *AJLH* 27 (1983), 330–53.

[Level and types of activity, with an appendix on statutes of labor, 1349–1445.]

677. ———. "The Custody of Children in English Manorial Courts." *L & HR* 3 (1985), 333–48.

[Mostly pre-1377, but treats interesting problems that do not vary much afterwards.]

678. Coleman, Olive. "What Figures? Some Thoughts on the Use of Information by Medieval Governments." In item 18. Pp. 96–112.

[How accessible were data to various parties?]

679. Condon, Margaret M. "A Wiltshire Sheriff's Notebook, 1464–65." In item 50. Pp. 409–29.

[A year in the public life of one George Darell.]

680. Crowder, C. M. D. "Peace and Justice around 1400: A Sketch." In item 75. Pp. 53–81.

[How they were treated in sermons, petitioned for in Parliament, and practiced in some specific instances.]

681. Crowley, D. A. "The Later History of Frankpledge." *BIHR* 48 (1975), 1–15.

[A neglected topic in late medieval history.]

682. Cuttino, G. P. *English Medieval Diplomacy.* Bloomington, Ind., 1985.

[A survey and discussion of methods and government agencies, moving through crises and problems. Chapter 1 is a general discussion; ch. 4 treats the Hundred Years War.]

683. Danbury, Elizabeth. "The Decoration and Illumination of Royal Charters in England, 1250–1500: An Introduction." In item 55. Pp. 157–79.
[Examples and illustrations; an unusual approach.]

684. Dobson, R. B., ed. *York City Chamberlains' Account Rolls, 1396–1500*. Publications of the Surtees Society, vol. 192 (1980 for 1978 and 1979).
[Appendix of York mayors and chamberlains.]

685. Donahue, Charles, Jr. "Lyndwood's Gloss *propriarum uxorum*: Marital Property and the *Ius Commune* in Fifteenth-Century England." In *Europäisches Rechtsdenken in Geschichte und Gegenwart. Festschrift für Helmut Coing zum 70. Geburtstag.* Edited by Norbert Horn in conjunction with Klaus Luig and Alfred Sollner. 2 vols. Munich, 1982. Vol. 1, pp. 19–37.

686. Drury, J. Linda. "Durham Palatinate Forest Law and Administration, Especially in Weardale up to 1400." *Arch Ael*, 5th ser., 6 (1978), 87–105.
[Varying levels of episcopal effectiveness in this area of administration.]

687. Elvey, E. M., ed. and intro. *The Courts of the Archdeaconry of Buckingham, 1483–1523.* Buckinghamshire Record Society, no. 19 (1975).
[Transcripts of court business, with numerous wills.]

688. Garay, Kathleen E. "Women and Crime in Later Medieval England: An Examination of the Evidence of the Courts of Gaol Delivery, 1388 to 1409." *Florilegium* 1 (1979), 87–109.

689. Gardiner, Dorothy M., ed. and intro. *A Calendar of Early Chancery Proceedings Relating to West Country Shipping, 1388–1493.* Devon and Cornwall Record Society, n.s., vol. 21 (1976).
[Economic, diplomatic, and political questions all covered.]

690. Garratt, H. J. H. *Derbyshire Feet of Fines 1323–1546.* Derbyshire Record Society, vol. 11 (1985).
[Garratt calendared; valuable introduction to this type of document by Carole Rawcliffe. The volume continues the Society's publications of 1885–96.]

691. Gervers, Michael. "The Medieval Cartulary Tradition and the Survival of Archival Material as Reflected in the English Hospitaller Cartulary of 1442." *MS* 37 (1975), 504–14.
[Codicology; how the materials were transmitted and assembled into a single cartulary at Hospitaller headquarters.]

692. ———. *The Hospitaller Cartulary in the British Library (Cotton MS Nero E VI): A Study of the Manuscript and Its Composition with a Critical Edition of Two Fragments of Earlier Cartularies for Essex.* Pon-

tifical Institute of Mediaeval Studies, Studies and Texts, 50. Toronto, 1981.
[Explains how earlier materials were put together into one large cartulary.]

693.   ———, ed. *The Cartulary of the Knights of St. John of Jerusalem in England: Secunda Camera, Essex.* Records of Social and Economic History, n.s., 6. Oxford and New York, 1982.
[For the British Academy. Reviewed by W. Reedy, *Speculum* 60 (1985), 979–82.]

694.   Gordon-Kelter, Janice. "The Lay Presence: Chancery and Privy Seal Personnel in the Bureaucracy of Henry VI." *Med Pros* 10/1 (Spring 1989), 53–74.
[With a table of clerks and an analysis of social status.]

695.   Gray, Charles M. "Plucknett's 'Lancastrian Constitution'." In item 5. Pp. 195–230.
[Four case studies re-examined to show how T. F. T. Plucknett misread the Year Books in his effort to correct William Stubbs.]

696.   Green, Thomas A. "The Jury and the English Law of Homicide, 1200–1600." *Michigan Law Review* 74 (1976), 414–99.
[Full treatment, virtually a short book.]

697.   Griffiths, Ralph A. "Public and Private Bureaucracies in England and Wales in the Fifteenth Century." *TRHS*, 5th ser., 30 (1980), 109–30.

698.   ———. "Bureaucracy and the English State in the Later Middle Ages." In *Prosopographie et genèse de l'Etat moderne. Actes de la table ronde.* Edited by Françoise Autrand. Collection de l'Ecole normale supérieure de jeunes filles, no. 30. CNRS. Paris, 1986. Pp. 53–65.

699.   Guy, John A. "The Development of Equitable Jurisdiction, 1450–1550." In item 53. Pp. 80–86.

700.   Hairsine, P. B., and R. C. Hairsine. "Exchequer Warrants for Issues: Another Source for Yorkist History." *Ricardian* 8/100 (March 1988), 2–8.

701.   Harding, Alan. "The Revolt against the Justices." In item 46. Pp. 165–93.
        [Against the gentry and their growing involvement in the machinery of the royal bench and judiciary.]

702.   Haren, Michael J., ed. *Calendar of Entries in the Papal Registers Relating to Great Britain and Ireland: Papal Letters,* 15: *Innocent VIII: Lateran Registers 1484–1492.* General editor, Leonard E. Boyle. The Stationer's Office for the Irish Manuscripts Commission. Dublin, 1978.
        [Good introduction on administration by Boyle. This major source is now concluded for the medieval period. Anne P. Fuller edited vol. 16, for 1492–98 (Dublin, 1986).]

703.   Harris, B. E., and Dorothy J. Clayton. "Criminal Procedure in Cheshire in the Mid-Fifteenth Century."
Lancashire & Cheshire 128 (1978), 161–72.
[Follows the fate of a group of felons indicted in
1464.]

704.   Harriss, Gerald L. "Theory and Practice in Royal Taxation: Some Observations." *EHR* 97 (1982), 811–19.
[A critical comment on J. Alsop's views on Tudor
taxation ("The Theory and Practice of Tudor
Taxation," *EHR* 97 [1982], 1–30).]

705.   ———. "Marmaduke Lumley and the Exchequer Crisis
of 1446–49." In item 75. Pp. 143–78.
[Valuable details of a case study of a conservative exchequer under pressure.]

706.   Harris, Mary, ed. "The Account of the Great House-
hold of Humphrey, First Duke of Buckingham, for the
Year 1452–3." *Camden Miscellany 28.* Camden Fourth
Ser., vol. 29. Royal Historical Society, 1984. Pp. 1–57.
[Introduction by J. M. Thurgood, pp. 2–8. Edited
from a manuscript in the Staffordshire Record
Office.]

707.   Haslop, T. A. "English Seals in the 13th and 14th
Centuries." In item 1. Pp. 114–17.

708.   Hector, L. C. "Reports, Writs, and Records in the
Common Bench in the Reign of Richard II." In item
50. Pp. 267–88.

709. Hector, L. C., and Michael J. Hager, eds. *Year Books of Richard II: 8–10 Richard II, 1385–1387.* Year Book Ser., vol. 4. Ames Foundation, 1987.

710. Helmholz, R. H. "Infanticide in the Province of Canterbury during the Fifteenth Century." *History of Childhood Quarterly* 2 (1975), 379–90. Reprinted in item 42. No. 9, pp. 157–68.

711. ———. "Ethical Standards for Advocates and Proctors in Theory and Practice." In *Proceedings of the Fourth International Congress of Medieval Canon Law, Toronto, 21–25 August, 1972.* Edited by Stephan Kuttner. Bibliotheca Apostolica Vaticana, Monumenta Iuris Canonici, Ser. C, Subsidia, vol. 5. Vatican City, 1976. Pp. 283–99. Reprinted in item 42. No. 3, pp. 41–57.

712. ———. "Writs of Prohibition and Ecclesiastical Sanctions in the English Courts Christian." *Minnesota Law Review* 60 (1976), 1011–33. Reprinted in item 42. No. 5, pp. 55–99.

713. ———. "Support Order, Church Courts, and the Rule of *Filius Nullius*: A Reassessment of the Common Law." *Virginia Law Review* 63 (1977), 431–48. Reprinted in item 42. No. 10, pp. 169–86.

714. ———. "The Roman Law of Guardianship in England, 1300–1600." *Tulane Law Review* 52 (1978), 223–57. Reprinted in item 42. No. 12, pp. 211–45.

715. ———. "The Early Enforcement of Uses." *Columbia Law Review* 79 (1979), 1503–13. Reprinted in item 42. No. 18, pp. 341–530.

716. ———. "Crime, Compurgation, and the Courts of the Medieval Church." *L & HR* 1 (1983), 1–26. Reprinted in item 42. No. 7, pp. 119–44.
[How ecclesiastical courts dealt with criminal cases.]

717. ———. "Legitimacy in English Legal History." *Illinois Law Review* (1984), 659–74. Reprinted in item 42. No. 13, pp. 247–62.
[Changing views of children's rights to a share of parental estates.]

718. ———, ed. *Select Cases on Defamation to 1600.* Publications of the Selden Society, vol. 101 (1985).
[Cases chosen from ecclesiastical, local, and king's courts.]

719. ———. "Canon Law and English Common Law." A lecture to the Selden Society. London, 1986. In item 42. No. 1, pp. 1–19.
[Areas of contact and suggestions for future work.]

720. ———. "The Sons of Edward IV: A Canonical Assessment of the Claim That They Were Illegitimate." In item 35. Pp. 91–103.
[Richard's case against the children may hold water, unattractive as it is to us.]

721.   ———. "Usury and the Medieval English Church Courts." *Speculum* 61 (1986), 364–80. Reprinted in item 42. No. 17, pp. 323–39.
[Canon law and legal practice were in reasonable accord.]

722.   Holland, Maurice J., ed. *Year Books of Richard II: 7 Richard II, 1383–1384.* Year Books Ser., vol. 3. Ames Foundation, 1989.

723.   Hollis, Daniel W. "The Crown Estate, 1000–1600: A Historiographical Essay." *BSM* 8/2 (no. 23, Summer 1978), 27–40.

724.   Hornsby, Joseph A. "Was Chaucer Educated at the Inns of Court?" *Chaucer Rev* 22 (1987–88), 255–68.
[Maybe the Inns of Chancery; in the late fourteenth century the Inns of Court as yet had little educational structure.]

725.   ———. *Chaucer and the Law.* Norman, Okla., 1988.
[What the literary corpus shows about canon, civil, and criminal jurisdictions.]

726.   Horrox, Rosemary, ed. "Financial Memoranda of the Reign of Edward V: Longleat Miscellaneous Manuscript Book II." *Camden Miscellany 29.* Camden Fourth Ser., vol. 34. Royal Historical Society, 1987. Pp. 197–244.
[Primarily compiled for the Exchequer; shows the need to raise money to hold Calais and defend the realm.]

727. Hunnisett, Roy F. "English Chancery Records." *JSA* 5/3 (April 1975), 158–68.
[Classes, categories, survivals, and curiosities, with many late medieval examples.]

728. Ingram, Martin. "Spousal Litigation in the English Ecclesiastical Courts, c 1350–c 1640." In *Marriage and Society: Studies in the Social History of Marriage*. Edited by R. B. Outhwaite. London, 1981. Pp. 35–57.
[Also New York, 1982. The (Europa) Social History of Human Experience. Mostly Tudor data, but suggestive for the dynamics of late medieval marriage as well, pro and con.]

729. *Calendar of Inquisitions Post Mortem and Other Analogous Documents Preserved in the Public Record Office*, 16: *7–15 Richard II (1384–92)*. HMSO, 1975 (for 1974).
[Compiled M. C. B. Dawes, with index by M. R. Devine, H. I. Jones, and M. J. Post.]

730. *Calendar of Inquisitions Post Mortem and Other Analogous Documents Preserved in the Public Record Office*, 17: *15–23 Richard II*. HMSO, 1988.
[See item 741 for the next volume in chronological order.]

731. Ives, E. W. " 'Agaynst taking awaye of Women': The Inception and Operation of the Abduction Act of 1487." In item 52. Pp. 21–49.
[The tale of Margaret Kebell: executive action triumphed over common law.]

732. ———. "Crime, Sanctuary, and Royal Authority under Henry VIII: The Exemplary Sufferings of the Savage Family." In item 5. Pp. 296–320.
[Although the murder was in 1516, the quarrels go back to divisions before Bosworth.]

733. ———. "The Common Lawyers." In item 17. Pp. 181–217.
[The training and the intellectual role they played.]

734. ———. *The Common Lawyers of Pre-Reformation England: Thomas Kebell, A Case Study.* Reprinted, Holmes Beach, Fla., 1986; Cambridge and New York, 1983.
[Cambridge Studies in English Legal History. The man and the legal system, both well explicated.]

735. Jefferies, Peggy. "The Medieval Use as Family Law and Custom: The Berkshire Gentry in the 14th and 15th Centuries." *Southern* 1 (1979), 45–69.
[Mostly lesser gentry relied on uses; those of higher status had other strategies.]

736. Jones, Michael K. "L'imposition illégale de taxes en 'Normandie anglaise': une enquête gouvernementale en 1446." In item 25. Pp. 461–68.

737. Kimball, Elisabeth G. "Commissions of the Peace for Urban Jurisdiction in England, 1327–1485." *Proceed-*

ings of the American Philosophical Society, vol. 121 (1977). Pp. 448–74.

738. ———, ed. *Oxfordshire Sessions of the Peace in the Reign of Richard II*. Oxfordshire Record Society, vol. 53 (1983 for 1979–80).
[Documents, with English summaries, plus a discussion of the Bampton uprising of 1398.]

739. Kirby, J. L., ed. *Calendar of Signet Letters of Henry IV and Henry V (1399–1422)*. HMSO, 1978.

740. ———, ed. *Abstracts of Feet of Fines Relating to Wiltshire, 1377–1509*. Wiltshire Record Society, vol. 41 (1986 for 1985).
[Following older volumes published by the Society, covering the reigns of Edwards I–III.]

741. ———, ed. *Calendar of Inquisitions Post Mortem and Other Analogous Documents Preserved in the Public Record Office, 18: 1–6 Henry IV (1399–1405)*. HMSO, 1987.
[Follows items 729 and 730; this major primary source has now, finally, reached the fifteenth century.]

742. Kittel, Ruth. "Women under the Law in Medieval England, 1066–1485." In *The Women of England: From Anglo-Saxon Times to the Present: Interpretive Bibliographical Essays*. Edited by Barbara Kanner. Hamden, Conn., 1979. Pp. 124–37.

743.   Lander, J. R. "The Yorkist Council, Justice and Public
Order: The Case of Straunge versus Kynaston." *Albion*
12 (1980), 1–22.
[The council's judicial role; a corrective to J. F.
Baldwin's old account.]

744.   ———. *English Justices of the Peace, 1461–1509.*
Gloucester and Wolfeboro, N.H., 1989.
[A link between the king's politics and his gov-
ernment at the local level.]

745.   Loengard, Janet S. "Legal History and the Medieval
Englishwoman: A Fragmented View." *L & HR* 4 (1986),
161–78.
[With a bibliography to survey recent work.]

746.   Madison, Kenneth G. "Some Unused Sources concern-
ing Litigation of Sir John Fastolf and John Paston III."
Iowa State Journal of Research 56 (1981), 159–75.
[Covers some Paston letters in U.S. archives
(Univ. of Illinois and Harvard).]

747.   McGregor, Margaret, ed. *Bedfordshire Wills Proved in
the Prerogative Court of Canterbury 1383–1548.* Publications of the Bedfordshire Historical Record Society,
vol. 58 (1979).
[Some English calendaring, with useful notes.]

748.   McIntosh, Marjorie K. "Central Court Supervision of
the Ancient Demesne Manor of Havering, 1200–1625."
In item 53. Pp. 87–93.

749.   McKay, W. P. *Clerks in the House of Commons, 1363–1989: A Biographical List.* House of Lords Record Office, Occasional Publications 3. HMSO, 1989.
[Most of the material is after 1485.]

750.   Meekings, C. A. F. "Thomas Kerver's Case, 1444." *EHR* 90 (1975), 331–46.
[Elaborate legal and political complications, with a treason conviction and then a pardon.]

751.   ———. "A King's Bench Bill Formulary." *JLH* 6 (1985), 86–104.
[Circa 1460: how bills were formulated when the defendent was in the marshal's custody.]

752.   Mertes, Kate. "The *Liber Niger* of Edward IV: A New Version." *BIHR* 54 (1981), 29–39.
[Cambridge Record Office, MS. DDM 64, compared here with A. R. Myers's edition of 1959.]

753.   ———. *The English Noble Household, 1250–1600: Good Governance and Politic Rule.* Oxford and New York, 1988.
[Family, Sexuality, and Social Relations in Past Time series. Thorough survey of the problem and of current scholarly views; useful statistics in appendices.]

754.   Millon, David. "Ecclesiastical Jurisdiction in Medieval England." *University of Illinois Law Review* (1984), 621–38.

755. Milsom, S. F. C. *The Legal Framework of English Feudalism: The Maitland Lectures Given in 1972.* Reprinted, Holmes Beach, Fla., 1986; Cambridge and New York, 1976.

[Cambridge Studies in English Legal History. Given at Cambridge. Major treatment. Reviewed by P. Hyams, *EHR* 93 (1978), 856–61.]

756. ———. *Historical Foundations of the Common Law.* 2nd ed. London and Boston, 1981.

[First published in 1969 (London). Basic recent survey volume.]

757. Neville, Cynthia J. "Gaol Delivery in the Border Counties, 1439–1459: Some Preliminary Observations." *Northern* 19 (1983), 45–60.

[The law's delay and its many loopholes.]

758. ———. "Border Law in Late Medieval England." *JLH* 9 (1988), 335–56.

[Gaol delivery in the North, 1439–59; efforts to compile and codify border law, with case illustrations.]

759. Norfolk Record Office. *Norfolk Peculiar Jurisdictions: Index to Probate Records 1416–1857 Compiled by Staff of the Norfolk Record Office [;] Index of Marriage Licence Bonds 1624–1860.* Norfolk Genealogy, vol. 16. Norfolk & Norwich Genealogical Society, 1984.

[Pages 3–13 for probate records 1416–1600.]

760.   Owen, A. E. B. "A Scrivener's Notebook from Bury St. Edmunds." *Archives* 14, no. 61 (September 1979), 16–22. [Cambridge University Library, MS. Add. 7318; contracts and twenty-four previously unknown wills.]

761.   Owen, Dorothy M. "The Practicing Canonist: John Lydford's Notebook." As item 711.
[Lydford's notebook was edited by Owen and published in 1974 by the Historical Manuscripts Commission and the Devon and Cornwall Record Society.]

762.   Palmer, Robert C. *The County Courts of Medieval England, 1150–1350*. Princeton, 1982.
[Important and useful study of a tangled area.]

763.   Payling, Simon J. "Law and Arbitration in Nottinghamshire, 1399–1461." In item 72. Pp. 140–60.
[Local give-and-take.]

764.   Post, J. B. "Courts, Councils, and Arbitrators in the Ladbroke Manor Dispute, 1382–1400." In item 50. Pp. 289–339.
[The long fight by the Catesby family to control land in Warwickshire.]

765.   ———. "Sir Thomas West and the Statute of Rapes, 1382." *BIHR* 53 (1980), 24–30.
[Study of family opposition to abduction and elopements.]

766.   ———. "Equitable Resorts before 1450." In item 53.
Pp. 68–79.

767.   ———. "Local Jurisdiction and Judgment of Death in
Later Medieval England." *Criminal Justice History* 4
(1983), 1–21.
[Indictments at quarter sessions and then trial
at the assizes were becoming customary for
felonies.]

768.   ———. "The Evidential Value of Approvers' Appeals:
The Case of William Rose, 1389." *L & HR* 3 (1985),
91–100.
[Extended delays.]

769.   ———. "The Justice of Criminal Justice in Late Fourteenth Century England." *Criminal Justice History* 7
(1986), 33–49.
[Approvers could spin out cases, among other
cracks in the legal system.]

770.   ———. "Crime in Late Medieval England: Some Historical Limitations." *Continuity and Change* 2 (1987),
211–24.
[The value of our sources and a look at some recent literature.]

771.   ———. "Jury Lists and Juries in the Late Fourteenth
Century." In *Twelve Good Men and True: The Crim-
inal Trial Jury in England, 1200–1800.* Edited by
J. S. Cockburn and Thomas A. Green. Princeton, 1988.
Pp. 65–77.

[How to get enough suitable men to appear, and how they were likely to behave once empaneled.]

772. Powell, Edward. "Social Research and the Use of Medieval Criminal Records." *Michigan Law Review* 79 (1981), 767–78.

773. ———. "Arbitration and the Law of England in the Late Middle Ages." *TRHS*, 5th ser., 33 (1983), 49–67.
[The wide use of arbitration: its value and popularity.]

774. ———. "The King's Bench in Shropshire and Staffordshire in 1414." In item 53. Pp. 94–103.

775. ———. "Proceedings before the Justices of the Peace at Shrewsbury in 1414: A Supplement to the Shropshire Peace Roll." *EHR* 99 (1984), 535–50.
[Addenda to Elisabeth Kimball's 1959 edition of this material.]

776. ———. "Settlement of Disputes by Arbitration in Fifteenth Century England." *L & HR* 2 (1984), 21–43.
[Case studies and an argument for the popularity of arbitration.]

777. ———. "The Restoration of Law and Order." In item 36. Pp. 53–74.
[Proceedings of 1414 served as the model for imposing peace on the counties.]

778. ———. "The Administration of Criminal Justice in Late Medieval England: Peace Sessions and Assizes." In *The Political Context of Law: Proceedings of the Seventh British Legal History Conference, Canterbury, 1985.* Edited by Richard Eales and David Sullivan. London and Ronceverte, W.Va., 1987. Pp. 49–59.
[List of circuit court judges appointed to peace commissions, 1351–94, and the control of the JPs.]

779. ———. "Jury Trial at Gaol Delivery in the Late Middle Ages: The Midland Circuit, 1400–1429." As item 771. Pp. 78–116.
[Examines the concept of the "self-informing" jury, with statistical information on jurors, cases, frequency of service, social origins, outcome of trials, etc.]

780. ———. *Kingship, Law, and Society: Criminal Justice in the Reign of Henry V.* Oxford and New York, 1989.
[General treatment and much case material from county proceedings.]

781. Pugh, Ralph B. "Early Registers of English Outlaws." *AJLH* 27 (1983), 319–329.
[Assesses the value of the sources and the frequency of punishment.]

782. Raban, Sandra. *Mortmain Legislation and the English Church, 1279–1500.* Cambridge Studies in Medieval Life and Thought, 3rd ser., vol. 17. Cambridge and New York, 1982.

783.   Ramsey, Nigel. "Retained Legal Counsel, c. 1275–1475." *TRHS*, 5th ser., 35 (1985), 95–112.
[A growing practice, but refers to practice of only limited importance.]

784.   Reeves, Albert Compton. *Purveyors and Purveyance for the Households of the Lancastrian and Yorkist Kings.* Notre Dame, Ind., 1983.
[Anthroscience Minigraph Series. The scope of this perennial problem, plus a list of the known purveyors.]

785.   Richardson, Malcolm. "Henry V, the English Chancery, and Chancery English." *Speculum* 55 (1980), 726–50.
[The Chancery played a key role in promoting standard English as the norm for governmental and popular usage.]

786.   Richter, Janice Gordon (s.v. Gordon-Kelter). "Education and Association: The Bureaucrat in the Reign of Henry VI." *JMH* 12 (1986), 81–96.
[How Chancery careers were built.]

787.   Rose, Susan, ed. *The Navy of the Lancastrian Kings: Accounts and Inventories of William Soper, Keeper of the King's Ships, 1422–1427.* Publications of the Navy Records Society, vol. 123 (1982).

788.   Roxburgh, Ronald F. "Lincoln's Inn of the Fourteenth Century." *LQR* 94 (1978), 363–82.
[A survey of buildings as well as of the development of the legal institution and schools.]

789. ———. "Lincoln's Inn in the Fifteenth Century." *LQR* 96 (1980), 51–72.

790. Sayles, George O. "A Fifteenth-Century Law Reading in English." *LQR* 96 (1980), 569–80.
["Earliest professional legal text in English": c. 1450, with text printed from a miscellany for law students, including a gloss on Magna Carta.]

791. [No entry.]

792. Sinclair, Alexandra. "The Great Berkeley Law-Suit Revisited, 1417–39." *Southern* 9 (1987), 34–50.
[The arbitration of 1425, and how efforts to settle ran counter to a host of powerful interests.]

793. Smith, Charles W. "Some Trends in the English Royal Chancery, 1377–1483." *Med Pros* 6/1 (Spring 1985), 69–94.
[The appearance and rise of laity in the service.]

794. ———. "A Conflict of Interest? Chancery Clerks in Private Service." In item 72. Pp. 176–91.
[The practice of serving two masters was forbidden in 1406 because of problems it caused.]

795. Somerville, Robert, Sir, ed. "Ordinances for the Duchy of Lancaster." *Camden Miscellany 26.* Camden Fourth Ser., vol. 14. Royal Historical Society, 1975. Pp. 1–29.
[Late fifteenth-century, in English.]

796. Stagg, D. J., ed. *A Calendar of New Forest Documents: The Fifteenth to the Seventeenth Centuries.* Hampshire

Record Ser., vol. 5. Hampshire Record Office for the Hampshire County Council, 1983.
[With appendices of officers and warders.]

797. Storey, Robin L. "Clergy and Common Law in the Reign of Henry IV." In item 50. Pp. 341–408.
[Statutes, indictments, petitions, and praemunire adjudication.]

798. ———. "Gentleman-Bureaucrats." In item 17. Pp. 90–129.
[Important study of careers, mobility, and consciousness, with some brief biographical notes.]

799. Sutton, Anne. "The Administration of Justice Whereunto We Be Professed." *Ricardian* 4/53 (June 1976), 4–15.
[Richard's policies were mostly a continuation of his brother's.]

800. Sutton, Anne F., and P. W. Hammond, eds. *The Coronation of Richard III: The Extant Documents.* Gloucester and New York, 1984; Gloucester, 1983.
[An elaborate and useful edition, with attention to costumes and ritual in addition to the *ordo* and a discussion of the constitutional issues. Discussed at length by Cecil H. Clough, "Review Article," *Ricardian* 6/85 (June 1984), 346–52.]

801. Virgoe, Roger. "The Parliamentary Subsidy of 1450." *BIHR* 55 (1982), 125–38.
[Much heat; less money than in 1436.]

802.   ———. "A Norwich Taxation List of 1451." *Norfolk* 40
(1988), 145–54.
[One hundred sixty-three people, with incomes
from £2–£200; the list published (from PRO Lay
Subsidies, E 179/238/78).]

803.   ———. "The Benevolence of 1481." *EHR* 104 (1989),
25–45.

804.   Walker, Sue Sheridan. "Free Consent and Marriage of
Feudal Wards in Medieval England." *JMH* 8 (1982),
123–34.

805.   ———. "Common Law Juries and Feudal Marriage
Customs in Medieval England: The Pleas of Ravish-
ment." *University of Illinois Law Review*, no. 3 (1984),
705–18.
[These two articles are among the author's contributions to a full legal delineation of medieval
marriage; most of her work is pre-1377.]

806.   Whittle, Stephen J., transcriber, and G. R. Price, ed. *A
Transcript of the Court Rolls of Yeadon, 1361–1476:
With the Early Rentals and Accounts of Esholt Priory,
Charters, Deeds and Associated Material to 1500 A.D.,
Dissolution Rentals and Accounts.* Skipton, North
Yorks., 1984; Draughton, 1984.
[Use the translation with care.]

807.   Whittick, Christopher. "The Role of the Criminal Appeal in the Fifteenth Century." In item 33. Pp. 55–72.

[The appeal was more important and persistent than the older scholarly literature suggests, though there was almost no chance of an actual trial by combat.]

808.   Zell, Michael L. "Fifteenth and Sixteenth Century Wills as Historical Sources." *Archives* 14, no. 62 (1979), 67–74.
[General discussion and useful observations.

VI. SOCIAL AND ECONOMIC HISTORY

809. Aers, David. *"Piers Plowman* and Problems in the Perception of Poverty: A Culture in Transition." *Leeds Studies in English*, n.s. 14 (1983), 5–25.

810. Archer, Rowena E. "Rich Old Ladies: The Problem of Late Medieval Dowagers." In item 69. Pp. 15–35.
[Aristocratic case studies.]

811. Archibald, Marion M. "A 15th Century English Gold Hoard from an Unknown Site." *Coin Hoards* 3 (1979), 724–27.
[From Harrogate: twelve gold coins buried before 1490.]

812. ———. "The Queenhithe Hoard of Late Fifteenth-Century Forgeries." *BNJ* 50 (1980), 61–66.
[A 1980 find of 495 pennies: fakes of Edward IV, from 1490–1500; metallurgical analysis by M. R. Cowell.]

813. Astill, G. G. "Economic Changes in Later Medieval England: An Archaeological Review." In item 7. Pp. 217–47.
[Interdisciplinary treatment: pottery, village settlement patterns, coins, etc.]

814.   Attreed, Lorraine. "From *Pearl* Maiden to Tower Prin-
        ces: Towards a New History of Medieval Childhood."
        JMH 9 (1983), 43–58.
        [Popular perceptions of how Richard III's mis-
        treatment of the princes hurt his image.]

815.   Awty, Brian G. "The Continental Origins of Wealden
        Ironworkers, 1451–1544." *EcHR*, 2nd ser., 34 (1981),
        524–39.
        [Mostly they were French, with numbers peak-
        ing in the 1520s.]

816.   Bailey, Mark. "Blowing Up Bubbles: Some New Demo-
        graphic Evidence for the Fifteenth Century?" *JMH* 15
        (1989), 347–58.
        [Not convinced by item 909: the administrative
        context of the register makes it less reliable
        than E. D. Jones indicates.]

817.   Barron, Caroline M. "The 'Golden Age' of Women in
        Medieval London." *Reading* 15 (1989), 35–58.
        [Good times, before the decline of Tudor days.]

818.   Beauroy, Jacques. "Family Patterns of Bishops Lynn
        Will-Makers in the Fourteenth Century." In *The
        World We Have Gained: Histories of Population and
        Social Structure: Essays Presented to Peter Laslett on
        His Seventieth Birthday*. Edited by Lloyd Bonfield,
        Richard M. Smith, and Keith Wrightson. Oxford,
        1986. Pp. 23–42.
        [The strength of the nuclear family.]

819. Belaubre, Jean. "Deux monstres sacrés de la numis-
matique du XVᵉ siècle; le 'Noble à la Rose' de
Edouard IV et le 'Fort' de Guyenne de Charles de
France." *Le Club Français de la Médaille*, Bulletin
55–56 (1977), 180–85.

820. Bennett, Michael J. "Sources and Problems in the
Study of Social Mobility: Cheshire in the Later Middle
Ages." *Lancashire & Cheshire* 128 (1978), 59–95.
[Case studies of men and families on the way up
and how they tried to consolidate their gains.]

821. ———. "*Sir Gawain and the Green Knight* and the
Literary Achievement of the North-West Midlands:
The Historical Background." *JMH* 5 (1979), 63–89.

822. ———. "Spiritual Kinship and the Baptismal Name in
Traditional European Society." In *Principalities,
Powers, and Estates: Studies in Medieval and Early
Modern Government and Society.* Edited by L. O.
Frappell. Adelaide, 1979. Pp. 1–13.

823. ———. *Community, Class, and Careerism: Cheshire
and Lancashire Society in the Age of Sir Gawain and
the Green Knight.* Cambridge Studies in Medieval Life
and Thought, 3rd ser., vol. 18. Cambridge and New
York, 1983.
[Important study of regional society: families,
mobility, political ties, and local culture.]

824. ———. "Careerism in Late Medieval England." In
item 72. Pp. 19–39.
[Avenues of mobility *and* their limitations.]

825.   Black, Maggie. *Food and Cooking in Medieval Britain: History and Recipes.* Historic Buildings and Monuments Commission for England. London, 1985.

826.   Blair, Claude, John Blair, and R. Brownsword. "An Oxford Brasier's Dispute of the 1390s: Evidence for Brass-Making in Medieval England." *AJ* 66 (1986), 81–90.
[A contract of 1392 (from PRO Exchequer miscellany) sheds light on the industry.]

827.   Blanchard, Ian. "Labour Productivity and Work Psychology in the English Mining Industry, 1400–1600." *EcHR*, 2nd ser., 31 (1978), 1–24.
[Farmer-miners yielded to full-time miners; appendices on production and productivity.]

828.   Blunt, Christopher E. "Privy-marking and the Trial of the Pyx." In *Studies in Numismatic Method Presented to Philip Grierson.* Edited by C. N. L. Brooke, B. H. I. H. Stewart, J. G. Pollard, and R. Volk. Cambridge and New York, 1983. Pp. 225–30.
[The discretion allowed the masters makes precise dating impossible.]

829.   Bowers, J. M. *"Piers Plowman* and the Unwillingness to Work." *Mediaevalia* 9 (1983), 239–491.
[A sage reminder that Piers *was* a plowman.]

830.   Bridbury, A. R. *Economic Growth: England in the Later Middle Ages.* Reprint, Westport, Conn., 1983;

reprinted with a new introduction, Brighton, 1975; New York, 1975.

[First published 1962 (London). Revised version of lively argument setting forth the case for economic growth.]

831. ———. *Medieval English Clothmaking: An Economic Survey.* Pasold Research Fund. Pasold Studies in Textile History, 4. London, 1982.

[Revisionary: questions both the usual way we read the evidence and the customary interpretations of the health and size of the industry. Though mostly pre-1377, chs. 6–7 and the appendices cover the later Middle Ages.]

832. Britnell, Richard H. "The Pastons and Their Norfolk." *AgHR* 36 (1988), 132–44.

[What the family letters tell about estate management and economic decisions, as well as about a slump of the 1460s.]

833. Brown, Henry Phelps, Sir, and Sheila V. Hopkins. *A Perspective of Wages and Prices.* London and New York, 1981.

[Reprinting of four classic articles from *Economica*, 1955–61.]

834. Butcher, Andrew F. "The Economy of Exeter College, 1400–1500." *Oxon* 44 (1979), 38–52.

["A triumph of parsimony"; with tabular data on income and expenditure.]

835.   Butlin, R. A. "The Late Middle Ages, c. 1350–1500." In *An Historical Geography of England and Wales.* Edited by R. A. Dodgshon and R. A. Butlin. London and New York, 1978. Pp. 119–50.
[Summary statement touching demography and regional economic variations.]

836.   Cantor, Leonard. "Castles, Fortified Houses, Moated Homesteads, and Monastic Settlements." In item 16. Pp. 126–53.

837.   ———. "Forests, Chases, Parks, and Warrens." In item 16. Pp. 56–85.

838.   Cattermole, Paul. "A Fourteenth Century Contract for Carpenter's Work at Aswellthorpe Church." *Norfolk* 40 (1989), 297–302.
[The carpenter received 17½ marks in an agreement of 1398 to build a roof and two doors; the contract is transcribed and translated.]

839.   Childs, Wendy R. *Anglo-Castilian Trade in the Later Middle Ages.* Manchester, 1978; Totowa, N.J., 1978.
[The standard treatment of the topic.]

840.   ———. "England's Iron Trade in the Fifteenth Century." *EcHR*, 2nd ser., 34 (1981), 25–47.
[Customs accounts show growing imports, largely from Spain.]

841.   Chorley, J. P. H. "The English Assize of Cloth: A Note." *BIHR* 59 (1986), 125–30.

[Fifteenth-century data and the regulations covering lengths of cloth.]

842.   Clark, Elaine. "Some Aspects of Social Security in Medieval England." *Journal of Family History* 7 (1982), 307–32.
[Contractual agreements to support the elderly.]

843.   Coss, Peter R., ed. *The Langley Cartulary*. Publications of the Dugdale Society, vol. 32 (1980).
[A Harleian MS (BL MS. Harley 7) about a secular family, *tempore* Edward IV; 567 items, many from the fifteenth century.]

844.   Crook, David. "Derbyshire and the English Rising of 1381." *HR* 60 (1987), 9–23.
[Local records and the role of the Statham brothers.]

845.   Curry, Anne E. "Cheshire and the Royal Demesne, 1399–1422." *Lancashire & Cheshire* 128 (1978), 113–38.
[Welsh wars and declining revenues led to an effort to mobilize resources.]

846.   Darby, Henry C., R. E. Glassock, J. Sheail, and G. R. Versey. "The Changing Geographical Distribution of Wealth in England: 1086–1334–1525." *JHG* 5 (1979), 247–62.
[Domesday Book and lay subsidies pinpoint growth.]

847. Davis, Ralph. "The Rise of Antwerp and Its English Connection, 1406–1510." In item 18. Pp. 2–20.
[In the context of Hanse relations and as a land-trade center.]

848. Delaney, Sheila. "Sexual Economics, Chaucer's Wife of Bath, and *The Book of Margery Kempe*." *Minnesota Review* 5 (1978), 104–15.

849. Dickinson, John C. "Three Pre-Reformation Documents concerning South Cumbria." *Cumberland & Westmorland* 86 (1986), 129–39.
[Two wills (1457 and 1508) and an ecclesiastical deed (1418).]

850. Dobson, R. B., and J. Taylor, comps. *Rymes of Robyn Hood: An Introduction to the English Outlaw*. 2nd ed., Gloucester, 1989.
[Good introduction, by topics, with a foreword on Robin Hood historiography and editorial reflections since the 1976 (London; Pittsburgh) editions. Collection of Robin Hood literature, medieval and more recent.]

851. Dockray, Keith. "The Troubles of the Yorkshire Plumptons." *History Today* 27 (July 1977), 459–66.

852. ———. "Why Did Fifteenth-Century English Gentry Marry?: The Pastons, Plumptons, and Stonors Reconsidered." In item 54. Pp. 61–80.
[No single motive or strategy fits all cases.]

853. Dyer, Christopher. "English Diet in the Later Middle Ages." In item 7. Pp. 191–216.
[Social contrasts and improving consumption and nutrition by the fifteenth century.]

854. ———. "Les régimes alimentaires en Angleterre, XIIIeme–XVeme siècles." In *Manger et boire au moyen âge. Actes de Colloque de, Nice, 15–17 octobre 1982*, 1: *Aliments et société*; 2: *Cuisine, manières du table, régimes alimentaires*. Translated, collected, and presented by Denis Menjot. 2 vols. Publications of the Faculté des lettres et sciences humaines de Nice, nos. 27–28, 1st ser. Paris, 1984. Vol. 1, pp. 263–74.
[From the Centre d'Etudes médiévales de Nice.]

855. ———. "The Social and Economic Background to the Rural Revolt of 1381." In item 46. Pp. 9–42.
[Social changes and the clash between prosperity, expectations, and reaction.]

856. ———. "The Consumer and the Market in the Later Middle Ages." *EcHR*, 2nd ser., 62 (1989), 305–27.
[Social strata and the ties between supply and demand.]

857. ———. *Standards of Living in the Later Middle Ages: Social Change in England c.1200–1520.* Cambridge and New York, 1989.
[Cambridge Medieval Textbooks. Valuable synthesis, well-sprinkled with case studies and detailed data, many from archival materials.]

858. Dymond, David. "A Fifteenth Century Building Contract from Suffolk." *VA* 9 (1978), 10–22.
[From 1473: an oak-framed building, no longer extant, by the Stour.]

859. Dymond, David, and Roger Virgoe. "The Reduced Population and Wealth of Early Fifteenth Century Suffolk." *Suffolk* 36 (1986), 73–100.
[Tax subsidies and physical evidence are in accord.]

860. Faith, Rosamund J. "The 'Great Rumor' of 1377 and Peasant Ideology." In item 46. Pp. 43–75.
[The strength of peasant sentiment about ancient rights and their popular culture.]

861. ———. "The Class Struggle in Fourteenth-Century England." In *People's History and Socialist Theory*. Edited by Raphael Samuel. London and Boston, 1986. Pp. 50–80.
[History Workshop Series. Also London and Boston (1981); Amsterdam (1981), listed without subtitle; Barcelona, translated as *Historia popular y teoria socialista* (1984). Causes of discontent and the tradition of resistance of organization. See also item 1230.]

862. Fraser, C. M., ed. *Northern Petitions Illustrative of Life in Berwick, Cumbria and Durham in the Fourteenth Century*. Publications of the Surtees Society, vol. 194 (1982).
[Only a few of the texts are post-1377.]

863.   Fryde, E. B. "The English Cloth Industry and Trade with the Mediterranean, c. 1370–c. 1530." In *Atti della seconda Settimana di studio (10–16 aprile 1970): Produzione, commercio e consumo dei panni di lana (nei secoli XII–XVIII)*. Edited by Marco Spallanzani. Pubblicazioni - Istituto internazionale di storia economica F. Datini, Prato: Ser. 2, Atti delle settimane di studi e altri convegni, 2. Florence, 1976. Pp. 343–63. Reprinted in item 26. No. 15.

864.   ———. "The Financial Policies of the Royal Governments and Popular Resistance to Them in France and England, c. 1270–c. 1420." *Revue belge de philologie et d'histoire*, 57 (1978), 824–60. Reprinted in item 26. No. 1.

865.   Fudge, John. "Anglo-Baltic Trade and the Hanseatic Commercial System in the Late Fifteenth Century." In *Britain and the Northern Seas: Some Essays: Papers Presented at the Fourth Conference of the Association for the History of the Northern Seas, Dartington, Devon, 16–20 September 1985*. Edited by Walter E. Minchinton. Pontefract, 1988. Pp. 11–19.
        [A survey, with an attempt at some new statistics on the volume and value of the trade.]

866.   Giles, Colum. *Rural Houses of West Yorkshire, 1400–1830*. West Yorkshire Metropolitan County Council and Royal Commission on Historical Monuments, Supplementary Ser., 8. HMSO, 1986.

[Serious coffeetable book: gentry houses, 1400–
1550, pp. 1–25; those of the yeomanry, pp.
26–47.]

867.   Glennie, Paul. "The Transition from Feudalism to
Capitalism as a Problem for Historical Geography."
JHG 13 (1987), 296–302.
[Review of the controversy, some bibliography,
and some sharp criticisms. See item 8.]

868.   Goldberg, P. J. P. "Female Labour, Service, and Marriage in the Late Medieval Urban North." *Northern* 22
(1986), 18–38.
[Service, the trades, and the declining economic
prospects outside of marriage.]

869.   ———. "Marriage, Migration, Servanthood, and the
Life-Cycle in Yorkshire Towns of the Later Middle
Ages: Some York Cause Paper Evidence." *Continuity
and Change* 1 (1986), 141–69.
[Depositions and ecclesiastical litigation telling
of mobility, demography, and social structure.]

870.   ———. "Mortality and Economic Change in the Diocese of York, 1390–1514." *Northern* 24 (1988), 38–55.
[A mortality series, with bad years and worse
years.]

871.   ———. "Women in Fifteenth-Century Town Life." In
item 82. Pp. 107–28.
[Varied roles with a good deal of integration.]

872. Green, T. A. P. "The Great Courts or Parliaments of Devon Tinners, 1474–1786." *Devonshire* 119 (1987), 145–67.
[Early parliaments well treated; legislation to control the industry in the courts of 1474, 1494, and 1510.]

873. Grierson, Philip. "Coinage in The Cely Papers." In *Later Medieval Numismatics (11th–16th Centuries): Selected Studies.* Collected by Grierson. Collected Studies Ser., CS 98. London, 1979.
[Grierson published this useful paper in 1967, to unravel a complex tale of coins and coin values; now reprinted in this volume of his collected essays, twenty-two articles 1951–77.]

874. Haas, Louis. "Social Connections between Parents and Godparents in Late Medieval Yorkshire." *Med Pros* 10/1 (Spring 1989), 1–21.
[Naming patterns and social ties.]

875. Habberjam, Moira. "Harrington *v.* Saville: A Fifteenth Century Divorce Case." *Ricardian* 8/101 (June 1988), 50–60.

876. Hajnal, John. "Two Kinds of Pre-Industrial Household Formation System." In *Family Forms in Historic Europe.* Edited by Richard Wall, in collaboration with Jean Robin and Peter Laslett, SSRC Cambridge Group for the History of Population and Social Structure. Cambridge and New York, 1983. Pp. 65–104.

877. Hallum, H. E. "Age at First Marriage and Age at Death in the Lincolnshire Fenland, 1252–1478." *Population Studies* 39 (1985), 55–69.
[The European marriage pattern can be seen as the prevailing one, even before the plague.]

878. Hanawalt, Barbara A. "Childrearing among the Lower Classes of Late Medieval England." *JIH* 8 (1977), 1–22.

879. ———. "Keepers of Lights: Late Medieval English Parish Gilds." *JMRS* 14 (1984), 21–37.
[A survey of guild life and roles.]

880. ———. "Peasant Resistance to Royal and Seignorial Impositions." In item 63. Pp. 23–47.
[Oppression, exaction, and signs of resistance.]

881. ———. *The Ties That Bound: Peasant Families in Medieval England.* New York and Oxford, 1988; New York, 1986.
[A rich and sympathetic study, based largely on coroners' rolls.]

882. Hanham, Alison, ed. *The Cely Letters, 1472–1488.* EETS, o.s., no. 273 (1975).
[This major source now readily accessible; useful introduction.]

883. ———. "Profits on English Wool Exports, 1472–1544." *BIHR* 55 (1982), 139–47.
[Reasonable profits, but a complicated matter.]

884.   ———. *The Celys and Their World: An English Merchant Family of the Fifteenth Century.* Cambridge, 1986; Cambridge and New York, 1985.
[Drawn from the letters, with much information on trade and economic life.]

885.   Harper-Bill, Christopher. "The Labourer Is Worthy of His Hire?—Complaints about Diet in Late Medieval English Monasteries." In item 11. Pp. 95–107.
[What was eaten, at what costs, with a look at monastic alms.]

886.   Harris, E. J. "The Halfpence and Farthings of Richard II." *Numismatic Circular* 95 (1987), 325.
[Summary of types.]

887.   ———. "Halfpence of the Henry IV–V Period." *Numismatic Circular* 96 (1988), 79–80.
[Eighteen coins of seven types illustrated.]

888.   ———. "Odd Pence of Henry V." *Seaby Coin and Medal Bulletin* 846 (December 1989), 299–300.
[Pence are often neglected because of more glamorous coins.]

889.   Haslop, G. S. "A Selby Kitchener's Roll of the Early Fifteenth Century." *YAJ* 48 (1976), 119–33.
[For 1416–17; translated, with introduction.]

890.   Hatcher, John. *Plague, Population, and the English Economy, 1348–1530.* Economic History Society, 1977.

[Studies in Economic and Social History. A mixed tale, but well told and easy for students to use. R. B. Dobson reviews, *History* 63 (1978), 217–18.]

891. Herbert, Ailsa. "Herefordshire, 1413–61: Some Aspects of Society and Public Order." In item 31. Pp. 103–22.
[Violence and efforts to impose law and order.]

892. Hicks, Michael A. "St. Katherine's Hospital, Heytesbury: Prehistory, Foundation, and Re-foundations, 1408–1472." *Wiltshire* 78 (1984), 62–69.
[A fourteenth-century foundation, re-launched by Hungerfords in the fifteenth century.]

893. ———. "Chantries, Obits, and Almshouses: The Hungerford Foundations, 1325–1478." In item 11. Pp. 123–42.
[Detailed study of family activity.]

894. Hilton, Rodney H. "Social Concepts in the English Rising of 1381." In *Revolte und Revolution in Europa: Referate u. Protokolle d. Internat. Symposiums zur Erinnerung an d. Bauernkrieg 1525 (Memmingen, 24.–27. Marz 1975).* Edited by Peter Blickle. *Historische Zeitschrift*, Beiheft n.F., 4. Munich, 1975. Pp. 31–46. Reprinted in item 45. No. 17, pp. 216–26.
[The reprint is published as a translation of "Soziale Programme in Englische auf Stand von 1381").

895. ———. "Idéologie et order social." *L'Arc* 72 (1978), 32–37. Reprinted in item 45 as "Ideology and Social Order in Late Medieval England." No. 20, pp. 246–52.

896. ———. "Feudalism or *Féodalité* and *Seigneurie* in France and England." In item 507. Pp. 39–50. Reprinted in item 45. No. 18, pp. 227–38.
[Rejoinder by Jacques Le Goff, pp. 51–61, in the 1980 volume.]

897. ———. "Popular Movements in England at the End of the Fourteenth Century." In *Il Tumulto dei Ciompi: un momento di storia fiorentina ed europea.* Istituto Nazionale di Studi sul Rinascimento. Florence, 1981. Pp. 223–40. Reprinted in item 45. No. 11, pp. 152–64.

898. ———. "Medieval Market Towns and Simple Commodity Production." *Past and Present* 109 (1985), 3–23.
[Important corrective: smaller towns are generally neglected.]

899. ———. "Women Traders in Medieval England." In item 45. No. 16, pp. 205–15.
[Not previously published; a valuable reminder of an active world that the sources barely reveal.]

900. Hoffmann, Richard C. "Fishing for Sport in Medieval Europe: New Evidence." *Speculum* 60 (1985), 877–902.
[Thorough survey, with some fifteenth-century texts and amusing anecdotes.]

901.   Hollingsworth, T. H. "A Note on the Mediaeval Longevity of the Secular Peerage, 1350–1500." *Population Studies* 29 (1975), 155–59.

[Corrective to J. T. Rosenthal, *Population Studies* 27 (1973), 287–93, on aristocratic mortality.]

902.   Holmes, Nicholas, and David A. Walker. "A Henry VI/ Edward IV Mule Penny from the Leith Hoard." *BNJ* 58 (1988), 84–89.

[Perhaps struck in 1462, when Henry's return seemed possible.]

903.   Horden, Peregrine. "Review Article: A Discipline of Relevance: The Historiography of the Late Medieval Hospital." *Social History of Medicine* 1 (1988), 359–74.

[Discussion of M. Rubin (item 969) and others, approaching hospitals by way of the "supply side."]

904.   Houlbrooke, Ralph A. *The English Family, 1450–1700.* London and New York, 1984.

[In the series Themes in British Social History. A synthetic work surveying current scholarship, and a useful introduction to a large body of work and a large topic.]

905.   ———. "Women's Social Life and Common Action in England from the 15th Century to the Eve of the Civil War." *Continuity and Change* 1 (1986), 171–89.

[Little indication of feminist consciousness but a wide social role for women, including activism and protest.]

906.   Jefferies, P. J. "Social Mobility in the Fourteenth Century: The Example of the Chelreys of Berkshire." *Oxon* 41 (1976), 324–36.
[Case study of a familiar sort of family.]

907.   Jewell, Helen M. " 'The Bringing Up of Children in Good Learning and Manners': A Survey of Secular Educational Provision in the North of England, c. 1350–1550." *Northern* 18 (1982), 1–25.
[Details of schooling and endowments.]

908.   ———. "The Cultural Interests and Achievements of the Secular Personnel of the Local Administration." In item 17. Pp. 130–54.
[Wills, patronage, and educational concerns.]

909.   Jones, E. D. "Going Round in Circles: Some New Evidence for Population in the Later Middle Ages." *JMH* 15 (1989), 329–45.
[A look at the registers of Spalding Priory, 1470s: conclusions strongly disputed in item 816.]

910.   Karras, Ruth M. "The Regulation of Brothels in Later Medieval England." *Signs* 14 (1989), 399–433.
[A preview of the forthcoming full-length study.]

911.   Keen, Maurice. "Chaucer's Knight, the English Aristocracy, and the Crusades." In item 77. Pp. 45–61.
[Historical typicality and the probability of the knight's career as sketched for us.]

912. Kelly, Henry Ansgar. *Love and Marriage in the Age of Chaucer.* Ithaca, N.Y., 1975.
[Links between marriage and "courtly love."]

913. Kettle, A. J. " 'My Wife Shall Have It': Marriage and Property in the Wills and Testaments of Later Medieval England." In *Marriage and Property.* Edited by Elizabeth M. Craik. Aberdeen, 1984. Pp. 89–103.

914. Kirby, Joan W. "A Fifteenth-Century Family, the Plumptons of Plumpton, and Their Lawyers, 1461–1515." *Northern* 25 (1989), 106–19.
[A secret marriage and broken agreement opened the doors for a generation of costly litigation.]

915. Lacey, Kay. "The Production of 'Narrow Ware' by Silkwomen in Fourteenth and Fifteenth Century England." *Textile History* 18 (1987), 187–204.

916. Lessen, Marvin. "The Groats of Edward V." *BNJ* 53 (1983), 180–83.
[Adding to C. E. Blunt and C. A. Whitton (1948) and I. Stewart, item 985.]

917. Lloyd, T. H. *The English Wool Trade in the Middle Ages.* Cambridge and New York, 1977.
[Now the standard work. Reviewed by M. Prestwich, *EHR* 93 (1978), 388–90. See also items 931, 933.]

918. Maddern, Philippa. "Honour among the Pastons: Gender and Integrity in 15th-Century English Provincial Life." *JMH* 14 (1988), 357–71.

[Community orientation, with wide scope for women's involvement in public affairs.]

919.　Martin, G. H. "Road Travel in the Middle Ages: Some Journeys by the Warden and Fellows of Merton College, Oxford, 1315–1470." *Journal of Transport History*, n.s. 3 (1975–76), 159–78.
　　[Itineraries and estate visitations.]

920.　Mate, Mavis. "The Role of Gold Coinage in the English Economy, 1338–1400." *Num Chr*, 7th ser., 18 (1978), 126–41.
　　[Thorough discussion of the role and economic effect of gold coinage.]

921.　McClure, Peter. "Patterns of Migration in the Later Middle Ages: The Evidence of English Place-Name Surnames." *EcHR*, 2nd ser., 32 (1979), 167–82.
　　[Difficult sources support a tale of considerable localized migration.]

922.　McColly, William. "Why Chaucer's Knight Has No Coat of Arms." *ELN* 21/3 (1984), 1–6.
　　[Chaucer may have been frightened off by the Scrope and Grosvenor controversy over such matters.]

923.　McHardy, Alison K. "Some Late Medieval Eton College Wills." *J Eccl H* 28 (1977), 387–95.
　　[Types of bequests analyzed.]

924. McIntosh, Marjorie K. "Local Responses to the Poor in Late Medieval and Tudor England." *Continuity and Change* 3 (1988), 109–45.
[The problems worsened after 1465.]

925. Melis, Federigo. "The 'Nationality' of Sea-Borne Trade between England and the Mediterranean, around 1400." *Journal of European Economic History* 4 (1975), 359–80.
[Many southern participants, even in inland sites.]

926. Miskimin, Harry A. "Money and Money Movements in France and England at the End of the Middle Ages." In *Precious Metals in the Later Medieval and Early Modern Worlds.* Edited by J. F. Richards. Durham, N.C., 1983. Pp. 79–96.
[England had bullion deficiences.]

927. Mitchiner, Michael. "English Tokens, c. 1425 to 1673." *BNJ* 54 (1984), 86–163.

928. Mitchiner, Michael, and Anne Skinner. "English Tokens, c. 1200 to 1425." *BNJ* 53 (1983), 29–77.
[Lead replaced pewter around 1350.]

929. Monnas, L. "Silk Cloths Purchased for the Great Wardrobe of the Kings of England, 1325–1462." *Textile History* 20 (1989), 283–307.

930. Morgan, David A. L. "The Individual Style of the English Gentleman." In item 54. Pp. 15–35.

[The growth of self-consciousness and its out-
ward garments; important short paper on a topic
that is very hard to get a handle on.]

931.   Munro, John H. "Wool Price Schedules and the Qual-
ities of English Wools in the Later Middle Ages,
c. 1270–1499." *Textile History* 9 (1978), 118–69.
[Important survey by counties of prices in Calais
and the Low Country towns.]

932.   ———. "Bullionism and the Bill of Exchange in England, 1272–1663: A Study in Monetary Management
and Popular Prejudice." In *The Dawn of Modern
Banking*. Center for Medieval and Renaissance Studies, University of California, Los Angeles. New Haven,
1979. Pp. 170–215.

933.   ———. "Mint Policies, Ratios, and Outputs in the Low
Countries and England, 1335–1420: Some Reflections
on New Data." *Num Chr* 141 (1981), 71–116.
[No winner in the "Anglo-Flemish monetary war";
disagreement with T. Lloyd, item 917.]

934.   Niles, Philip. "Baptism and the Naming of Children in
Late Medieval England." *Med Pros* 3/1 (Spring 1982),
95–107.
[Godparents made the decision.]

935.   Nixon, Howard M. "Caxton, His Contemporaries, and
Successors in the Book Trade from Westminster Documents." *Library*, 5th ser., 31 (1976), 305–36.

936. North, J. J. *English Hammered Coinage*, 2: *Edward I to Charles I, 1272–1662*. 2nd rev. ed. London, 1975.
[All known types; pp. 47–80 for the later Middle Ages.]

937. Orme, Nicholas. "The Education of the Courtier." In item 77. Pp. 63–85. Reprinted in item 65. No. 8, pp. 153–75.
[Useful survey of lay training.]

938. ———, ed. and trans. *Table Manners for Children/ John Lydgate's Stans Puer ad Mensam*. Salisbury, 1989.
[Foreword by Lotte Hellinga, in this version (and facsimile) of the Caxton edition of 1476 in the Huntington Library. Limited edition (265, numbered).]

939. Owen, Charles A., Jr. "A Certein Nombre of Conclusions: The Nature and Nurture of Children in Chaucer." *Chaucer Rev* 16 (1981–82), 60–75.
[Ages of children, the contemporary idea of childhood, and parent-child relations.]

940. Penn, Simon A. C. "Female Wage-Earners in Late Fourteenth-Century England." *AgHR* 35 (1987), 1–14.
[Court records give much data: comparable pay and involvement throughout the labor force.]

941. Platts, Graham. *Land and People in Medieval Lincolnshire*. History of Lincolnshire, 4. History of Lincolnshire Committee for the Society for Lincolnshire History and Archaeology, 1985.

[Mostly to 1349, but general comments cover the
fifteenth century.]

942.   Pollard, Anthony J. "The Burghs of Brough Hall,
c. 1270–1574." North Yorkshire Record Office, 6 (1978).

943.   ———. "Richard Clervaux of Croft: A North-Riding
Squire in the Fifteenth Century." *YAJ* 50 (1978),
151–69.
[Family aggrandizement and consolidation of
land, not national politics, were of concern.]

944.   Poos, L. R. "Life Expectancy and 'Age of First Ap-
pearance' in Medieval Manorial Court Rolls." *Local
Population Studies* 37 (Autumn 1986), 45–52.
[Well above sixteen; perhaps in their twenties.]

945.   Post, J. B. "Faces of Crime in Later Medieval England." *History Today* 38 (January 1988), 18–24.

946.   Postan, M. M. "Feudalism and Its Decline: A Semantic
Exercise." In item 7. Pp. 73–87.
[The dangers of models that aim to be all-
inclusive.]

947.   Postles, David. "Early Coalmining at West Hallum."
Derbyshire 99 (1979), 221–32.
[References to activity in the 1390s.]

948.   Proudfoot, L. J. "The Extension of Parish Churches in
Medieval Warwickshire." *JHG* 9 (1983), 231–46.
[Their size is a useful guide to local population,
correlated with tax data and acreage.]

949. Raftis, James Ambrose. "Social Changes versus Revolution: New Interpretations of the Peasants' Revolt of 1381." In item 63. Pp. 3–22.
[Peasant culture in opposition to ruling-class hegemony.]

950. Reeves, A. Compton. "Histories of English Families in the 1970s." *Med Pros* 1/2 (Autumn 1980), 59–71.
[Survey of recent work.]

951. ———. *Delights of Life in Fifteenth-Century England*. Richard III Society, 1989.
[A talk on recreations and popular taste.]

952. Richmond, Colin. "The Expenses of Thomas Playter of Sotterley, 1459–60." *Suffolk* 35 (1981), 41–52.
[A Paston legal adviser; transcript of Magdalen College Fastolf MS paper, 71.]

953. ———. *John Hopton: A Fifteenth Century Suffolk Gentleman*. Cambridge and New York, 1981.
[A model study of the county gentry.]

954. ———. "Religion and the Fifteenth-Century English Gentleman." In item 23. Pp. 193–208.
[Major essay on lay religion and bourgeois consciousness.]

955. ———. "The Pastons Revisited: Marriage and the Family in Fifteenth-Century England." *BIHR* 58 (1985), 25–36.

[Some insights still to be found on such familiar ground; comments towards his full-length study of the family.]

956. ———. "The Sulyard Papers: The Rewards of a Small Family Archive." In item 84. Pp. 199–228.
[Family ups and downs, with some documents.]

957. ———. "Two Late Medieval Marriage Contracts from Staffordshire." In *Staffordshire Studies: Essays Presented to Denis Stuart.* Edited by Philip Morgan. Department of Adult and Continuing Education, University of Keele. Keele, 1987. Pp. 53–60.
[Lesser gentry; documents printed and discussed.]

958. ———. "When Did John Hopton Become Blind?" *HR* 60 (1987), 103–06.
[Probably by 1471; the truth behind excuses from duties.]

959. ———. "Hand to Mouth: Information Gathering and Use in England in the Later Middle Ages." *Journal of Historical Sociology* 1/3 (1988), 233–52.
[The Pastons: how they sent and received current information.]

960. Robertson, Donald W., Jr. " 'And For My Land Thus Hastow Mordred Me?': Land Tenure, the Cloth Industry, and the Wife of Bath." *Chaucer Rev* 14 (1979–80), 403–20.

[Margery Haynes, a real-life model of dower-collecting, spousal gifts, and land transfers.]

961. ———. "Chaucer and the 'Commune Profit': The Manor." *Mediaevalia* 6 (1980), 239–59.
[Literature looks at peasants, labor, and the local community.]

962. ———. "Chaucer and the Economic and Social Consequences of the Plague." In item 63. Pp. 49–74.
[Chaucer's social consciousness was stronger than is often argued.]

963. Rosenthal, Joel T. "Old Mens' Lives: Elderly English Peers, 1350–1500." *Mediaevalia* 8 (1982), 211–38.

964. ———. "Sir Richard Choke (d. 1483) of Long Aston." *Somerset* 127 (1982–83), 105–21.

965. ———. "Aristocratic Marriage and the English Peerage, 1350–1500: Social Institution and Personal Bond." *JMH* 10 (1984), 181–94.

966. ———. "Aristocratic Widows in Fifteenth Century England." In *Women and the Structure of Society: Selected Research from the Fifth Berkshire Conference on the History of Women.* Edited by Barbara J. Harris and Jo Ann K. McNamara. Durham, N.C., 1984. Pp. 36–47, 259–60.
[Duke Press Policy Studies.]

967. ———. "Heirs' Ages and Family Succession in Yorkshire, 1399–1422." *YAJ* 56 (1984), 87–94.

[An analysis of Yorkshire Inquisitions Post Mortem.]

968. ———. "Other Victims: Peeresses as War Widows, 1450–1500." *History* 72 (1987), 213–30.

969. Rubin, Miri. *Charity and Community in Medieval Cambridge.* Cambridge Studies in Medieval Life and Thought, 4th ser., 4. Cambridge and New York, 1987.
[Popular religious activity, benefaction, and the sense of community; a local study in a wider perspective. See item 903.]

970. Sass, Lorna J. *To the King's Taste: Richard II's Book of Feasts and Recipes Adapted for Modern Cooking.* New York, 1975.
[Metropolitan Museum of Art. Also, *To the King's Taste: Richard II's Book of Feasts and Recipes* (New York, 1984; London, 1976).]

971. Saul, Nigel. *Knights and Esquires: The Gloucestershire Gentry in the Fourteenth Century.* Oxford and New York, 1981.
[Oxford Historical Monographs. Important study of social structure and regional society, reaching the late fourteenth century.]

972. ———. "The Social Status of Chaucer's Franklin: A Reconsideration." *Medium Aevum* 52 (1983), 10–26.
[Status and mobility in literature and in "real life."]

973. ———. *Scenes from Provincial Life: Knightly Families in Sussex, 1280–1400*. Oxford and New York, 1986. [Sensitive study of gentry families that never rose to the very top: their strategies and their social world.]

974. Scattergood, V. John. "Fashion and Morality in the Late Middle Ages." In item 84. Pp. 255–72. [Sumptuary legislation and what literature tells us about fashion.]

975. Sheehan, Michael M. "Choice of a Marriage Partner in the Middle Ages: Development and Mode of Application of a Theory of Marriage." *Studies in Medieval and Renaissance History*, n.s. 1 (1978), 1–33.

976. ———. "Marriage Theory and Practice in the Conciliar Legislation and Diocesan Statutes of Medieval England." *MS* 40 (1978), 408–60.

977. ———. "The Wife of Bath and Her Four Sisters: Reflection on a Woman's Life in the Age of Chaucer." *Medievalia et Humanistica*, n.s. 13 (1985), 23–42.

978. ———. "Theory and Practice: Marriage of the Unfree and the Poor in Medieval Society." *MS* 50 (1988), 457–87. [Sheehan's papers, both those listed here and earlier essays, represent a major contribution towards the social (and canonical) history of medieval English marriage. They are being collected into a single volume.]

979. Shepherd, Geoffrey. "Poverty in *Piers Plowman.*" In item 7. Pp. 169–89.
[Deep ambiguity about poverty.]

980. Sherborne, James. *William Canynges, 1402–1474: Mayor of Bristol and Dean of Westbury College.* Bristol Branch, Historical Association, 1985.
[Biography: business ventures and spiritual life; a useful pamphlet.]

981. Smith, Richard M. "Modernization and the Corporate Medieval Village Community in England: Some Sceptical Reflections." In *Explorations in Historical Geography: Interpretative Essays.* Edited by Alan R. H. Baker and Derek Gregory. Cambridge Studies in Historical Geography, 5. Cambridge and New York, 1984. Pp. 140–79, 234–45.
[Theories and historiography to keep in mind in balancing the strengths of lordship and community.]

982. Smith, William. "Two Medieval Salisbury Wills." *JSA* 10/3 (1989), 118–22.
[From Salisbury Borough archives, one from 1406.]

983. Spufford, Peter ("Part I"), and Peter Woodhead ("Part II"). "Calais and Its Mint." In *Coinage in the Low Countries (880–1500): The Third Oxford Symposium on Coinage and Monetary History.* Edited by N. J. Mayhew. British Archaeological Reports, o.s. 3: International Ser., 54 (1979). Pp. 171–83; pp. 185–202.

[Woodhead gives details of the mint, its output, and the role of its money in England and on the Continent.]

984. Stephenson, M. J. "Wool Yields in the Medieval Economy." *EcHR*, 2nd ser., 41 (1988), 368–91.
[Fleece weights, based on the account rolls of the Winchester estates 1208–1454.]

985. Stewart, Ian. "The Dies of Edward V's Silver Coins." *BNJ* 50 (1980), 133–35.
[Late sun-and-rose coins; see item 916.]

986. Summerson, Henry. "Crime and Society in Medieval Cumberland." *Cumberland & Westmorland* 82 (1982), 111–24.
[Based on eyre and gaol delivery rolls.]

987. Vale, M. G. A. *Piety, Charity, and Literacy among the Yorkshire Gentry, 1370–1480.* Borthwick Papers, no. 50. York, 1976.
[The meshing of urban history and social behavior.]

988. Ware, T. G. Webb. "Dies and Designs: The English Gold Coinage, 1465–1485: Part I." *BNJ* 55 (1985), 95–133.
[Follows Blunt and Whitton, 1945–49, mostly on dies.]

989. Webster, Bruce. "The Community of Kent in the Reign of Richard II." *Arch Cant* 100 (1984), 217–29.
[Social structure, family and political activity.]

990. White, W. J. "Changing Burial Practices in Late Mediaeval England." *Ricardian* 4/63 (December 1978), 23–30.
[Embalming as a method declined in popularity in the fifteenth century.]

991. Williams, Daniel. "The Hastily Drawn Up Will of William Catesby, Esquire, 25 August 1485." *Leicestershire* 51 (1975–76), 43–52.

992. ———. "From Towton to Bosworth: The Leicestershire Community and the Wars of the Roses, 1461–85." *Leicestershire* 59 (1984–85), 27–43.
[Hastings was the focal point of stability and Yorkist loyalty; later, men turned against Richard.]

993. Wright, Susan M. *The Derbyshire Gentry in the Fifteenth Century.* Derbyshire Record Society, vol. 8 (1983).
[Social and economic survey, with some prosopography.]

VII. URBAN HISTORY

994. Alcock, N. W. "A Four-Part Indenture of 1388." *JSA* 7/4 (1983), 242–44.
[A Coventry lease, published with two photostats.]

995. Ashcroft, M. Y. "Snape in the Late Fifteenth Century." *North Yorkshire County Record Office Journal* 5 (1977), 20–58.

996. Astill, G. G. "Archaeology and the Smaller Town." *UHY* (1985), 46–53.
[Light on the question of urban decline in the later Middle Ages.]

997. Attreed, Lorraine. "Beggarly Bretons and Faynte-Harted Frenchmen: Age- and Class-Specific Mortality during London's Sweating Sickness of 1485." *Ricardian* 4/59 (December 1977), 2–16.
[The disease's heavy toll on the upper classes may have created openings for new men.]

998. ———. "The King's Interest: York's Fee Farm and the Central Government." *Northern* 17 (1981), 24–43.

999. ———. "Medieval Bureaucracy and York's Fee Farm during the 15th Century." *York Historian* 6 (1985), 24–31.

1000. Barley, Maurice W. "Town Defences in England and Wales after 1066." In item 10. Pp. 57–71.
[Mostly covering the High Middle Ages.]

1001. Barron, Caroline M. "London and the Crown, 1451–61." In item 43. Pp. 88–109.
[What government cost and who paid for it (with table of loans from Londoners).]

1002. ———. *Revolt in London: 11th to 15th June 1381.* London, 1981.
[Museum of the City of London. A close look at an exciting week.]

1003. ———. "The Parish Fraternities of Medieval London." In item 11. Pp. 13–37.
[A wide window into important aspects of urban life.]

1004. ———. "The Fourteenth Century Poll Tax Returns for Worcester." *Midland* 14 (1989), 1–29.
[Demography, occupational structure, household size, sex ratios, and an appendix on the taxation rates.]

1005. ———. "The Late Middle Ages: 1270–1520: Local History and Topography." In *The British Atlas of Historic Towns,* 3: *The City of London, from Prehistoric Times to c. 1520*. General editor, Mary D. Lobel, topographical editor, W. H. Johns. Oxford, 1989. Pp. 42–56. [Oxford University Press in conjunction with Historic Towns Trust. Also New York, 1989. In this volume Martha Carlin and Victor Belcher compiled the gazeteer, with historical notes for the two maps (from c. 1270 and c. 1520), pp. 63–99; see also item 1096.]

1006. Benedict, P. "Late Medieval and Early Modern Urban History in England." *Comparative Studies in Society and History* 28 (1986), 169–80.
[A review article of recent work and controversies.]

1007. Beresford, Maurice W. "Inclesmoor, West Riding of Yorkshire, circa 1407." In item 79. Pp. 147–61.

1008. Bigmore, Peter. "Villages and Towns." In item 16. Pp. 154–92.

1009. Blair, John. "Religious Gilds as Landowners in the Thirteenth and Fourteenth Centuries: The Example of Chesterfield." In item 71. Pp. 35–49.

1010. Blinkhorn, Steve, and Gabriel Newfield. "Charter of Freedom of St. Albans, 16th June 1381." In item 67. Pp. 123–26.
[Charter translated, with notes.]

1011. Bolton, James L. "The City and the Crown, 1456–61." *London Journal* 12/1 (Summer 1986), 11–24.

[Anti-alien riots of 1456 and the City's tilt towards the Yorkists.]

1012. Bridbury, Anthony R. "English Provincial Towns in the Later Middle Ages." *EcHR*, 2nd ser., 34 (1981), 1–24.
[Argues against the heavy emphasis on urban decline. For a critical response see item 1163, by R. Tittler, plus Bridbury's response.]

1013. Britnell, R. H. "Burghal Characteristics of Market Towns in Medieval England." *Durham University Journal* 42 (1981), 147–51.
[The similarities between market towns and boroughs.]

1014. ———. "The Oath Book of Colchester and the Borough Constitutions, 1372–1404." *Essex* 14 (1982), 94–101.
[A town memorandum book of the 1390s.]

1015. ———. "Colchester Courts and Court Records, 1310–1525." *Essex* 17 (1986), 133–40.
[A tally of sessions and a look at the business they handled.]

1016. ———. *Growth and Decline in Colchester, 1300–1525.* Cambridge and New York, 1986.
[Detailed, full-length study: prosperity peaked in the mid-fifteenth century.]

1017. Brooke, C. N. L. "The Churches of Medieval Cambridge." In *History, Society, and the Churches: Essays*

in Honour of Owen Chadwick. Edited by Derek Beales
and Geoffrey Best. Cambridge and New York, 1985.
Pp. 49–76.
[A survey of all the town's ecclesiastical buildings and their history.]

1018. Burgess, Clive. " 'By Quick and by Dead': Wills and
Pious Provision in Late Medieval Bristol." *EHR* 102
(1987), 837–58.
[Urban and religious history, well-woven into a
single fabric.]

1019. Butcher, A. F. "Rent, Population, and Economic
Change in Late-Medieval Newcastle." *Northern* 14
(1978), 67–77.
[Decline is the most likely theme.]

1020. ———. "Rent and the Urban Economy: Oxford and
Canterbury in the Later Middle Ages." *Southern* 1
(1979), 11–43.
[Following R. B. Dobson's lead (item 1030): some
improvement after 1450.]

1021. ———. "English Urban Society and the Revolt of
1381." In item 46. Pp. 84–111.
[The conditions that led to the rising in Canterbury: the town in the context of county and
rural society.]

1022. Butler, Lawrence. "The Evolution of Towns: Planted
Towns after 1066." In item 10. Pp. 32–48.
[Mostly planted before 1377.]

1023. Champion, Barbara A. "The Gilds of Medieval Beverley." In item 71. Pp. 51–66.

1024. Childs, Wendy R., ed. *The Customs Accounts of Hull, 1453–1490*. Record Ser., 144. Yorkshire Archaeological Society, 1986, for 1984.
[Itemized lists discussed for what they tell of Hull's economic life and prosperity.]

1025. Cobb, Harry S. "Cloth Exports from London and Southampton in the Late Fifteenth and Early Sixteenth Centuries: A Revision." *EcHR*, 2nd ser., 31 (1978), 601–09.
[London decline and Southampton boom in Henry VII's time.]

1026. Cocks, J. V. Somers. "Dartmoor, Devonshire: Late 15th and Early 16th Century." In item 79. Pp. 293–302.

1027. Cooper, C. R. H. "The Archives of the City of London Livery Companies and Related Organisations." *Archives* 16, no. 72 (1984), 323–53.
[A published lecture covering the sources and problems; touches on most of the major companies with extant records.]

1028. Cripps, Judith A. "Barholm, Greatford, and Stowe, Lincolnshire: Late 15th Century." In item 79. Pp. 263–88.

1029. Dale, Marian K. "The London Silkwomen of the Fifteenth Century." *Signs* 14 (1989), 489–501.

[Reprint of article from the *EcHR*, 1st ser., 4 (1933), 324–45; early and still valuable study of women in the urban workforce. This volume of *Signs* was subsequently published as *Sisters and Workers in the Middle Ages*, ed. Judith M. Bennett and Elizabeth Clark (Chicago, 1989).]

1030. Dobson, R. B. "Urban Decline in Late Medieval England." *TRHS*, 5th ser., 27 (1977), 1–22.
[Comprehensive survey of the evidence for decline and a caveat against a single pattern or answer; also see item 1020.]

1031. [No entry.]

1032. Dobson, R. B. "The Risings in York, Beverley, and Scarborough, 1380–1381." In item 46. Pp. 112–42.
[Town oligarchies exacerbated urban tension and oppression.]

1033. ———. "Yorkshire Towns in the Late Fourteenth Century." In *Miscellany: Volume 18 Part 1*. Publications of the Thoresby Society, vol. 59, pt. 1, no. 129 (1985). Pp. 1–21.
[Comparisons between large and small towns.]

1034. Douglas, Audrey. "Midsummer in Salisbury: The Tailors' Guild and Confraternity, 1444–1642." *Renaissance and Reformation* 25 (1989) 35–51.
[Festival, frivolity, and pageantry.]

1035. Dyer, Christopher. "Deserted Medieval Villages in the West Midlands." *EcHR*, 2nd ser., 35 (1982), 19–34.
[Long-term depopulation and out-migration.]

1036. Fox, Harold S. A. "Exeter, Devonshire: c. 1420." In item 79. Pp. 163–69.

1037. Girtin, T. *The Mark of the Sword: A Narrative History of the Cutlers' Company, 1189–1975*. London, 1975.
[Narrative story of a London company.]

1038. Goodall, Peter. "Chaucer's 'Burgesses' and the Aldermen of London." *Medium Aevum* 50 (1981), 284–92.
[A "petty bourgeois" perspective on town government can be seen in the General Prologue.]

1039. Gottfried, Robert S. "Bury St. Edmunds and the Population of Late Medieval Towns, 1270–1530." *JBS* 20 (1980), 1–31.

1040. ———. *Bury St. Edmunds and the Urban Crisis, 1290–1539*. Princeton, 1982.

1041. ———. "English Towns in the Later Middle Ages." *JIH* 19 (1988), 87–92.

1042. Green, Richard F. "Historical Notes of a London Citizen, 1483–88." *EHR* 96 (1981), 585–90.
[College of Arms MS. 2M6.]

1043. Grieve, H. E. P. "The Rebellion and the County Town." In item 59. Pp. 37–53.

[Chelmsford's contribution to and role in the excitement of 1381.]

1044. Guth, DeLloyd J. "Richard III, Henry VII, and the City: London Politics and the 'Dun Cow'." In item 32. Pp. 185–204.

[How the City prepared for another turn of Fortune's wheel after the battle of Bosworth.]

1045. Hadley, Guy. *Citizens and Founders: A History of the Worshipful Company of Founders, London, 1365–1975.* London, 1976.

1046. Hammer, Carl I., Jr. "The Town-Gown Confraternity of St. Thomas the Martyr in Oxford." *MS* 39 (1977), 466–76.

[An unusual link, lasting from 1349 until the dissolution under Edward VI.]

1047. ———. "Anatomy of an Oligarchy: The Oxford Town Council in the Fifteenth and Sixteenth Centuries." *JBS* 18 (Fall 1978), 1–27.

[More turnover and rotation than in many towns.]

1048. Harding, Vanessa. "The Two Cold Harbours of the City of London." *London Topographical Record* 24 (1980), ed. Ann L. Saunders, 11–29.

[Late medieval waterfront tenements.]

1049. Harvey, Barbara F. "Denham, Buckinghamshire, and Harefield, Middlesex, c. 1478." In item 79. Pp. 303–08.

1050. Harvey, John H. "Symbolic Plan of a City." In item 79. Pp. 342–43.

[The plan is found, BL Harley MS. 1808, fol. 45ᵛ.]

1051. ———. "Winchester, Hampshire, circa 1390." In item 79. Pp. 141–46.

1052. Harvey, Paul D. A. "Boarstall, Buckinghamshire, 1444 x 1446." In item 79. Pp. 211–20.

1053. ———. "Shouldham, Norfolk: 1440 x 1441." In item 79. Pp. 195–201.

1054. Hawes, Timothy, ed. *An Index to Norwich City Officers, 1453–1835*. Norfolk Record Society, vol. 52 (1989 for 1986).

[Also in the Norfolk Genealogy series, vol. 21, Norfolk & Norwich Genealogical Society, 1989. Mayors, sheriffs, aldermen of the thirteen wards, town recorders, and other officials.]

1055. Herbert, N. M., ed. *The 1483 Gloucester Charter in History*. Gloucester City Council and Gloucester Civic Trust. Gloucester, 1983.

[The charter is translated, pp. 9–15; Peter Clark, "A Poisoned Chalice? The 1483 Charter, City and County, 1483–1662"; R. A. Griffiths, "Richard III: King or Anti-King"; Herbert, "1483: Gloucester's Livelihood in the Middle Ages"; Susan Reynolds, "1483: Gloucester and Town Government in the Middle Ages."]

1056. Hilton, Rodney H. "The Small Towns and Urbanisation—Evesham in the Middle Ages." *Midland* 7 (1982), 1–8.
[Comparison of the town in the 1330s and 1520s argues for prosperity.]

1057. ———. "Towns in Societies—Medieval England." *UHY* (1982), 7–13.
[Importance of the links between urban and rural.]

1058. Holt, R. "Gloucester in the Century after the Black Death." *B & G AS* 103 (1985), 149–61.
[Still another tale of decline.]

1059. Homer, Ronald F. "The Medieval Pewterers of London, c. 1190–1457." *London & Middlesex* 36 (1985), 137–63.
[With references to the technology and the personnel.]

1060. Horrox, Rosemary. *The Changing Plan of Hull, 1290–1650: A Guide to Documentary Sources for the Early Topography of Hull*. City Council. Kingston upon Hull, 1978.

1061. ———. "Urban Patronage and Patrons in the Fifteenth and Sixteenth Century." In item 31. Pp. 145–66.
[The towns searched actively to find friends and protectors.]

1062.   ———, ed. *Selected Rentals and Accounts of Medieval Hull, 1293–1528*. Record Ser., vol. 141. Yorkshire Archaeological Society, 1983 for 1982.
[Chamberlain's account roll (1464–65) and rental of town's land (1465), printed in full.]

1063.   ———. "Richard III and London." *Ricardian* 6/85 (June 1984), 322–29.

1064.   ———. "The Urban Gentry in the Fifteenth Century." In item 82. Pp. 22–44.
[Ties between urban success, gentility, and landholding.]

1065.   Hull, Felix. "Memoranda from the Queenborough Statute Book, 1452–1556." In *A Kentish Miscellany*. Edited by F. Hull. Kent Records, vol. 21. London, 1979. Pp. 79–101.

1066.   ———. "Cliffe, Kent, Late 14th Century x 1408." In item 79. Pp. 99–105.

1067.   ———. "Isle of Thanet, Kent, Late 14th Century x 1414." In item 79. Pp. 119–26.

1068.   Hulton, Mary H. M. *"Company and Fellowship": The Medieval Weavers of Coventry*. Occasional Papers, no. 31. Dugdale Society, 1987.
[Mostly sixteenth-century.]

1069.   Jalland, Patricia. "The 'Revolution' in Northern Borough Representation in Mid-Fifteenth Century England." *Northern* 11 (1975), 27–51.

[Crown influence grew, as did the importance of winning parliamentary seats.]

1070.   James, Mervyn E. "Ritual, Drama, and Social Body in the Late Medieval English Town." *Past and Present* 98 (1983), 3–29.
[Valuable essay, informed by anthropology and the *Annales* school.]

1071.   James, T. B. "Administration and Aspiration: Some Southampton Property Owners, c. 1400–1600." *Proceedings of the Hampshire Field Club and Archaeological Society* 37 (1981), 55–62.

1072.   Jennings, John M. "The Distribution of Landed Wealth in the Wills of London Merchants, 1400–1450." *MS* 39 (1977), 261–80.
[With tables on categories of beneficiaries and quantitative data.]

1073.   Jones, Philip E. *The Butchers of London: A History of the Worshipful Company of Butchers of the City of London.* London, 1976.

1074.   ———. "Deptford, Kent and Surrey: Lambeth, Surrey: London, 1470–1478." In item 79. Pp. 251–62.

1075.   Keene, Derek. "Suburban Growth." In item 10. Pp. 71–82.

1076. ———. "Town into Gown: The Site of the College and Other College Lands in Winchester before the Reformation." In item 20. Pp. 37–73.
[Urban topography and economic history.]

1077. ———. "The Medieval Urban Environment in Documentary Records." *Archives* 16, no. 70 (1983), 137–44.
[The link between documentary evidence and the physical environment.]

1078. ———. "A New Study of London before the Great Fire." *UHY* (1984), 11–21.
[A description of the London reconstitution project.]

1079. ———. *Survey of Medieval Winchester.* Contribution by Alexander R. Rumble. 2 vols. Winchester Studies, 2. Oxford and New York, 1985.
[Major study of a city caught in a long decline. Volume 1 is a narrative, vol. 2 a detailed gazetteer with biographical entries and family trees; Rumble on personal names, 2:1405–11.]

1080. ———. "Medieval London and Its Region." *London Journal* 14 (1989), 99–111.
[Conference talk, with a note on London's population.]

1081. Kellaway, William. "John Carpenter's *Liber Albus*." *Guildhall* 3/2 (1978), 67–84.
[How the *Liber Albus* was assembled.]

1082. Kermode, Jennifer I. "The Merchants of Three Northern English Towns." In item 17. Pp. 7–48.
[Internal and external activity in York, Beverley, and Hull.]

1083. ———. "Urban Decline? The Flight from Office in Late Medieval York." *EcHR*, 2nd ser., 35 (1982), 179–98.
[Plenty were willing to serve, as the oligarchs replaced themselves.]

1084. ———. "Merchants, Overseas Trade, and Urban Decline: York, Beverley, and Hull, c. 1380–1500." *Northern* 23 (1987), 51–73.

1085. ———. "Obvious Observations on the Formation of Oligarchies in Late Medieval English Towns." In item 82. Pp. 87–106.
[How the ruling classes hung on.]

1086. Kettle, Ann J. "City and Close: Lichfield in the Century before the Reformation." In item 11. Pp. 158–69.
[Much closer ties than in some towns, e.g., Lincoln.]

1087. King, Edmund. "Peterborough, Mid- or Late-Fourteenth Century." In item 79. Pp. 83–87.

1088. Kirby, Joan W., ed. and intro. *The Manor and Borough of Leeds, 1425–1662: An Edition of Documents*. Publications of the Thoresby Society, vol. 57, no. 127 (1983 for 1981).

[Pages 1–22 are documents from before 1485; useful introduction, with statistical and biographical data in appendices.]

1089. ———. "The Rulers of Leeds: Gentry, Clothiers, and Merchants, c. 1425–1626." As item 1033. Pp. 22–49.
[How the oligarchy functioned, though we mostly see them after 1500.]

1090. Knowles, Michael David. "Clerkenwell and Islington, Middlesex: Mid-15th Century." In item 79. Pp. 221–28.

1091. Kowaleski, Maryanne. "Taxpayers in Late Fourteenth Century Exeter: The 1377 Murage Roll." *D & C N&Q* 34/6 (Autumn 1980), 217–22.
[A window into urban social stratification.]

1092. ———. "The Commercial Dominance of a Medieval Provincial Oligarchy: Exeter in the Late Fourteenth Century." *MS* 46 (1984), 355–84.
[Case studies of manipulation.]

1093. ———. "The 1377 Dartmouth Poll Tax." *D & C N&Q* 25/8 (Autumn 1985), 281–92.
[Analysis, with a list of taxpayers.]

1094. ———. "Women's Work in a Market Town: Exeter in the Late Fourteenth Century." In *Women and Work in Preindustrial Europe*. Edited by Barbara A. Hanawalt. Bloomington, Ind., 1986. Pp. 145–56.
[Though on Exeter, wider implications for social and economic history.]

1095.   Lacey, Kay E. "Women and Work in Fourteenth and Fifteenth Century London." In *Women and Work in Pre-Industrial England.* Edited by Lindsey Charles and Lorna Duffin. London and Dover, N.H., 1985. Pp. 24–82.
[In The Oxford Women's Series. Sanguine view of women's economic activities in a wide variety of roles and situations.]

1096.   Lobel, M. D., Joan C. Lancaster, and James Campbell, eds. *The British Atlas of Historic Towns, 2: Historic Towns: Atlas of the Historic Towns.* General editor, M. D. Lobel; typographical mapping editor, W. H. Johns. Oxford, 1975; New York, 1975.
[In conjunction with the Historic Towns Trust. Volume 1, 1969. In vol. 2, Lobel edited for Bristol and Cambridge, Lancaster for Coventry, Campbell for Norwich. A project of the International Commission for the History of Towns and the British Committee of Historic Towns. For vol. 3 see Barron, item 1005.]

1097.   Macfarlane, Alan, ed. *Records of An English Village: Earls Colne, 1400–1750.* 3 vols. Cambridge, 1980–81.
[The volumes cover church records, estate records, and records of secular government. Compiled and edited by Sarah Harrison, Charles Jardine, Tim King, Jessica King, and Cherry Bryant. A Social Science Research Council (SSRC) project, with the document sources available on microfiche.]

1098. Maddern, Philippa. "The Legitimation of Power: Riot and Authority in Fifteenth Century Norwich." *Pargeron*, n.s. 6 (1988), 65–84.
[Town-gown tension and a riot against the Black Monks in 1443.]

1099. Marsden, Peter. "The Medieval Ships of London." In *The Archaeology of Medieval Ships and Harbours in Northern Europe: Papers Based on Those Presented to an International Symposium on Boat and Ship Archaeology at Bremerhaven in 1979*. Edited by Sean McGrail. BAR International Ser., 66. Oxford, 1979. Pp. 83–92.
[Also National Maritime Museum, Greenwich, Archaeological Ser., no. 5 (Greenwich, 1979).]

1100. May, Peter. "Newmarket 500 Years Ago." *Suffolk* 33 (1975), 253–74.
[Topography and town life.]

1101. ———. "Newmarket and Its Market Court, 1399–1413." *Suffolk* 35 (1981), 31–39.
[Methods and results of quick commercial justice.]

1102. McDonnell, K. G. T. *Medieval London Suburbs*. London, 1978.
[Their growth and economic development, suburb by suburb.]

1103. McIntosh, Marjorie K. "Money Lending on the Periphery of London, 1300–1600." *Albion* 20 (1988), 557–71.

[Lively cash economy: wealthy tenants and landlords were all in the game.]

1104. McRee, Ben R. "Religious Gilds and the Regulation of
Behavior in Late Medieval Towns." In item 72. Pp.
108–22.
[Social control and the fight to maintain a good
reputation.]

1105. Moran, J. "Caxton and the City of London." *JPHS* 11
(1976), 81–91.

1106. Moss, Douglass. "Death in Fifteenth Century Tottenham." *Local Population Studies* 37 (Autumn 1986),
36–44.
[Reasonable longevity for those who reached
adulthood.]

1107. Moss, Douglass, and Ian Murray. "Signs of Change in
a Medieval Village Community." *London & Middlesex*
27 (1976), 280–87.
[Land turnover in Tottenham: small plots and a
good volume of exchange.]

1108. Murray, Jacqueline. "Kinship and Friendship: The
Perception of Family by Clergy and Laity in Late
Medieval London." *Albion* 20 (1988), 369–85.
[Consistory court materials.]

1109. Nightingale, Pamela. "Capitalism, Crafts, and Constitutional Change in Late Fourteenth Century London."
Past and Present 124 (1989), 3–35.

1110.   Orme, Nicholas. "The Kalendar Brethren of the City of Exeter." *Devonshire* 109 (1977), 153–69.

1111.   ———. "The Guild of Kalendars, Bristol." *B & G AS* 96 (1978), 32–52.
[The personnel and the institution, with lists of chaplains and guild property.]

1112.   ———. "Mortality in Fourteenth Century Exeter." *Medical History* 32 (1982), 195–203.
[Cathedral obits.]

1113.   Owen, Dorothy M., ed. *William Asshebourne's Book.* Norfolk Record Society, vol. 48 (1981).
[Printed and catalogued with *The Records of a Commission of Sewers for Wiggenhall, 1319–1324*, ed. A. E. B. Owen. The troubles and events in Lynn in 1415, as seen and recorded by the town clerk.]

1114.   ———, ed. *The Making of King's Lynn: A Documentary Survey.* British Academy, Records of Social and Economic History, n.s., 9. London, 1984.
[This is vol. 3 of the King's Lynn Archaeological Survey; long introduction, with many documents covering 1377–1485; especially strong on urban economic life.]

1115.   ———. "Clenchwarton, Norfolk: Late 14th Century or Early 15th Century." In item 79. Pp. 127–30.

1116.   Palliser, David M. "Sources for Urban Topography: Documents, Buildings, and Archaeology." In item 10. Pp. 1–7.

1117.   ———. "A Crisis in English Towns? The Case of York, 1460–1640." *Northern* 14 (1978), 108–25.
[Mostly post-Reformation.]

1118.   ———. "A Regional Capital as Magnet: Immigrants to York, 1477–1560." *YAJ* 57 (1985), 111–23.
[Mostly sixteenth-century; how many came, whence (and from how far).]

1119.   ———. "Urban Decay Revisited." In item 82. Pp. 1–21.
[Against a simple typology or aetiology.]

1120.   Phythian-Adams, Charles. "Jolly Cities, Goodly Towns: The Current Research for England's Urban Roots." *UHY* (1977), 30–39.
[Review article and bibliographic survey.]

1121.   ———. "Urban Decay in Late Medieval England." In *Towns in Societies: Essays in Economic History and Historical Sociology.* Edited by Philip Abrams and E. A. Wrigley. Cambridge, 1979; Cambridge and New York, 1978. Pp. 159–85.
[Past and Present Publications.]

1122.   ———. *Desolation of a City: Coventry and the Urban Crisis of the Late Middle Ages.* Cambridge and New York, 1979.

[Past and Present Publications. Perhaps the major monograph on a single town, and a strong statement of the case for decline and decay. Reviewed by R. B. Dobson, *History* 66 (1981), 123–25.]

1123. Platt, Colin. *The English Medieval Town*. London, 1986, 1979, 1976; New York, 1976.
[General treatment and well-informed: town size, plans, architecture, urban life, and other aspects.]

1124. ———. "The Evolution of Towns: Natural Growth." In item 10. Pp. 48–56.

1125. Platts, Graham. "Butterwick and the Poll Taxes of 1377 and 1380." *Lincolnshire* 24 (1989), 5–20.
[Details of households, residential patterns, and growing resistance.]

1126. Post, J. B. "A Fifteenth-Century Customary of the Southwark Stews." *JSA* 5/7 (April 1977), 418–28.
[Social control; the document is published.]

1127. Prescott, Andrew. "London in the Peasants' Revolt: A Portrait Gallery." *London Journal* 7/2 (1981), 125–43.
[High marks to the rebels' awareness. Also see James Bolton, "London and the Peasants' Revolt," ibid., pp. 123–24, calling attention to the six-hundredth anniversary.]

1128. Ralph, Elizabeth. "Bristol: c. 1480." In item 79. Pp. 309–16.

1129. Reddaway, T. F., and Lorna E. M. Walker. *The Early History of the Goldsmiths' Company, 1327–1509*. London, 1975.
[Prepared for publication with additional material including the first volume of the ordinances and statutes of the Worshipful Company of Goldsmiths, *The Book of Ordinances, 1478–83* (1975), by Walker.]

1130. Repina, L. P. "Burgerdom in Medieval England: The Main Problems and Stages." In *Studies in British History*. Moscow, 1984. Pp. 158–72.

1131. Reynolds, Susan. *An Introduction to the History of English Medieval Towns*. Reprinted with corrections, Oxford and New York, 1982; Oxford, 1977.
[A basic scholarly discussion and synthesis.]

1132. ———. "Decline and Decay in Late Medieval Towns: A Look at Some of the Concepts and Arguments." *UHY* (1980), 76–78.
[Balanced, with suggestions for future work.]

1133. ———. "Medieval Urban History and the History of Political Thought." *UHY* (1982), 14–23.
[Towns were nuclei of community self-consciousness.]

1134. ———. "Chertsey, Surrey and Laleham, Middlesex: Mid- or Late 15th Century." In item 79. Pp. 237–43.

1135. ———. "Staines, Middlesex: 1469 x circa 1477." In item 79. Pp. 245–50.

1136. Rigby, Stephen H. "Urban Decline in the Later Middle Ages: Some Problems in Interpreting the Statistical Evidence." *UHY* (1979), 46–59.
[Uncertainties attached to using the lay subsidies to determine size and wealth.]

1137. ———. "Boston and Grimsby in the Middle Ages: An Administrative Contrast." *JMH* 10 (1984), 51–66.
[Urban liberties and their link to economic development and health.]

1138. ———. "Urban Decline in the Later Middle Ages: The Reliability of the Non-Statistical Evidence." *UHY* (1984), 45–60.
[The difficulty of knowing whether to believe the towns' cries of poverty.]

1139. ———. "The Customs Administration at Boston in the Reign of Richard II." *BIHR* 58 (1985), 12–24.
[Are the returns a key to the volume and value of foreign trade? Maybe.]

1140. ———. " 'Sore Decay' and 'Fair Dwellings': Boston and Urban Decline in the Later Middle Ages." *Midland* 10 (1985), 47–61.
[Cloudy picture, but Boston seems (another) tale of decline.]

1141. ———. "Late Medieval Urban Prosperity: The Evidence of Lay Subsidies." *EcHR*, 2nd ser., 29 (1986), 411–16.

[A difference of opinion: see A. R. Bridbury, "Dr. Rigby's Comment: A Reply," ibid., pp. 417–22, and J. F. Hadwin, "From Dissonance to Harmony on the Late Medieval Town?" ibid., pp. 423–26.]

1142. ———. "Urban 'Oligarchy' in Late Medieval England." In item 82. Pp. 62–86.
[The general drift in hard times was towards more oligarchy.]

1143. Roberts, Eileen. "The Boundary of the Borough of St. Albans, and Its Significance in the Revolt." In item 67. Pp. 128–85.
[An elaborate topographical treatment of the reconstructed boundaries.]

1144. Rosser, Gervase. "The Essence of Medieval Urban Communities: The Vill of Westminster, 1200–1540." *TRHS*, 5th ser., 34 (1984), 91–112.
[Guilds and community activity in the shadow of the abbey.]

1145. ———. "The Town and Guild of Lichfield in the Late Middle Ages." *Transactions - South Staffordshire Archaeological and Historical Society*, 27 (1985–86), 38–47.
[The story before the license of 1387, and the institution after that.]

1146. ———. "The Guild of St. Mary and St. John the Baptist, Lichfield: Ordinances of the Late 14th Century." In *Collections for a History of Staffordshire.*

4th ser., vol. 13. Staffordshire Record Society, 1988.
Pp. 19–26.

[Ordinances published.]

1147.   ———. "London and Westminster: The Suburb in the
Urban Economy in the Later Middle Ages." In item
82. Pp. 45–61.

[Not such a strong distinction between city and
major suburb.]

1148.   ———. *Medieval Westminster, 1200–1540.* Oxford and
New York, 1989.

[Detailed treatment of an important community,
touching its internal life, the abbey, and relations with the City of London.]

1149.   Saul, Anthony. "The Herring Industry at Great Yarmouth, c. 1280–c. 1400." *Norfolk* 38 (1981), 33–43.

[Serious decline by the late fourteenth century;
includes the organization of the herring trade.]

1150.   ———. "English Towns in the Late Middle Ages: The
Case of Great Yarmouth." *JMH* 8 (1982), 75–88.

[Every index points to prolonged decline.]

1151.   Scattergood, V. John. "Chaucer in the Suburbs." In
*Medieval Literature and Antiquities: Studies in Honour
of Basil Cottle.* Edited by Myra Stokes and T. L.
Burton. Woodbridge and Wolfeboro, N.H., 1987. Pp.
145–62.

[What light Chaucer sheds on urbanization and the problems of town government and public order.]

1152.   Schofield, John. *The Building of London: From the Conquest to the Great Fire.* London, 1983.
[British Museum, with Museum of London. A Colonnade Book.]

1153.   Schofield, John, and Tony Dyson. *Archaeology of the City of London: Recent Discoveries of the Department of Urban Archaeology, Museum of London.* City of London, Archaeological Trust. London, 1980.
[Good guide to recent digs and finds.]

1154.   Slater, Terry R. "The Urban Hierarchy in Medieval Staffordshire." *JHG* 11 (1985), 115–37.
[Lay subsidies as the source: size, wealth, population, and migration.]

1155.   ———. "English Medieval Town Planning." In *Urban Historical Geography: Recent Progress in Britain and Germany.* Edited by Dietrich Denecke and Gareth Shaw. Cambridge Studies in Historical Geography, 10. Cambridge and New York, 1988. Pp. 93–105, 363–66.
[A quick overview, with an interest in plot sizes and patterns.]

1156.   Smith, William. "A Medieval Archive from Trinity Hospital, Salisbury." *Archives* 14, no. 69 (1983), 39–46.
[Of value for urban history, with some examples.]

1157. Stevens, K. F., ed. *The Brokage Books of Southampton for 1477–8 and 1527–8*. Southampton Records Ser., vol. 28. Southampton, 1985.
[T. E. Olding, trans., the material from 1477–78.]

1158. Sutton, Anne. "The City of London and the Coronation of Richard III." *Ricardian* 4/63 (December 1978), 2–8.

1159. Swanson, Heather. *Building Craftsmen in Late Medieval York*. Borthwick Institute of Historical Research, Borthwick Papers, no. 63. York, 1983.
[The craft and the personnel.]

1160. ———. "The Illusion of Economic Structure: Craft Guilds in Late Medieval English Towns." *Past and Present* 121 (1985), 29–48.
[He who controlled trade, controlled urban political decisions.]

1161. ———. *Medieval Artisans: An Urban Class in Late Medieval England*. Oxford, 1989; Oxford and New York, 1989.
[Using wills to explore their links to town government and their own culture; also valuable on urban economic life.]

1162. Titow, Jan Z. "The Decline of the Fair of St. Giles, Winchester, in the Thirteenth and Fourteenth Centuries." *Nottingham* 31 (1987), 58–75.
[Mostly tabular data, now interpreted to tell a sad tale.]

1163.   Tittler, Robert. "Late Medieval Urban Prosperity."
        EcHR, 2nd ser., 37 (1984), 551–54.
        [Argument with A. R. Bridbury (item 1012); in
        favor of a picture of urban decline: Bridbury's
        response, "Late Medieval Urban Prosperity: A
        Rejoinder," ibid., pp. 555–56.]

1164.   Urry, William. "Canterbury, Kent: Late 14th Century
        x 1414." In item 79. Pp. 107–17.

1165.   Waters, Gwen. *King Richard's Gloucester: Life in a
        Medieval Town*. London, 1983.
        [A short attempt at a rounded picture, with a
        discussion of Richard III's charter of 1483.]

1166.   Weinstein, Rosemary. "Medieval Houses in St. Giles,
        Cripplegate, and St. Botolphs, Bishopsgate." *London
        Topographical Record* 25 (1985), ed. Ann L. Saunders,
        13–32.
        [Much late-medieval building.]

1167.   White, Eileen. *The St. Christopher and St. George
        Guild of York*. University of York, Borthwick Papers,
        no. 72. York, 1987.
        [History of the guild and its role in urban life.]

VIII. RURAL, AGRARIAN, AND MANORIAL HISTORY

1168.   Bailey, Mark. "The Rabbit and the Medieval East
Anglian Economy." *AgHR* 36 (1988), 1–20.
[Cultivated as a commercial animal, good on
poor land; poaching problems.]

1169.   ———. *A Marginal Economy? East Anglian Breckland
in the Later Middle Ages.* Cambridge Studies in
Medieval Life and Thought, 4th ser., 12. Cambridge
and New York, 1989.
[Chapters 4–5 cover 1300–1540: a tale of crisis,
decline, and some recovery.]

1170.   Baker, Alan R. H. "Changes in the Later Middle
Ages." In *A New Historical Geography of England
before 1600.* Edited by H. C. Darby. Cambridge and
New York, 1976. Pp. 186–247.
[Originally published (1973) in hardcover, this
edition covers chs. 1–6; judicious and valuable
summary.]

1171.   Barley, Maurice W. "Sherwood Forest, Nottingham-
shire: Late 14th or Early 15th Century." In item 79.
Pp. 131–39.
[Details of a local map.]

1172. Barton, Paul. "Manorial Economy and Society in Shenly Park." In item 67. Pp. 4–53.
[Village topography on the eve of the Peasants' Rebellion.]

1173. Birrell, Jean, ed. "The *Status Maneriorum* of John Catesby, 1385 and 1386." In *Miscellany I*. Edited by Robert Bearman. Publications of the Dugdale Society, vol. 31 (1977). Pp. 15–28.
[Manorial accounting, based on PRO SC6/1041/10.]

1174. Blanchard, Ian. "Industrial Employment and the Rural Land Market." In item 80. Pp. 227–75.
[The issues of economic history, transported to the countryside and the rural labor question.]

1175. Brenner, Robert. "Agrarian Class Structure and Economic Development in Pre-Industrial Europe." *Past and Present* 70 (1976), 30–75.
[The first challenge in what became the "Brenner Debate" about the decline of manorial Europe and the causes of change; contributions eventually collected in item 8.]

1176. ———. "The Agrarian Roots of European Capitalism." In item 8. Pp. 213–327.
[Brenner's final say in this important controversy.]

1177. Britnell, R. H. "The Langley Survey of Durham Bishopric Estates, 1418–21." *Arch Ael*, 5th ser., 16 (1988), 213–21.

[The value and problems of the survey as a source for manorial economic and administrative history; PRO SC12/21/29.]

1178. Brooks, Nicholas P. "The Organization and Achievement of the Peasants of Kent and Essex in 1381." In *Studies in Medieval History Presented to R. H. C. Davis.* Edited by Henry Mayr-Harting and R. I. Moore. London and Ronceverte, W.Va., 1985. Pp. 247–70.
[Perhaps they were well organized, highly disciplined, and with a canny eye to the deployment of resources.]

1179. Brown, Ann. "London and North-West Kent in the Late Middle Ages: The Development of a Land Market." *Arch Cant* 92 (1976), 145–55.
[The predecessors of today's commuters and land and estate developers.]

1180. Campbell, Bruce M. S. "Agricultural Progress in Medieval England: Some Evidence from Eastern Norfolk." *EcHR*, 2nd ser., 36 (1983), 26–46.
[From bailiffs' accounts: high productivity.]

1181. ———. "Arable Productivity in Medieval England: Some Evidence from Norfolk." *Journal of Economic History* 43 (1983), 379–404.
[Covers 1268–1430: the crop yields of sixty-two demesne holdings, with caveats and an argument for the need to accept diversity.]

1182. ———. "The Complexity of Manorial Structures in Medieval Norfolk: A Case Study." *Norfolk* 39 (1986), 225–61.
[Tenurial complexity and the changing nature of lordship to the late fourteenth century.]

1183. ———. "Population Changes and the Genesis of Common Fields on a Norfolk Manor." *EcHR*, 2nd ser., 32 (1986), 174–92.
[Martham: population growth triggered so much more.]

1184. ———. "The Diffusion of Vetches in Medieval England." *EcHR*, 2nd ser., 41 (1988), 193–208.
[Main increase in planting, 1375–99. Also see C. R. J. Currie, "Early Vetches in Medieval England: A Note," ibid., pp. 114–16, for thirteenth-century references.]

1185. ———. "Towards an Agricultural Geography of Medieval Europe." *AgHR* 36 (1988), 87–98.
[A review article covering Langdon, item 1221.]

1186. Campey, Lucille H. "Medieval Village Plans in the County of Durham: An Analysis of Reconstructed Plans Based on Medieval Documentary Sources." *Northern* 25 (1989), 60–87.
[Based on a Durham bursar's rental of 1400.]

1187. Carpenter, Christine. "The Fifteenth-Century English Gentry and Their Estates." In item 54. Pp. 36–60.
[Control and consolidation warred with the urge to take risks.]

1188.   Cooper, J. P. "In Search of Agrarian Capitalism."
Past and Present 80 (1978), 20–65. Reprinted in item 8.
Pp. 138–91.
[In disagreement with R. Brenner.]

1189.   Coward, Harold. "The Wowwall: Some Aspects of Government and Land-Drainage Early in the Fifteenth
Century." *Somerset* 124 (1979–80), 151–58.
[Efforts to control floods could split local communities.]

1190.   Croot, Patricia, and David Parker. "Agrarian Class
Structure and the Development of Capitalism: France
and England Compared." *Past and Present* 78 (1978),
37–47. Reprinted in item 8. Pp. 79–90.
[A contribution to the "Brenner Debate."]

1191.   DeWindt, Anne R. "Peasant Power Structure in Fourteenth Century Kings Ripton." *MS* 38 (1976), 236–67.
[The activities of the families of the village.]

1192.   ———. "A Peasant Land Market and Its Participants:
Kings Ripton, 1280–1400." *Midland* 4 (1978), 142–59.
[Considerable freedom to alienate, dispose by
will, and other such devices.]

1193.   DeWindt, Edwin Brezette. *The Liber Gersumarum of
Ramsey Abbey: A Calendar and Index of B.L. Harley
MS 445.* Pontifical Institute of Mediaeval Studies,
Subsidia Mediaevalia, 7. Toronto, 1976.
[A world in motion, mostly 1398–1458; opens the
window on over 4300 entries of peasants' activ-
ities.]

1194.   Drury, J. Linda. "Early Settlement in Stanhope Park, Weardale, 1406–79." *Arch Ael*, 5th ser., 4 (1976), 139–49.
[The leasing of grazing rights enables us to follow the tale.]

1195.   Dyer, Christopher. *Lords and Peasants in a Changing Society: The Estates of the Bishopric of Worcester, 680–1540*. Cambridge and New York, 1980.
[Past and Present Publications. A major monograph on economy and regional development. Criticized on demography by J. Hatcher, *AgHR* 32 (1984), 96–97.]

1196.   ———. *Warwickshire Farming 1349–c. 1520: Preparations for Agricultural Revolution*. Dugdale Society Occasional Papers, no. 27 (1981).

1197.   ———. "Changes in the Link between Families and Land in the West Midlands in the Fourteenth and Fifteenth Centuries." In item 80. Pp. 305–11.
[These two papers are important case studies, showing local conditions as the possible basis for larger interpretations.

1198.   ———. "Changes in the Size of Peasant Holdings in Some West Midland Villages, 1400–1500." In item 80. Pp. 277–94.

1199.   ———. "Changes in Diet in the Late Middle Ages: The Case of Harvest Workers." *AgHR* 36 (1988), 21–37.
[Better food at the end of the period; Sedgeford, Norfolk, the main data base.]

1200. Faith, Rosamund J. "Berkshire, Fourteenth and Fifteenth Centuries." In item 39. Pp. 106–77.
[Updating and expanding her seminal work from the *AgHR*, 1966.]

1201. Farmer, David. "Grain Yields on the Winchester Manors in the Later Middle Ages." *EcHR*, 2nd ser., 30 (1977), 555–66.
[Late fourteenth-century rise in productivity.]

1202. ———. "Grain Yields on Westminster Abbey Manors, 1271–1410." *Canadian Journal of History/Annales canadiennes d'histoire* 18 (1983), 331–47.
[Good sources tell a tale of contracting acreage and better yields.]

1203. Field, R. K. "Migration in the Later Middle Ages: The Case of the Hampton Lovett Villeins." *Midland* 8 (1983), 29–48.
[Mostly local migration.]

1204. Fox, Harold S. A. "The Chronology of Enclosure and Economic Development in Medieval Devon." *EcHR*, 2nd ser., 28 (1975), 181–202.
[Beware single explanations or the reliance on a single chronological framework.]

1205. Glennie, Paul. "In Search of Agrarian Capitalism: Manorial Land Markets and the Acquisition of Land in the Lea Valley." *Continuity and Change* 3 (1988), 11–40.
[The persistance of copyhold over leasehold; individual holdings traced.]

1206. Hare, J. N. "Durrington: A Chalkland Village in the Later Middle Ages." *Wiltshire* 74 (1979–80), 137–47.
[Prosperity until the mid-fifteenth century.]

1207. ———. "The Demesne Lessees of Fifteenth Century Wiltshire." *AgHR* 29 (1981), 1–15.
[Leasing came late, mostly to prosperous peasants of the locality.]

1208. ———. "The Monks as Landlords: The Leasing of the Monastic Demesnes in Southern England." In item 11. Pp. 82–94.
[A diverse picture, with sharp contrasts even in one particular region.]

1209. Harvey, Barbara F. *Westminster Abbey and Its Estates in the Middle Ages.* Oxford, 1977.
[Chapters 9–11, from 1348; the movement away from villeinage and towards custom and leasing, well illustrated in this important study.]

1210. Hatcher, John. "Mortality in the Fifteenth Century: Some New Evidence." *EcHR*, 2nd ser., 39 (1986), 19–38.
[On the monks of Christ Church Priory, Canterbury, and towards the construction of a model life table.]

1211. Hilton, R. H. *The English Peasantry in the Later Middle Ages: The Ford Lectures for 1973 and Related Studies.* Oxford, 1979, 1975.
[The lectures, pp. 3–110, and important papers on social structure, rents, and peasant economic status.]

1212.   ———. "Reasons for Inequality among Medieval Peasants." *Journal of Peasant Studies* 5 (1977–78), 271–84. Reprinted in item 45. Pp. 139–51.
[An overview, with emphasis on a shifting in the land-labor ratio.]

1213.   ———. "A Crisis of Feudalism." *Past and Present* 80 (1978), 3–19. Reprinted in item 8. Pp. 119–37.
[Taking sides (largely with Brenner, against the neo-Malthusians) in the "Brenner Debate."]

1214.   Hogan, M. Patricia. "Clays, *Culturae*, and the Cultivator's Wisdom: Management Efficiency at Fourteenth Century Wistow." *AgHR* 36 (1988), 117–31.
[Decision-making, centering around the need to choose a strategy for cropping.]

1215.   Howell, Cicely. "Stability and Change, 1300–1700: The Socio-Economic Context of the Self-Perpetuating Family Farm in England." *Journal of Peasant Studies* 2 (1974–75), 468–82.
[The complicated development of the "commercial family farm."]

1216.   ———. "Peasant Inheritance Customs in the Midlands, 1280–1700." In *Family and Inheritance: Rural Society in Western Europe, 1200–1800*. Edited by Jack Goody, Joan Thirsk, and E. P. Thompson. Cambridge and New York, 1976. Pp. 112–55.
[Past and Present Publications. Also Cambridge, 1979; Cambridge and New York, 1978. The long transition from the traditional to the more stratified society.]

1217. ————. *Land, Family, and Inheritance in Transition: Kibworth Harcourt, 1280–1700.* Cambridge and New York, 1983.
[Model of detailed local study. Reviewed by J. M. W. Bean, *JBS* 24 (1985), 375–81.]

1218. Hurst, J. G. "The Changing Medieval Village in England." In item 70. Pp. 27–62.
[The diversity of shape and form.]

1219. Jones, Andrew. "A Dispute between the Abbey of Ramsey and Its Tenants." *EHR* 91 (1976), 341–43.
[Customary tenants vs. the abbot.]

1220. ————. "Bedfordshire: Fifteenth Century." In item 39. Pp. 178–251.
[Scholarship drawn from his 1975 thesis; careful localized analysis.]

1221. Langdon, John. *Horses, Oxen, and Technological Innovation: The Use of Draught Animals in English Farming from 1066 to 1500.* Cambridge and New York, 1986.
[Past and Present Publications. See review article, item 1185.]

1222. Lomas, R. A. "The Priory of Durham and Its Demesnes in the Fourteenth and Fifteenth Centuries." *EcHR*, 2nd ser., 31 (1978), 339–53.
[Economic needs governed policies of demesne cultivation: follows (and corrects) E. M. Halcrow, *EcHR*, 1954–55.]

1223.   ———. "A Northern Farm at the End of the Middle Ages: Elvethall Manor, Durham, 1443/4–1513/14." *Northern* 18 (1982), 26–53.
[Considerable fifteenth-century prosperity.]

1224.   ———. "South-East Durham: Late Fourteenth and Fifteenth Centuries." In item 39. Pp. 252–327.

1225.   Mate, Mavis. "Agrarian Economy after the Black Death: The Manors of Canterbury Cathedral Priory, 1348–91." *EcHR*, 2nd ser., 37 (1984), 341–54.
[The crisis led to a pruning of resources and better management.]

1226.   ———. "Property Investment by Canterbury Cathedral Priory, 1250–1400." *JBS* 23 (1984), 1–21.

1227.   ———. "Pastoral Farming in South-East England in the Fifteenth Century." *EcHR*, 2nd ser., 40 (1987), 523–36.
[Many fluctuations, some from external causes, some from agricultural and pastoral ones.]

1228.   McIntosh, Marjorie Keniston. *Autonomy and Community: The Royal Manor of Havering, 1200–1500*. Cambridge Studies in Medieval Life and Thought, 4th ser., 5. Cambridge and New York, 1986.
[Important case study of community growth and change, on the outer edge of London.]

1229.   McLean, Teresa. *Medieval English Gardens*. London, 1989, 1981; New York, 1981.

[General treatment, covering food production, flowers, and aesthetics and horticultural design.]

1230.   Medick, Hans. "The Transition from Feudalism to Capitalism: Renewal of the Debate." As item 861. Pp. 120–30.
[With an eye on Brenner (item 8) and Immanuel Wallerstein.]

1231.   Owen, A. E. B. "Deeping Fen, Lincolnshire: Late 15th Century." In item 79. Pp. 289–91.

1232.   ———. "Isle of Ely, Cambridgeshire and Holland, Lincolnshire: Late 14th Century." In item 79. Pp. 89–98.

1233.   Pollard, Anthony J. "The North-Eastern Economy and the Agrarian Crisis of 1438–1440." *Northern* 25 (1989), 88–105.
[Severe crisis, with shortish ups and downs; much material from Lord Fitzhugh's manors.]

1234.   Poos, L. R. "The Rural Population of Essex in the Later Middle Ages." *EcHR*, 2nd ser., 38 (1985), 515–30.
[Fifteenth-century stagnation, based on frankpledge and tithing unit sources.]

1235.   Postan, Michael M., and John Hatcher. "Population and Class Relations in Feudal Society." *Past and Present* 78 (1978), 24–37. Reprinted in item 8. Pp. 64–78.
[In the "Brenner Debate," against Brenner's views.]

1236. Postles, David. "The Oseney Abbey Flock." *Oxon* 49
(1984), 141–52.
[Demesne diminished, but not the flocks; accounts of 1476–77, the main source.]

1237. Raban, Sandra. *The Estates of Thorney and Crowland: A Study in Medieval Monastic Land Tenure.* University of Cambridge, Department of Land Economy, Occasional Paper No. 7. Cambridge, 1977.

1238. Raftis, J. A. *A Small Town in Late Medieval England: Godmanchester, 1278–1400.* Pontifical Institute of Mediaeval Studies, Studies and Texts, 53. Toronto, 1982.
[Mostly demographic, with an interest in economic and social structure.]

1239. Razi, Zvi. *Life, Marriage, and Death in a Medieval Parish: Economy, Society, and Demography in Halesowen, 1270–1400.* Cambridge and New York, 1980.
[Past and Present Publications. Reviewed by Marjorie K. McIntosh, *Speculum* 56 (1981), 906–09.]

1240. ———. "Family, Land, and the Village Community in Later Medieval England." *Past and Present* 93 (1981), 3–36.
[The data from Halesowen argue for strong family interaction; an important article, often cited as one of the richer case studies.]

1241. ———. "The Erosion of the Family-Land Bond in the Late Fourteenth and Fifteenth Centuries: A Methodological Note." In item 80. Pp. 295–304.

1242. Rees, Una. "The Leases of Haughmond Abbey, Shropshire." *Midland* 8 (1983), 14–28.
[Leasing was predominant from 1320 on.]

1243. Riden, Philip. "An Early Fifteenth Century Chesterfield Rental." *Derbyshire* 95 (1975), 6–11.
[Document transcribed.]

1244. Rowley, Trevor. "Medieval Field Systems." In item 16. Pp. 25–55.

1245. Snape, M. G. "Durham: 1440 x 1445." In item 79. Pp. 203–09.

1246. ———. "Durham: 1439 x circa 1442." In item 79. Pp. 189–94.

1247. ———. "Witton Gilbert, County Durham: Mid-Fifteenth Century." In item 79. Pp. 229–35.

1248. Snape, M. G., and B. K. Roberts. "Tursdale Beck, County Durham: circa 1430 x 1442." In item 79. Pp. 171–87.

1249. Styles, Dorothy. "A Financial Account of St. Mary's, Warwick: Michaelmas, 1410–Michaelmas, 1411." As item 1173. Pp. 138–58.
[A final balance of £281, as in the Warwick Record Office account, edited here.]

1250. Symons, David. "Weobley Castle and Northfield in 1424." *Transactions of the Buckingham and Warwickshire Archaeological Society*, 93 (1983–84), 45–56.

[A survey of the year, with list of tenants and
holdings.]

1251. Tomkins, M. "The Manor of Park in the Fourteenth
Century." In item 67. Pp. 55–81.
[With the charter of 1377.]

1252. Unwin, Tim. "Rural Marketing in Medieval Nottinghamshire." *JHG* 7 (1981), 231–51.
[Distances between markets, and why they were
formed and why some did well.]

1253. Waites, Bryan. "Pastoral Farming on the Duchy of
Lancaster's Pickering Estate in the Fourteenth and
Fifteenth Centuries." *YAJ* 49 (1977), 77–86.
[Mostly sheep; good organization strengthened
the manor's political contribution.]

1254. Watkin, Andrew. "Cattle Grazing in the Forest of
Arden in the Later Middle Ages." *AgHR* 37 (1989),
12–25.
[The positive effect of pastoral economy on the
region.]

1255. Williams, C. L. Sinclair. "A Rental of the Manor of
East Malling, A.D. 1410." As item 1065. Pp. 27–78.
[Introduction, an English calendar, notes on
place names.]

1256. Williams, Michael. "Marshland and Waste." In item
16. Pp. 86–125.
[The course of colonization and settlement.]

IX. THE CHURCH AND RELIGIOUS HISTORY

1257. Archer, Margaret, ed. *The Register of Bishop Philip Repingdon, 1405-1419, 3: Memoranda, 1414-1419.* Publications of the Lincoln Record Society, vol. 74 (1982).
[The earlier volumes, 57 and 58 of the Lincoln Record Society, were published in 1963.]

1258. Aston, Margaret. "Lollardy and Literacy." *History* 62 (1977), 347–71. Reprinted in item 6. Pp. 193–217.
[How the Lollards worked to link themselves with literature and literate followers.]

1259. ———. "Lollard Women Priests?" *J Eccl H* 31 (1980), 441–61. Reprinted in item 6. Pp. 49–70.
[The mere possibility sufficed to horrify their enemies.]

1260. ———. "William White's Lollard Followers." *CHR* 68 (1982), 469–97. Reprinted in item 6. Pp. 71–99.
[Largely devoted to a review and discussion of Tanner, item 1519.]

1261. ———. " 'Caim's Castles': Poverty, Politics, and Disendowment." In item 23. Pp. 45–81.
[Wyclif's dislike of the mendicants and various proposals to disendow them.]

1262.   ———. "Devotional Literacy." In item 6. Pp. 101–33.

1263.   ———. "Lollards and Images." In item 6. Pp. 135–92. [These two papers are newly printed in this volume of Aston's collected essays.]

1264.   ———. "Wyclif and the Vernacular." In item 49. Pp. 281–330.
[What others, e.g., Pecock, thought of the resorting to the vernacular; two vernacular confessions printed.]

1265.   Atkinson, Clarissa W. *Mystic and Pilgrim: The Book and the World of Margery Kempe*. Ithaca, N.Y., 1985, 1983.

1266.   Baker, Derek. "Old Wine in New Bottles: Attitudes to Reform in Fifteenth Century England." In *Renaissance and Renewal in Christian History: Papers Read at the Fifteenth Summer Meeting and the Sixteenth Winter Meeting of the Ecclesiastical History Society*. Edited by Derek Baker. Studies in Church History, 14. Ecclesiastical History Society, 1977. Pp. 193–211.
[Some late examples of monastic efforts towards ecclesiastical reform.]

1267.   Ball, R. M. "Thomas Cyrcetur, a Fifteenth Century Theologian and Preacher." *J Eccl H* 37 (1986), 205–39.
[The second generation of anti-Lollard propaganda.]

1268. Barker, Eric E., ed. *The Register of Thomas Rother-ham, Archbishop of York, 1480-1500.* Canterbury and York Society, vol. 69 (1976).
[Cover title, *Diocesis Eboracencis, registrum Thome Rotherham.* Reviewed by R. B. Dobson, *J Eccl H* 28 (1977), 416–17.]

1269. Barker, Paula S. Datsko. "The Motherhood of God in Julian of Norwich's Theology." *Downside* 100 (1982), 290–304.
[The strength of maternal imagery as a pillar of redemption and love.]

1270. Barratt, Alexandra. "Works of Religious Instruction." In item 24. Pp. 413–32.
[A survey of recent work.]

1271. Beer, Frances, ed. *Julian of Norwich's Revelations of Divine Love: The Shorter Version Ed. from B.L. Add. MS 37790.* Middle English Texts, 8. Heidelberg, 1978.

1272. Blair, John. "Religious Gilds as Landowners." In item 71. Pp. 35–49.

1273. Blake, N. F., ed. *Quattuor Sermones.* Middle English Texts, 2. Heidelberg, 1975.
[Printed by William Caxton, 1483.]

1274. Blamires, Alcuin. "The Wife of Bath and Lollardy." *Medium Aevum* 58 (1989), 224–42.
[Argues for a serious Lollard dimension to her views on marriage and remarriage.]

1275. Bosse, Roberta B. "Margery Kempe's Tarnished Reputation: A Reassessment." *14th Century English Mystics Newsletter* 5/1 (1979), 9–19.
[Saints' lives were her model.]

1276. Boyd, Anne. *Life in a Medieval Monastery: Durham Priory in the Fifteenth Century.* Cambridge, 1987.
[Cambridge Introduction to World History series, for children and casual readers. First published as *The Monks of Durham: Life in a Fifteenth-Century Monastery* (Trevor Cairns, general editor; Anna Mieke, drawings; Reg Piggott, maps, Cambridge Introduction to the History of Mankind series: Topic Books [Cambridge and New York, 1975]); then as *Life in a Fifteenth-Century Monastery*, A Cambridge Topic Book [Minneapolis, 1979].]

1277. Boyle, Leonard E. "Aspects of Clerical Education in Fourteenth Century England." In *The Fourteenth Century.* Edited by Paul E. Szarmach and Bernard S. Levy. ACTA - Center for Medieval and Early Renaissance Studies, State University of New York at Binghamton, vol. 4. Binghamton, N.Y., 1977. Reprinted in Boyle's collected papers, *Pastoral Care, Clerical Education and Canon Law, 1200–1400.* Collected Studies Ser., CS135. London, 1981. Pp. 19–32.
[Treats the use of *cum ex eo* licenses and efforts to improve the quality of clerical education and training.]

1278.   Bradley, Ritamary. "Christ, the Teacher, in Julian's *Showings*: The Biblical and Patristic Traditions." In item 27. Pp. 127–42.
[How she fits into a long religious and intellectual tradition.]

1279.   ———. "Julian of Norwich: Writer and Mystic." In *An Introduction to the Medieval Mystics of Europe: Fourteen Original Essays*. Edited by Paul E. Szarmach. Albany, N.Y., 1984. Pp. 195–216.
[Positive assessment of whether she was "really" a mystic.]

1280.   ———. "Perception of Self in Julian of Norwich's *Showings*." *Downside* 104 (1986), 227–39.
[A unity in Christ, not a male-female hierarchy.]

1281.   ———. "Julian on Prayer." In item 64. Vol. 2, pp. 291–304.

1282.   Brady, M. Teresa. "Lollard Sources and 'The Pore Caitif'." *Traditio* 44 (1988), 389–418.

1283.   ———. "Lollard Interpolations and Omissions in Manuscripts of 'The Pore Caitif'." In item 76. Pp. 183–203.
[Traces the history of the manuscripts and discusses the indications and thrust of Lollard editorial decisions.]

1284.   Brockwell, Charles W., Jr. "Answering 'the Known Men': Bishop Reginald Pecock and Richard Hooker." *Church History* 49 (1980), 125–46.

[Similarity of responses to non-conformity, but no argument for direct influence of Pecock on Hooker.]

1285. ————. *Bishop Reginald Pecock and the Lancastrian Church: Securing the Foundations of Cultural Authority.* Texts and Studies in Religion, vol. 25. Lewiston, N.Y., 1985.
[An intellectual history of a baffling figure.]

1286. Brundage, James A. "English-Trained Canonists in the Middle Ages: A Statistical Analysis of a Social Group." In *Law-Making and Law-Makers in British History: Papers Presented to the Edinburgh Legal History Conference, 1977.* Edited by Alan Harding. Studies in History, no. 22. Royal Historical Society, 1980. Pp. 64–78.
[Who they were, how many, and what they contributed.]

1287. Burgess, Clive. " 'For the Increase of Divine Service': Chantries in the Parish in Late Medieval Bristol." *J Eccl H* 36 (1985), 46–65.
[Their obligations and the levels of endowment they received.]

1288. ————. "A Service for the Dead: The Form and Function of the Anniversary in Late Medieval Bristol." *B & G AS* 105 (1987), 183–211.
[This neglected liturgical institution can tell about the popularity of the doctrine of purgatory.]

1289.   Burton, Janet E., ed. *The Cartulary of the Treasurer of York Minster, and Related Documents.* University of York, Borthwick Institute of Historical Research, Borthwick Texts and Calendars, Records of the Northern Province, 5. York, 1978.
[From York Minster Library MS. M2(3)a, fols. 1–16ᵛ.]

1290.   Carey, Hilary M. "Devout Literate Laypeople and the Pursuit of the Mixed Life in Later Medieval England." *JRH* 14 (1986–87), 361–81.
[The new "tradition," especially among women; puts Ms. Kempe into a wider context.]

1291.   Carpenter, Christine. "The Religion of the Gentry of Fifteenth-Century England." In item 84. Pp. 53–74.
[Chantries, ritual, education, and individualism.]

1292.   Carson, T. E. "The Problem of Clerical Irregularities in the Late Medieval Church: An Example from Norwich." *CHR* 72 (1986), 185–200.
[Pluralism and absenteeism: real but not rampant.]

1293.   Cattermole, Paul, and Simon Cotton. "Medieval Parish Church Building in Norfolk." *Norfolk* 38 (1983), 235–79.
[Church by church, with amounts spent, as a guide to popular religiosity.]

1294. Catto, Jeremy. "Religion and the English Nobility in the Later Fourteenth Century." In *History & Imagination: Essays in Honour of H. R. Trevor-Roper.* Edited by Hugh Lloyd-Jones, Valerie Pearl, and Blair Worden. London, 1981. Pp. 43–55.
[Also New York, 1982. Survey of aristocratic support, with an eye for liturgical concerns, astrology, and Lollardy.]

1295. ———. "John Wyclif and the Cult of the Eucharist." In *The Bible in the Medieval World: Essays in Memory of Beryl Smalley.* Edited by Katherine Walsh and Diana Wood. Studies in Church History, Subsidia, 4. Ecclesiastical History Society, 1985. Pp. 269–86.
[The centrality of the doctrine, and how it concerned the professionals and the popular preachers.]

1296. ———. "Religious Change under Henry V." In item 36. Pp. 97–115.
[Piety, orthodoxy, and some steps to build unity.]

1297. ———. "Some English Manuscripts of Wyclif's Latin Works." In item 49. Pp. 353–59.
[They suggest an audience that reached beyond just Lollards and Hussites.]

1298. Catto, Jeremy, Pamela Gradon, and Anne Hudson, eds. *Wyclif and His Followers: An Exhibition to Mark the 600th Anniversary of the Death of John Wyclif: December 1984 to April 1985.* Oxford, 1984.
[Bodleian Library.]

1299.   Cigman, Gloria, ed. "Middle English Sermons in Manuscript: *Ubi Sunt.*" *Medieval Sermon Studies Newsletter* 3 (1978–79), 5–7.

1300.   Clark, J. P. H. *"Fiducia* in Julian of Norwich." *Downside* 99 (1981), 97–108, 214–29.
[A difficult issue to trace historically.]

1301.   ———. "Nature, Grace, and the Trinity in Julian of Norwich." *Downside* 100 (1982), 203–20.
[A development within the Augustinian tradition.]

1302.   ———. "Predestination in Christ According to Julian of Norwich." *Downside* 100 (1982), 79–91.
[Her doctrine and its relationship to the views of Duns Scotus.]

1303.   Cleve, Gunnel. "Semantic Dimensions in Margery Kempe's 'Whyght Clothys'." *Mystics Quarterly* 12 (1986), 162–70.

1304.   Cloake, John. "The Charterhouse of Sheen." *Surrey Archaeological Collections* 71 (1977), 145–98.
[The building of Henry V: groundplans and designs.]

1305.   Colchester, L. S., ed. and trans. *Wells Cathedral: Fabric Accounts, 1390–1600.* Friends of Wells Cathedral. Wells, 1983.

1306.   ———. *Documents of the Vicars Choral of Wells, 1348–1600.* Privately printed. Wells, 1986.

1307.   ——, intro. and trans. *Wells Cathedral: Escheators'*
Accounts, 1369–1600, 1: *1369–1474*; 2: *1480–1600*.
2 vols. Privately printed. Wells, 1988.

1308.   Colledge, Edmund, and James Walsh. "Editing Julian
of Norwich's *Revelation*: A Progess Report." *MS* 38
(1976), 404–27.
[Summarizes her biography, literary expression,
and religiosity.]

1309.   ——, eds. *A Book of Showings to the Anchoress*
Julian of Norwich. 2 vols. Pontifical Institute of
Mediaeval Studies, Studies and Texts, no. 35. Toronto,
1978.
[Full scholarly treatment of text and compre-
hensive introduction.]

1310.   Crawford, Anne. "The Piety of Late Medieval English
Queens." In item 11. Pp. 48–57.
[Survey of the group; they get mixed grades.]

1311.   Crowder, C. M. D. "Four English Cases Determined in
the Roman Curia during the Council of Constance,
1414–1418." *Annuarium Historiae Conciliorum* 12
(1980), 315–411; 13 (1981), 67–145.
[Tale of a quarrel between Merton College and
New College; many documents from college archives and from St. Paul's are transcribed.]

1312.   Cummings, Charles. "The Motherhood of God According to Julian of Norwich." In item 64. Vol. 2, pp.
305–14.
[Looks at the sources of her theology.]

1313. Davies, C. S. L. "Bishop John Morton, the Holy See, and the Accession of Henry VII." *EHR* 102 (1987), 2–30.
[Morton's efforts on Henry's behalf and the value of church support.]

1314. Davies, R. G. "Alexander Neville, Archbishop of York, 1374–1388." *YAJ* 47 (1975), 87–101.
[Biographical: did he deserve his bad reputation?]

1315. ———. "The Episcopate and the Political Crisis in England of 1386–88." *Speculum* 51 (1976), 659–93.
[As a group the bishops played the moderating role.]

1316. ———. "After the Execution of Archbishop Scrope: Henry IV, the Papacy, and the English Episcopate, 1405–08." *BJRL* 59 (1976–77), 40–74.
[Another case study of Henry's infelicitous touch in episcopal appointments.]

1317. ———. "A Contested Appointment to the Bishopric of Bath and Wells, 1400–1." *Somerset* 121 (1976–77), 67–76.
[The Bowet-Clifford contest, and Henry IV's heavy hand.]

1318. ———. "Martin V and the English Episcopate, with Particular Reference to His Campaign for the Repeal of the Statute of Provisors." *EHR* 92 (1977), 309–44.
[Papal authority was still important in episcopal appointments.]

1319.   ———. "The Episcopate." In item 17. Pp. 51–89.
[Covers 1375–1461, emphasizing the diversity
found within the ranks.]

1320.   ———. "The Attendance of the Episcopate in English
Parliaments, 1376–1461." *Proceedings of the American
Philosophical Society* 129/1 (March 1985), 30–81.
[Every parliament is covered, with tables show-
ing each bishop's record and each diocese's
record of attendance.]

1321.   Davis, Virginia. "The Rule of St. Paul, the First
Hermit, in Late Medieval England." In *Monks, Her-
mits, and the Ascetic Tradition: Papers Read at the 1984
Summer Meeting and the 1985 Winter Meeting*. Edited
by W. J. Sheils. Studies in Church History, 22.
Ecclesiastical History Society, 1985. Pp. 203–14.
[A small cult but gaining popular interest
through the fifteenth century.]

1322.   ———. "Rivals for Ministry? Ordinations of Secular
and Regular Clergy in Southern England c.1300–1500."
In *The Ministry: Clerical and Lay: Papers Read at the
1988 Summer Meeting and the 1989 Winter Meeting*.
Edited by W. J. Sheils and Diana Wood. Studies in
Church History, 26. Ecclesiastical History Society,
1989. Pp. 99–109.
[Low recruitment levels and anti-mendicant feel-
ing; the proportion of clerics in orders rose between 1349 and 1450.]

1323.   Dobson, Barrie. "The Later Middle Ages, 1215–1500."
In *A History of York Minster*. Edited by G. E. Aylmer
and Reginald Cant. Oxford, 1977. Pp. 44–109.
[Reprinted with corrections, Oxford, 1979. Internal history, finances, personnel, politics, and
the church's urban role and popularity; also see
item 1835.]

1324.   ———. "The Residentiary Canons of York in the Fifteenth Century." *J Eccl H* 30 (1979), 145–74.
[Administration and some prosopography for
thirty-four of the canons.]

1325.   ———. "Cathedral Chapters and Cathedral Cities:
York, Durham, and Carlisle in the Fifteenth Century."
Northern 19 (1983), 15–44.
[Succinct survey, emphasis on administration.]

1326.   Doyle, A. I. "Publication by Members of the Religious
Orders." In item 30. Pp. 109–23.
[Their literary activities, and how such works
reached a wider audience.]

1327.   Dunning, Robert W. "The Building of Syon Abbey."
Ancient Monuments, n.s. 25 (1981), 16–26.

1328.   ———. "Patronage and Promotion in the Late-Medieval
Church." In item 31. Pp. 167–80.
[West Country cases of new men.]

1329.   ———. "The Abbey of the Princes: Athelney Abbey,
Somerset." In item 32. Pp. 295–303.

1330.   Eberly, Susan. "Margery Kempe, St. Mary Magdalene, and Patterns of Contemplation." *Downside* 107 (1989), 209–23.
[Medieval images of the Magdalene and their effect on Margery's models and definition of spirituality.]

1331.   Ellis, Roger. *Syon Abbey: The Spirituality of the English Bridgettines.* Analecta Cartusiana, 68, 2. Salzburg, 1984. Pp. 1–123.
[A history of the house and an exposition of St. Bridgette's rule.]

1332.   Evans, G. R. "Wyclif on Literal and Metaphorical." In item 49. Pp. 259–66.
[On how scripture should be read.]

1333.   Fleming, Peter W. "Charity, Faith, and the Gentry of Kent, 1422–1529." In item 69. Pp. 36–58.
[Useful analysis of two hundred wills.]

1334.   Fletcher, Alan J. "John Mirk and the Lollards." *Medium Aevum* 56 (1987), 217–24.
[Mirk wrote to offer a work that could be used against Lollards.]

1335.   Fletcher, Alan J., and S. Powell. "The Origins of a Fifteenth Century Sermon Collection: mss Harley 2247 and Royal 18 B xxv." *Leeds Studies in English*, n.s. 10 (1978), 74–96.

1336.   Forde, Simon. "Theological Sources Cited by Two
Canons of Repton: Philip Repyngdon and John Eyton."
In item 49. Pp. 419–28.
[How the strains of Wycliffite thought spread
and became altered.]

1337.   ———. "Nicholas Hereford's Ascension Day Sermon,
1382." *MS* 51 (1989), 205–41.
[The sermon's text and its place in academic
quarrels over Wyclif.]

1338.   Foss, David B. "From God as Mother to Priest as
Mother: Julian of Norwich and the Movement for the
Ordination of Women." *Downside* 104 (1986), 214–26.
[She stopped short, though she emphasized the
"motherhood of god."]

1339.   ———. " 'Overmuch blaming of the Clergy's Wealth':
Pecock's Exculpation of Ecclesiastical Endowment." In
*The Church and Wealth: Papers Read at the 1986
Summer Meeting and the 1987 Winter Meeting.* Edited
by W. J. Sheils and Diana Wood. Studies in Church
History, 24. Ecclesiastical History Society, 1987. Pp.
155–60.
[Why Pecock believed in and defended ecclesi-
astical property.]

1340.   ———. "John Mirk's *Instructions for Parish Priests.*"
As item 1322. Pp. 131–40.
[Analysis of the contents of this "delightfully
readable text."]

1341. Frankforter, A. Daniel. "The Reformation and the Register: Episcopal Administration of Parishes in Late Medieval England." *CHR* 63 (1977), 204–24.
[Bishops were mostly attentive and concerned with parishioners' needs.]

1342. Fries, Maureen. "Margery Kempe." As item 1279. Pp. 217–35.
[Defends Margery Kempe against a bad press.]

1343. Genet, Jean-Philippe. "Wyclif et Les Lollards." *Historiens et géographes* 294 (1983), 869–86.

1344. Gillespie, Vincent. "Vernacular Books of Religion." In item 30. Pp. 317–44.
[Survey of what was being produced and available.]

1345. Goodman, A. E. "The Piety of John Brunham's Daughter of Lynn." In *Medieval Women: Dedicated & Presented to Professor Rosalind M. T. Hill on the Occasion of Her Seventieth Birthday*. Edited by Derek Baker; introduction, Christopher N. L. Brooke; bibliography, John Fuggles. Studies in Church History, Subsidia, 1. Ecclesiastical History Society, 1978. Pp. 347–58.
[Also 1984. Sensible appraisal of Margery Kempe, with an eye to her social and urban background.

1346. ———. "Religion and Warfare in the Anglo-Scottish Marches." In *Medieval Frontier Societies*. Edited by Robert Bartlett and Angus MacKay. Oxford and New York, 1989. Pp. 245–66.

[No single thread, as the church mediated hostilities and fitted into the fabric of border life.]

1347. Gradon, Pamela, ed. *English Wycliffite Sermons.* Vol. 2. Oxford, 1988.
[Follows Hudson's edition of vol. 1 (item 1396).]

1348. Gransden, Antonia. "The History of Wells Cathedral, c. 1090–1547." In *Wells Cathedral: A History.* Edited by L. S. Colchester. Shepton Mallet, 1982. Pp. 24–51.

1349. Greatrex, Joan, ed. *The Register of the Common Seal of the Priory of St. Swithun, Winchester, 1345–1497.* Hampshire Record Ser., vol. 2. Hampshire County Council, 1978.
[Daily life, mostly reported via English calendaring of entries.]

1350. ———, ed. *Account Rolls of the Obedientiaries of Peterborough.* Publications of the Northamptonshire Record Society, vol. 33 (1984).
[On behalf of the Dean and Chapter of Peterborough. Also vol. 2 in the Anthony Mellows Memorial Trust series. Shows the complicated world of ecclesiastical administration and finances, and of the duties of the many kinds of officials connected to a great house.]

1351. Green, J. Patrick. "The Elevation of Norton Priory, Cheshire, to the Status of Mitred Abbey." *Lancashire & Cheshire* 128 (1978), 97–112.
[The house was elevated in status, 1391: the negotiations and diplomacy that paved the way.]

1352.   Greenway, Diana E. "Cathedral Clergy in England and Wales: *Fasti Ecclesiae Anglicanae.*" *Med Pros* 1/1 (Spring 1980), 15–22.
[A report on the vast and invaluable project.]

1353.   Haines, Roy M. "Church, Society, and Politics in the Early Fifteenth Century as Viewed from an English Pulpit." In *Church Society and Politics: Papers Read at the Thirteenth Summer Meeting and the Fourteenth Winter Meeting.* Edited by Derek Baker. Studies in Church History, 12. Ecclesiastical History Society, 1975. Pp. 143–57.
[Contemporary affairs, as reflected in twenty-five sermons in Bodley MS. 649.]

1354.   ———. "Reginald Pecock: A Tolerant Man in an Age of Intolerance." In *Persecution and Toleration: Papers Read at the Twenty-second Summer Meeting and the Twenty-third Winter Meeting.* Edited by W. J. Sheils. Studies in Church History, 21. Ecclesiastical History Society, 1984. Pp. 125–37.
[Why he was seen as a threat, with a look at some of the historiography about him.]

1355.   ———. *Ecclesia Anglicana: Studies in the English Church of the Later Middle Ages.* Toronto, 1989.
[Argues for good organization, vitality, and intellectual growth.]

1356.   Hanna, Katharine A., ed. *The Cartularies of South-wick Priory.* Pt. 2. Hampshire Record Ser., vol. 10. Hampshire County Council, 1989.
[Only a few entries after 1377.]

1357. Hargreaves, Henry. "Popularizing Biblical Scholarship:
The Role of the Wycliffite *Glossed Gospels.*" In *The
Bible and Medieval Culture.* Edited by W. Lourdaux
and D. Verhelst.   Mediaevalia Lovaniensia, ser. 1,
studia 7. Louvain, 1979. Pp. 171–89.
[The popularity and influence of vernacular biblical scholarship.]

1358. Harley, Marta Powell, ed. and trans. *A Revelation of
Purgatory by an Unknown, Fifteenth-Century Woman
Visionary: Introduction, Critical Text, and Translation.*
Studies in Women and Religion, vol. 18. Lewiston,
N.Y., 1985.
[A northern text.]

1359. Harper, R. I. "A Note on Corrodies in the Fourteenth
Century." *Albion* 15 (1983), 95–101.
[As utilized by William Courtenay and Thomas
Arundel.]

1360. Harper-Bill, Christopher. "The Priory and Parish of
Folkestone in the Fifteenth Century." *Arch Cant* 93
(1977), 195–200.
[Town-gown tension and some local crises.]

1361. ———. "Archbishop John Morton and the Province of
Canterbury, 1486–1500." *J Eccl H* 29 (1978), 1–21.
[Mostly looking at administrative practices (and
cases).]

1362. ———. "The *Familia*, Administrators, and Patronage
of Archbishop John Morton." *JRH* 10 (1979), 236–52.
[An early Tudor tale that begins in the 1470s.]

1363. ———. "Cistercian Visitation in the Late Middle Ages: The Case of Hailes Abbey." *BIHR* 53 (1980), 103–14.

1364. ———. "Monastic Apostacy in Late Medieval England." *J Eccl H* 32 (1981), 1–18.

1365. Harriss, Gerald L. "Henry Beaufort, 'Cardinal of England'." In item 84. Pp. 111–27.
[His motives for seeking the red hat.]

1366. Hartzell, Karl D. "Diagrams of Liturgical Ceremonies." In item 79. Pp. 339–41.
[BL Add. MS. 57534 discussed but not depicted.]

1367. Harvey, Margaret. "Ecclesia Anglicani, Cui Ecclesiastes Noster Christus Vos Preficit: The Power of the Crown in the English Church during the Great Schism." In *Religion and National Identity: Papers Read at the Nineteenth Summer Meeting and the Twentieth Winter Meeting.* Edited by Stuart Mews. Studies in Church History, 18. Ecclesiastical History Society, 1982. Pp. 229–41.
[How royal power grew until by 1408 it dictated the European policies of the English church and churchmen.]

1368. ———. *Solutions to the Schism: A Study of Some English Attitudes 1378 to 1409.* Kirchengeschichtliche Quellen und Studien, Bd. 12. St. Ottilien, 1983.

1369. ———. "John Whethamstede, the Pope and the General Council." In item 11. Pp. 108–22.

[The sources for Whethamstede's treatment of these topics.]

1370. ———. "The Benefice as Property: An Aspect of Anglo-Papal Relations during the Pontificate of Martin V, 1417–31." As item 1339. Pp. 161–73.
[Provisors, reform, and the realities of papal power.]

1371. ———. "Lollardy and the Great Schism: Some Contemporary Perceptions." In item 49. Pp. 385–96.
[Viewpoints of the 1390s.]

1372. Hayes, Rosemary C. E. "The Pre-Episcopal Career of William Alnwick, Bishop of Norwich and Lincoln." In item 72. Pp. 90–107.
[A careerist and an active government servant.]

1373. Heath, Peter. "Urban Piety in the Later Middle Ages: The Evidence of Hull Wills." In item 23. Pp. 209–34.
[Strong religious interest and many signs of a new burst of lay piety.]

1374. Heffernan, Thomas J. "Sermon Literature." In item 24. Pp. 177–207.

1375. Heimmel, Jennifer P. *"God is our Mother": Julian of Norwich and the Medieval Image of Christian Feminine Divinity*. Institut für Anglistik und Amerikanistik, Universität Salzburg, Salzburg Studies in English Literature, Elizabethan & Renaissance Studies, 92:5. Salzburg, 1982.

1376.   Herold, Vilem. "Wyclifs Polemik Gegen Ockhams Auf-
fassung der Platonischen Ideen und Ihr Nachklang in
der Tschechischen Hussitischen Philosophie." In item
49. Pp. 185–215.

1377.   Hicks, Michael A. "The Piety of Margaret, Lady
Hungerford (d. 1478)." *J Eccl H* 38 (1987), 19–38.
[An active lady and a good case study.]

1378.   Higgs, Laquita. "Margery Kempe: 'Whete-breed or
Barly-breed'?" *Mystics Quarterly* 18 (1987), 57–64.
[Asceticism compared to "the realities of the con-
dition of the married woman."]

1379.   Hirsch, John C. "Author and Scribe in *The Book of
Margery Kempe.*" *Medium Aevum* 44 (1975), 145–50.
[Gives the scribe a good deal of credit for shaping the tale as it was preserved and transmitted.]

1380.   ———. *The Revelations of Margery Kempe; Para-
mystical Practices in Late Medieval England.* Medieval and Renaissance Authors, vol. 10. Leiden and
New York, 1989.

1381.   Hobbs, Mary, trans. *Register of the Vicars Choral of
Wells Cathedral, 1393–1534.* Wells, n.d.
[A pamphlet.]

1382.   Hockey, Frederick. *Beaulieu, King John's Abbey: A
History of Beaulieu Abbey, Hampshire, 1204–1538.*
London, 1976.

[Covers fifteenth-century efforts to restore order and regular conduct.]

1383. Hogg, James. *Mount Grace Charterhouse and Late Medieval English Spirituality.* Analecta Cartusiana, 82, Collectanea Cartusiensia, 3. Salzburg, 1980. Pp. 11–44.

1384. ———. "The Contribution of the Brigittine Order to Late Medieval English Spirituality." Analecta Cartusiana, 35. Salzburg, 1983. Pp. 153–74.

1385. ———. "Everyday Life in a Contemplative Order in the Fifteenth Century." In item 28. Pp. 62–76.
[Life in a charterhouse.]

1386. Holbrook, Sue Ellen. "Order and Coherence in *The Book of Margery Kempe.*" In *The Worlds of Medieval Women: Creativity, Influence, Imagination.* Edited by Constance H. Berman, Charles W. Connell, and Judith Rice Rothschild. Literary and Historical Perspectives of the Middle Ages, vol. 2. Morgantown, W.Va., 1985. Pp. 97–112.

1387. Horn, Joyce M., ed. *The Register of Robert Hallum, Bishop of Salisbury, 1407–17.* 2 vols. Canterbury and York Society, pt. 145, vol. 72 (1977–78, 1978–79).
[English calendar and good indices.]

1388. Horner, Patrick J. "A Sermon on the Anniversary of the Death of Thomas Beauchamp, Earl of Warwick." *Traditio* 34 (1978), 381–401.

[Published from Laud MS. misc. 706: sermon delivered within ten to twenty years of Thomas's death in 1401.]

1389. Horsfield, Robert A. " 'The Pomander of Prayer': Aspects of Late Medieval English Carthusian Spirituality and Its Lay Audience." In item 76. Pp. 205–27.

1390. Hosker, P. "The Stanleys of Lathom and Ecclesiastical Patronage in the North-West of England during the Fifteenth Century." *Northern* 18 (1982), 212–29.
[It increased apace with their political reach.]

1391. Hudson, Anne. "The Debate on Bible Translation, Oxford, 1401." *EHR* 90 (1975), 1–18. Reprinted in item 48. No. 5, pp. 67–84.
[Corrects Deanesley; a Vienna MS, probably by Ullerston rather than by Purvey.]

1392. ———. "A Neglected Wycliffite Text." *J Eccl H* 29 (1978), 257–77. Reprinted in item 48. No. 4, pp. 43–66.
[Commentary of 1390 on the Apocalypse.]

1393. ———, ed. and intro. *Selections from English Wycliffite Writings.* Cambridge and New York, 1981; Cambridge, 1978.
[A representative short reader, covering numerous aspects of the topic, with notes on each selection.]

1394. ———. "John Purvey: A Reconsideration of the Evidence for His Life and Writing." *Viator* 12 (1981), 355–80. Reprinted in item 48. No. 6, pp. 85–110.

[His development, consistency, and contemporary reputation.]

1395. [No entry.]

1396. Hudson, Anne, ed. *English Wycliffite Sermons.* Vol. 1. Oxford, 1983.
[An important contribution to Wycliffite scholarship. Reviewed by R. B. Dobson, *J Eccl H* 35 (1984), 271–74. For vol. 2 see item 1347; vol. 3 (ed. Hudson), 1990; vol. 4, forthcoming.]

1397. ———. " 'No Newe Thyng': The Printing of Medieval Texts in the Early Reformation Period." In item 29. Pp. 74–89. Reprinted in item 48. No. 15, pp. 227–48.

1398. ———. "Wycliffite Prose." In item 24. Pp. 249–70.

1399. ———. "A Wycliffite Scholar of the Early Fifteenth Century." As item 1295. Pp. 301–15.
[An academic author? Cotton Titus D. v, *Tractatus de oblacione Iugis Sacrificii.*]

1400. ———. "Wycliffism and the English Language." In item 56. Pp. 85–103.

1401. ———. "Wycliffism in Oxford, 1381–1411." In item 56. Pp. 67–84.

1402. ———. *The Premature Reformation: Wycliffite Texts and Lollard History.* Oxford and New York, 1988.
[Major discussion of social as well as religious and theological aspects; looks to Lollard heritage

in early Reformation thought. Reviewed by
Michael Wilks, *Albion* 21 (1989), 620–22.]

1403. ———. "Lollard Book Production." In item 30. Pp.
125–42.
[Covers the scope and purpose of a wide variety
of items produced by the movement.]

1404. Hudson, Anne, and H. L. Spencer. "Old Author, New
Work: The Sermons of Ms. Longleat 4." *Medium
Aevum* 53 (1984), 220–38.
[Anti-Lollard work by a friar; call for an edition
of the text.]

1405. Hughes, Jonathan. *Pastors and Visionaries: Religion
and Secular Life in Late Medieval Yorkshire.* Woodbridge and Wolfeboro, N.H., 1988.
[Religious character of the nobility, eremetic
movements, pastoral care, and religious literature; attempts a full profile of regional religion
and religiosity.]

1406. Hussey, S. S. "The Audience for the Middle English
Mystics." In item 76. Pp. 109–22.

1407. Jantzen, Grace M. *Julian of Norwich: Mystic and
Theologian.* New York, 1988; London, 1987.
[Biography and exposition.]

1408. Jeffrey, David Lyle, ed. and trans. *The Law of Love:
English Spirituality in the Age of Wyclif.* Grand
Rapids, Mich., 1988.

[Selections from some lesser-known pieces and from Purvey and Mirk, as well as Walter Hilton, Julian, Margery, etc.]

1409. Jewell, Helen M. "English Bishops as Educational Benefactors in the Late Fifteenth Century." In item 23. Pp. 146–67.
[A positive assessment of episcopal activity and benefaction. Also see item 1493.]

1410. John-Julian, Father, O.J.N., ed. and trans. *A Lesson of Love: The Revelations of Julian of Norwich.* New York, 1988.
[Prepared for devotional, not scholarly, use.]

1411. Johnston, Alexandra F. "The Guild of Corpus Christi and the Procession of Corpus Christi in York." *MS* 38 (1976), 372–84.
[Its role in public piety; the city council ran the fraternity.]

1412. Jolliffe, P. S. "Two Middle English Tracts of the Contemplative Life." *MS* 37 (1975), 85–121.
[BL Add. MSS 37790 and 37049: fifteenth-century and of Carthusian provenance, published here and compared with *Cloud* and the *Scale of Perfection*.]

1413. Kaufman, Peter I. "Henry VII and Sanctuary." *Church History* 53 (1984), 465–76.
[Henry VII did not plan an assault on the church's liberty or power.]

1414.   Keen, Maurice. "The Influence of Wyclif." In item 56.
Pp. 127–45.

1415.   ———. "Wyclif, the Bible, and Transubstantiation."
In item 56. Pp. 1–16.

1416.   Keiser, George R. " 'To Knawe God Almyghtyn': Robert Thornton's Devotional Book." Analecta Cartusiana,
106, 2. Salzburg, 1984. Pp. 103–29.
[How the mid-fifteenth-century book was com-
posed.]

1417.   ———. "The Mystics and Early English Printers: The
Economics of Devotionalism." In item 28. Pp. 9–26.
[Though Caxton had not printed such materials,
De Worde was quite happy to do so.]

1418.   Kenny, Anthony. *Wyclif.* Oxford and New York, 1985.
[A volume in the Past Masters series. Short introduction; sets Wyclif in an Ockhamist tradition and largely concerned with his philosophy
and theology.]

1419.   ———. "The Realism of the *De Universalibus.*" In
item 56. Pp. 17–29.

1420.   ———. "Wyclif." *PBA* 72 (1986), 91–113.
[A summary of his ideas and their "afterlife."]

1421.   Kreider, Alan. *English Chantries: The Road to Dissolution.* Harvard Historical Studies, vol. 97. Cambridge, Mass., 1979.

1422. Kretzman, Norman. "Continuations, Indivisibles, and Change in Wyclif's Logic of Scripture." In item 56. Pp. 31–65.

1423. Lagorio, Valerie M. "Defensorium contra Oblectratores: A 'Discerning' Assessment of Margery Kempe." In *Mysticism: Medieval & Modern.* Edited by V. M. Lagorio. Institut für Anglistik und Amerikanistik, Universität Salzburg, Salzburg Studies in English Literature, Elizabethan & Renaissance Studies, 92:20. Salzburg, 1986. Pp. 29–49.

1424. Lang, Judith. " 'The Goodly Wylle' in Julian of Norwich." *Downside* 102 (1984), 163–73.
[How Julian worked to merge her will with Christ's will, plus the role of grace.]

1425. Lawrance, N. A. H., ed. *Fasti Parochiales, 5: Deanery of Buckrose.* Yorkshire Archaeological Society, Record Ser., 143 (1985, for 1983).
[Follows earlier volumes in the series, 85 (1933), 107 (1943), 129 (1967), 133 (1971).]

1426. Leff, Gordon. "Wyclif and Hus: A Doctrinal Comparison." In item 56. Pp. 105–25.

1427. ———. "The Place of Metaphysic in Wyclif's Theology." In item 49. Pp. 217–32.

1428. Llewelyn, Robert, ed. *Julian Woman of Our Day.* Mystic, Conn., 1987; London, 1985.

[Not historically oriented; essays on Julian's value by Elizabeth R. Abbard, A. M. Allchin, Ritamary Bradley, Richard Harries, Kenneth Leech, Llewelyn, Michael McLean, Anna M. Reynolds, and John Swanson.]

1429. Lochrie, Karma. *"The Book of Margery Kempe*: The Marginal Woman's Quest for Literary Authority." *JMRS* 16 (1986), 33–55.
[Margery's book was meant to legitimate her life and visions.]

1430. Logan, F. Donald. "Archbishop Thomas Bourgchier Revisited." In item 11. Pp. 170–88.
[A survey of his administrative formulary book (Queen's College Library, Oxford, MS. 54).]

1431. Lomas, R. A., and A. J. Piper, eds. *Durham Cathedral Priory Rentals*, 1: *Bursar's Rentals*. Publications of the Surtees Society, vol. 198 (1989).
[(The first three parts are pre-1377.) Part 4 covers the bursar's rental, 1396–97; pt. 5, the rental book, 1495–96; transcripts with a gazetteer of the estates.]

1432. Longley, Katharine M., comp. *Ecclesiastical Cause Papers at York: Dean and Chapter's Court, 1350–1843.* University of York, Borthwick Institute of Historical Research, Borthwick Texts and Calendars, Records of the Northern Province, 6. York, 1980.

1433. Lorenz, Bernadette. "The Mystical Experience of Julian of Norwich, with Reference to the Epistle to the Hebrews (Chapter ix): Semiotic and Psychoanalytic Analysis." Translated by Yvette Guillou. In item 27. Pp. 161–81.
[For the already-converted.]

1434. Lovatt, Roger. "Henry Suso and the Medieval Mystical Tradition in England." In item 27. Pp. 47–62.
[In the Exeter Medieval Texts and Studies series. Suso's *Horlogium* was known but much diluted by its translation and in its transmission.]

1435. Lucas, Elona K. "The Emigmatic, Threatening Margery Kempe." *Downside* 105 (1987), 294–305.
[A look at some historiographical treatments.]

1436. Lupton, Lewis. *Wyclif's Wicket: Sign of a Credible Faith.* London, 1984.
[Volume 16 of *A History of the Geneva Bible.* Old-fashioned discussion.]

1437. Luscombe, David. "Wyclif and Hierarchy." In item 49. Pp. 233–44.
[Wyclif argues for hierarchy, following Denis the pseudo-Areopagite.]

1438. Maisonneuve, Roland. "Margery Kempe and the Eastern and Western Tradition of the 'Perfect Fool'." In item 27. Pp. 1–17.

1439. McEntire, Sandra. "Walter Hilton and Margery Kempe: Tears and Compunction." As item 1423. Pp. 49–57.

1440. McHardy, A. K. "The Alien Priories and the Expulsion of Aliens from England in 1378." As item 1353. Pp. 133–41.
[The Commons' petition of October 1377 as a chapter in a longer story.]

1441. ———, comp. *The Church in London, 1375–1392.* London Record Society, vol. 13 (1977).
[Entries calendared in English, covering poll taxes, a survey of ecclesiastical property, and Courtenay's *Acta*, 1375–81.]

1442. ———. "Liturgy and Propaganda in the Diocese of Lincoln during the Hundred Years War." As item 1367. Pp. 215–27.
[With an appendix of special prayers read from pulpits, 1342–1435.]

1443. ———. "The English Clergy and the Hundred Years War." In *The Church and War: Papers Read at the Twenty-first Summer Meeting and the Twenty-second Winter Meeting.* Edited by W. J. Sheils. Studies in Church History, 20. Ecclesiastical History Society, 1983. Pp. 171–78.
[The clergy backed the war, both with taxes and ideological support.]

1444. ———. "Clerical Taxation in Fifteenth Century England: The Clergy as Agents of the Crown." In item 23. Pp. 168–92.

[Appendix: clerical taxes granted by convocation.]

1445.   ———. "The Lincolnshire Clergy in the Later 14th Century." In item 66. Pp. 145–51.
[As revealed from tax returns, 1377–81.]

1446.   ———. "Ecclesiastics and Economics: Poor Clerks, Prosperous Laymen, and Proud Prelates in the England of Richard II." As item 1339. Pp. 129–37.
[Lay subsidy rolls as a source for a look at the unbeneficed clergy.]

1447.   ———. "Careers and Disappointments in the Late-Medieval Church: Some English Evidence." As item 1322. Pp. 111–30.
[How unbeneficed clergy coped, found employment, and viewed their future career prospects.]

1448.   ———. "The Effects of War on the Church: The Case of the Alien Priories in the Fourteenth Century." In item 55. Pp. 277–95.
[Long, steady, sad tale of decline and harrassment, mostly pre-1377.]

1449.   McNab, Bruce. "Obligations of the Church in English Society: Military Arrays of the Clergy, 1369–1418." In item 638. Pp. 295–314, 516–22.
[Clerical military service and fundraising.]

1450.   Mertes, R. G. K. A. "The Household as a Religious Community." In item 72. Pp. 123–39.
[Also covered in her full treatment, item 753.]

1451. Moran, Jo Ann Hoeppner. "Clerical Recruitment in the Diocese of York, 1340–1530: Data and Commentary." *J Eccl H* 34 (1983), 19–54.
[Fluctuating numbers, but not a tale of serious decline.]

1452. Mudroch, Vaclav. *The Wyclyf Tradition.* Edited by Albert Compton Reeves. Athens, Oh., 1979.
[Concentrates on Wyclif's European reputation and interpretation.]

1453. Mueller, Ivan J., ed. John Wyclif. *Tractatus de universalibus.* 2 vols. Oxford and New York, 1985.
[In vol. 2, *On Universals*, note the translation by Anthony Kenny and introduction by Paul Vincent Spade. Mainly concerned to establish a text, but with a long introduction on the problem of universals. See also I. Mueller, "A Lost *Summa* of John Wyclif," in item 49, pp. 179–83.]

1454. Mueller, Janet M. "Autobiography of a New 'Creatur': Female Spirituality, Selfhood, and Authorship in *The Book of Margery Kempe.*" In *Women in the Middle Ages and the Renaissance: Literary and Historical Perspectives.* Edited and introduced by Mary Beth Rose. Syracuse, N.Y., 1986. Pp. 155–71.

1455. Mumford, W. F. "The Monks of Wenlock Priory." *Proceedings of the Shropshire Archaeological Society* 60 (1975–76), 97–111.
[Names and brief biographies of 160 men, out of the medieval monastic population of about 500.]

1456. Murray, Hugh. "Heraldry of the See of York." *York Historian* 8 (1988), 11–24.
[The coats-of-arms of the bishops, with church sites where arms are still to be seen.]

1457. Needham, Paul. *The Printer & the Pardoner: An Unrecorded Indulgence Printed by William Caxton for the Hospital of St. Mary Rounceval, Charing Cross.* Washington, D.C., 1986.
[Library of Congress. A commission of 1480, with the text in facsimile and model scholarly editing.]

1458. Nichols, John A. "Medieval Cistercian Nunneries and English Bishops." In item 64. Vol. 1, pp. 237–49.
[Some warnings about the problematic value of visitation records as a source when not checked against other information.]

1459. Nolan, Barbara. "Nicholas Love." In item 24. Pp. 83–95.
[The "Mirrour of the Blessed Lyf of Jesu" from c. 1400–10.]

1460. Orme, Nicholas. "A Bristol Library, for the Clergy." *B & G AS* 96 (1978), 33–52. Reprinted in item 65. No. 12, pp. 208–19.

1461. ———. *The Minor Clergy of Exeter Cathedral, 1300–1548: A List of Minor Officers, Vicars Choral, Annuellars, Secondaries and Choristers.* Exeter, 1980.
[Exemplary local study.]

1462. ———. "Education and Learning at a Medieval English Cathedral: Exeter, 1380–1548." *J Eccl H* 32 (1981), 265–83. Reprinted in item 65. No. 11, pp. 189–207.

[A reasonably well-educated clergy.]

1463. ———. "The Medieval Chantries of Exeter Cathedral." *D & C N&Q*, pt. 1, 34/8 (Autumn 1981), 319–26; pt. 2, 35/1 (Spring 1982), 12–21; pt. 3, 35/2 (Autumn 1982), 67–71.

[Covering all the chantries in the cathedral church.]

1464. ———. "The Medieval Clergy of Exeter Cathedral, Part I. The Vicars and Annuellars." *Devonshire* 113 (1981), 79–102; "Part II. The Secondaries and Choristers." Ibid. 115 (1983), 79–100.

[The focus is more administrative than prosopographical.]

1465. ———. "Indulgences in the Diocese of Exeter, 1100–1536." *Devonshire* 120 (1988), 15–32.

[With list of recipient churches.]

1466. ———. "A Medieval Almshouse for the Clergy: Clyst Gabriel Hospital, near Exeter." *J Eccl H* 39 (1988), 1–15.

[A small place; statistics on mortality and length of residence.]

1467. Panichelli, Debra S. "Finding God in the Memory: Julian and the Loss of the Visions." *Downside* 104 (1986), 299–317.

1468.   Parker, Geoffrey. "The Medieval Hermitage of Grafton
        Regis." *Northamptonshire Past and Present* 6 (1981–
        82), 247–52.
        [The Wydville family as patrons of a house now
        gone except for what can be found by subter-
        ranean digs.]

1469.   Partner, Nancy. " 'And Most of All for Inordinate Love':
        Desire and Denial in *The Book of Margery Kempe*."
        Thought 64 (1989), 254–67.
        [That she was an hysteric is no reason to dis-
        miss her lightly.]

1470.   Pearson, Samuel C., Jr. "Margery Kempe: Her *Book*,
        Her Faith, Her World." *ABR* 32 (1981), 365–77.

1471.   Pelphrey, Brant. *Love Was His Meaning: The Theology
        and Mysticism of Julian of Norwich*. Institut für
        Anglistik und Amerikanistik, Universität Salzburg,
        Salzburg Studies in English Literature, Elizabethan &
        Renaissance Studies, 92:4. Salzburg, 1982.

1472.   ———. *Christ our Mother: Julian of Norwich*. The
        Way of the Christian Mystics, vol. 7. Wilmington,
        Del., 1989.

1473.   Peters, Brad. "The Reality of Evil within the Mystic
        Vision of Julian of Norwich." *Mystics Quarterly* 13
        (1987), 195–202.

1474.   Platt, Colin. *The Parish Churches of Medieval Eng-
        land*. London, 1981.

[Good synthesis and survey; much material covering the years after 1348.]

1475. Plumb, Derek. "The Social and Economic Spread of Rural Lollardy: A Reappraisal." In *Voluntary Religion: Papers Read at the 1985 Summer Meeting and the 1986 Winter Meeding.* Edited by W. J. Sheils and Diana Wood. Studies in Church History, 23. Ecclesiastical History Society, 1986. Pp. 111–29.
[Much on the early sixteenth century, but also a look at the subsidy rolls of 1424–25.]

1476. Pollard, William F. "Mystical Elements in a Fifteenth Century Prayer Sequence: 'The Festis and the Passion of Oure Lord Ihesa Crist'." In item 28. Pp. 47–61.
[Written by a sister, at another's request; much feminine expression.]

1477. Porter, Roy. "Margery Kempe and the Meaning of Madness." *History Today* 38 (February 1988), 39–44.
[A medical historian's reading of Margery's book and life.]

1478. Powell, Susan, ed. *The Advent and Nativity Sermons from a Fifteenth-Century Revision of John Mirk's Festial: Ed. from B.L. MSS Harley 2247, Royal 18 B xxv, and Gloucester Cathedral Library 22.* Middle English Texts, 13. Heidelberg, 1981.

1479. ———. "A New Dating of John Mirk's Festial." *Notes and Queries,* n.s. 29 (1982), 487–89.
[1380s or early 1390s.]

1480. Proudfoot, L. J. "Parochial Benefices in Late Medieval Warwickshire: Patterns of Stability and Change, 1291 to 1535." In *Field and Forest: An Historical Geography of Warwickshire and Worcestershire*. Edited by T. R. Slater and P. J. Jarvis. Norwich, 1982. Pp. 203–30.
[Parochial church incomes did not change much over the years; many variables and cyclical factors roughly evened out.]

1481. Pyper, Rachel. "An Abridgement of Wyclif's *De Mandatis Divinis*." *Medium Aevum* 52 (1983), 306–10.
[MS. Laud misc. 524, Bodleian, summarized; a source of orthodox material.]

1482. Reeves, Albert Compton. "William Booth, Bishop of Coventry and Lichfield (1447–52)." *Midland* 3 (1975), 11–29.
[See his fuller study, in item 290.]

1483. Renna, Thomas. "Wyclif's Attacks on the Monks." In item 49. Pp. 267–80.
[His hostility and the older roots of these views.]

1484. Revell, Peter, comp. *Fifteenth-Century English Prayers and Meditations: A Descriptive List of Manuscripts in the British Library*. Garland Reference Library of the Humanities, vol. 19. New York, 1975.
[Three hundred fifty-five manuscripts covered.]

1485. Reynolds, Anna M. " 'Courtesy' and 'Homeliness' in the *Revelations* of Julian of Norwich." *14th Century English Mystics Newsletter* 5/2 (1979), 15ff.

1486. Richards, Mary P. "Some Fifteenth Century Calendars from Rochester Diocese." *Arch Cant* 102 (1985), 71–85.
[The calendars reveal the degree of consensus about holy days and local cults, along with their popularity.]

1487. Riehle, Wolfgang. *The Middle English Mystics*. Translated by Bernard Standring. London and Boston, 1981.
[Revised translation of *Studien zur englischen Mystik des Mittelalters unter besonderer Berücksichtigung ihrer Metaphorik* (Heidelberg, 1977).]

1488. ———. "Research and the Medieval English Mystics." In *Genres, Themes, and Images in English Literature: From the Fourteenth to the Fifteenth Century: The J. A. W. Bennett Memorial Lectures, Perugia, 1986*. Edited by Piero Boitani and Anna Torti. Tübinger Beitrage zur Anglistik, 11. Tübingen, 1988. Pp. 141–55.
[The fifth series of the lectures. A survey of various research problems and why they are of enduring interest.]

1489. Robertson, Craig A. "The Tithe-Heresy of Friar William Russell." *Albion* 8 (1976), 1–16.
[A murky affair: a sermon and a long trial before Chichele.]

1490. Rodes, Robert E., Jr. *Ecclesiastical Administration in Medieval England: The Anglo-Saxons to the Reformation*. Notre Dame, Ind., 1977.

1491. ——. *Lay Authority and Reformation in the English Church: Edward I to the Civil War.* Notre Dame, Ind., 1982.

[Along with item 1490, in the university press's series This House I Have Built.]

1492. Rogers, Daniel J. "Psychotechnological Approaches to the Teachings of the *Cloud*-Author and to the *Showings* of Julian of Norwich." In item 27. Pp. 143–60.

[Maybe.]

1493. Rosenthal, Joel T. "Lancastrian Bishops and Educational Benefaction." In item 11. Pp. 199–211.

[On this topic see also Jewell, item 1409.]

1494. Rouse, Richard H., and Mary A. Rouse. "The Franciscans and Books: Lollard Accusation and the Franciscan Response." In item 49. Pp. 369–84.

[Lollard allegations that Franciscans were anti-intellectual hurt the friars and their public image.]

1495. Rubin, Miri. "Corpus Christi Fraternities and Late Medieval Piety." As item 1475. Pp. 97–109.

[Their role in shaping lay piety.]

1496. Ryder, Andrew. "A Note on Julian's Visions." *Downside* 96 (1978), 299–304.

[Glosses her tale and compares her with Richard Rolle.]

1497. Sacks, David H. "The Demise of the Martyrs: The Feasts of St. Clement and St. Katherine in Bristol, 1400–1600." *Social History* 11 (1986), 141–69.

[A civic carnival tradition that came to an end for obvious reasons.]

1498. Sargent, Michael G. "Contemporary Criticism of Richard Roll." Analecta Cartusiana, 55. Salzburg, 1981. Pp. 160–205.

[Especially in Thomas Basset's *Defensiorium contra oblectractores*, c. 1400; the text printed here.]

1499. ———. "Bonaventura English: A Survey of Middle English Prose Translations of Early Franciscan Literature." As item 1416. Pp. 145–76.

1500. Saul, Nigel. "The Religious Sympathies of the Gentry in Gloucestershire, 1200–1500." *B & G AS* 98 (1980), 99–112.

[Shifting currents of lay piety.]

1501. Schmidtke, James A. " 'Saving' by Faint Praise: St. Birgitta of Sweden, Adam Easton, and Medieval Antifeminism." *ABR* 33 (1982), 149–61.

[Easton defended her in the canonization process in the 1380s.]

1502. Smith, Kirk S. "An English Conciliarist? Thomas Netter of Walden at the Councils of Pisa and Constance." In *Popes, Teachers, and Canon Law in the Middle Ages.* Edited by James Ross Sweeney and

Stanley Chodorow. Foreword by Stephan Kuttner. Ithaca, N.Y., 1989. Pp. 290–99.

1503. Smith, Waldo E. L. *The Register of Richard Clifford, Bishop of Worcester, 1401–1407: A Calendar.* Pontifical Institute of Mediaeval Studies, Subsidia Mediaevalia, 6. Toronto, 1976.
[Valuable, but entries are heavily calendared.]

1504. Smith, William. "A Register from Reading Abbey." *JSA* 7/8 (1985), 513–25.
[Handlist of transactions, 1450–1511.]

1505. Spencer, Brian. "King Henry of Windsor and the London Pilgrim." In item 13. Pp. 235–64.
[Pilgrim badges as a key to lay piety and to religion as important urban business.]

1506. Spencer, Helen L. "A Fifteenth Century Translation of a Late Twelfth-Century Sermon Collection." *Review of English Studies*, n.s. 28 (1977), 257–67.

1507. ———. "The Fortunes of a Lollard Sermon-Cycle in the Later Fifteenth Century." *MS* 48 (1986), 352–96.
[Cambridge: Sidney Sussex College 74.]

1508. Stargardt, Ute. "The Beguines of Belgium, the Dominican Nuns of Germany, and Margery Kempe." In item 41. Pp. 277–313.
[Continental parallels and a look at European scholarship.]

1509. Storey, Robin L. "Recruitment of English Clergy in the Period of the Conciliar Movement." *Annuarium Historiae Conciliorum* 7 (1975), 290–313.
[The difficulties of recruiting: low stipends and men in regular orders always pushing forward.]

1510. ———. "Episcopal King-Makers in the Fifteenth Century." In item 23. Pp. 82–98.
[The careers of Thomas Arundel and Thomas Bourgchier.]

1511. Styles, Dorothy, ed. "A Financial Account of St. Mary's, Warwick, Michaelmas 1410–Michaelmas 1411." As item 1173. Pp. 138–58.

1512. Swanson, R. N. "Papal Letters among the Ecclesiastical Archives of York, 1378–1415." *Borthwick Institute Bulletin* 1/4 (York, 1978), 165–93.
[English précis of fifty-five items in the *Calendar of Papal Letters*, plus thirty-seven of uncertain status.]

1513. ———. "Archbishop Arundel and the Chapter of York." *BIHR* 54 (1981), 254–57.
[Arundel had limited control over internal matters.]

1514. ———. *A Calendar of the Register of Richard Scrope, Archbishop of York, 1398–1405*. Parts 1, 2. University of York, Borthwick Institute of Historical Research, Texts and Calendars, Records of the Northern Province, 8, 11. York, 1981–85.

[Part 1 is mostly ordinations: a valuable source now made accessible.]

1515. ———. "Thomas Holme and His Chantries." *York Historian* 5 (1984), 3–7.
[Two late fourteenth-century chantries and an inventory of 1428.]

1516. ———. "Episcopal Income from Spiritualities in Later Medieval England: The Evidence for the Diocese of Coventry and Lichfield." *Midland* 13 (1988), 1–20.
[An overlooked and not insignificant source of income.]

1517. ———. "Lichfield Chapter Acts, 1433–61." In *Collections for a History of Staffordshire.* Staffordshire Record Ser., 4/13 (1988), 26–46.
[Admissions to the chapter, some clerical wills, a few chapter ordinances.]

1518. ———. *Church and Society in Late Medieval England.* Oxford and New York, 1989.
[Scholarly general treatment; emphasizes the unity between the church and lay society.]

1519. Tanner, Norman P., ed. *Heresy Trials in the Diocese of Norwich, 1428–31.* Camden Fourth Ser., vol. 20. Royal Historical Society, 1977.
[Spine title, *Norwich Heresy Trials, 1428–31.* From Westminster Diocesan Archives MS.B.2. Important material for the later Lollards.]

1520. ———. *The Church in Late Medieval Norwich, 1370–1532.* Pontifical Institute of Mediaeval Studies, Studies and Texts, 66. Toronto, 1984.
[Valuable synthetic study of a regional church; see Aston's comments, item 1260.]

1521. ———. "The Reformation and Regionalism: Further Reflections on the Church in Late Medieval Norwich." In item 82. Pp. 129–47.
[Strong popular piety opened the door for the Reformation.]

1522. Theilmann, John M. "Communitas among Fifteenth Century Pilgrims." *Historical Reflections / Réflexion Historiques* 3 (1984), 253–70.
[Social control and popular enthusiasm.]

1523. ———. "Medieval Pilgrims and the Origins of Tourism." *Journal of Popular Culture* 20 (1987), 93–102.

1524. Thomson, David. "Two Lists of Fifteenth Century Feasts in the Diocese of Hereford." *J Eccl H* 34 (1983), 584–90.

1525. [No entry.]

1526. Thomson, John A. F. " 'The Well of Grace': Englishmen and Rome in the Fifteenth Century." In item 23. Pp. 99–114.
[English cases on appeal.]

1527. ———. "Orthodox Religion and the Origins of Lollardy." *History* 74 (1989), 39–55.

[Contemporary thought and the line between heresy and orthodoxy.]

1528. Thomson, Williell R. "An Unknown Letter by John Wyclyf in Manchester, John Rylands University Library Ms. English 86." *MS* 43 (1981), 531–36.
[With a plate of the text: discussion of Matthew 21:2.]

1529. ———. *The Latin Writings of John Wyclyf: An Annotated Catalogue*. Pontifical Institute of Mediaeval Studies, Subsidia Mediaevalia, 14. Toronto, 1983.
[To complete the vast project begun by S. Harrison Thomson.]

1530. ———. "*Manuscripta Wyclifiana Desiderato*: The Potential Contribution of Missing Latin Texts of Our Image of Wyclif's Life and Works." In item 49. Pp. 343–51.
[Gloss on his thoughts in preparing item 1529.]

1531. Tillotson, John H., ed. and trans. *Monastery and Society in the Late Middle Ages: Selected Account Rolls from Selby Abbey, Yorkshire, 1398–1537*. Woodbridge and Wolfeboro, N.H., 1988.
[The rolls produced by the various categories of ecclesiastical and estate officials.]

1532. ———. *Marrick Priory: A Nunnery in Late Medieval Yorkshire*. University of York, Borthwick Papers, no. 75. York, 1989.
[Small house and small economy, with accounts in translation.]

1533.   Timmins, T. C. B., ed. *The Register of John Chandler, Dean of Salisbury, 1404–17.* Wiltshire Record Society, vol. 39 (1983).
[Items calendared; mostly the findings of three visitations.]

1534.   Trench, T. W. "The Tomb of Archbishop Scrope in York Minster." *YAJ* 61 (1989), 95–102.
[Probably not buried in St. Stephen's chapel.]

1535.   Tuck, J. Anthony. "Carthusian Monks and Lollard Knights: Religious Attitude at the Court of Richard II." *Studies in the Age of Chaucer, Proceedings*, no. 1 (1984). Knoxville, 1985. Pp. 149–61.
[Compares the "Lollard Knights" with similar aspects of Carthusian thought, showing the wide gamut of court religious thinking.]

1536.   Tuma, George Wood. *The Fourteenth Century English Mystics: A Comparative Analysis.* 2 vols. Institut für Englische Sprache und Literatur, Universität Salzburg, Salzburg Studies in English Literature, Elizabethan & Renaissance Studies, 61–62. Salzburg, 1977.
[Richard Rolle, Walter, *Cloud*, Julian, and Margery: exposition and theological doctrines.]

1537.   Vinje, Patricia Mary. *An Understanding of Love According to the Anchoress Julian of Norwich.* Institut für Anglistik und Amerikanistik, Universität Salzburg, Salzburg Studies in English Literature, Elizabethan & Renaissance Studies, 92:8. Salzburg, 1983.

1538. Von Nolken, Christina. "Julian of Norwich." In item 24. Pp. 97–108.

1539. ———. "An Unremarked Group of Wycliffite Sermons in Latin." *Modern Philology* 83 (1986), 233–49.

1540. ———. "Another Kind of Saint: A Lollard Perception of John Wyclif." In item 49. Pp. 429–43.
[How the movement came to see Wyclif as a saint and a martyr.]

1541. ———. "Notes on Lollard Citations of John Wyclif's Writings." *Journal of Theological Studies*, n.s. 39 (1988), 411–37.
[Cites and compares passages in *Florentum/ Rosarium.*]

1542. Wall, John. "Penance as Poetry in the Late Fourteenth Century." In *Medieval English Religious and Ethical Literature: Essays in Honour of G. H. Russell.* Edited by Gregory Kratzmann and James Simpson. Cambridge and Dover, N.H., 1986. Pp. 179–91.
[Penance in Chaucer and *Sir Gawain*; the roots of the doctrine.]

1543. Walsh, Katherine. "Wyclif's Legacy in Central Europe in the Late Fourteenth and Early Fifteenth Centuries." In item 49. Pp. 397–417.
[As regarded in Prague, Vienna, etc.]

1544. Warren, Ann K. "Old Forms with New Meanings: Changing Perceptions of Medieval English Anchorites." *Fifteenth-Century Studies* 5 (1982), 209–21.

1545. ———. "The Nun as Anchoress: England, 1100–1500." In item 64. Vol. 1, pp. 197–212.

1546. ———. *Anchorites and Their Patrons in Medieval England.* Berkeley, 1985.
[General treatment, but much late medieval material.]

1547. Weissman, Hope P. "Margery Kempe in Jersalem: *Hysteria Compassio* in the Late Middle Ages." In *Acts of Interpretation: The Text in Its Contexts, 700–1600: Essays on Medieval and Renaissance Literature in Honor of E. Talbot Donaldson.* Edited by Mary J. Carruthers and Elizabeth D. Kirk. Norman, Okla., 1982. Pp. 201–17.
[On the difficult fight with and to transcend carnality.]

1548. Wilks, Michael. "Royal Priesthood: The Origins of Lollardy." In *The Church in a Changing Society: Conflict —Reconciliation or Adjustment? Proceedings of the CIHEC-Conference in Uppsala, August 17–21, 1977.* Department of Church History, Faculty of Theology, Uppsala University. Publications of the Swedish Society of Church History, n.s., 30. Uppsala and Stockholm, 1978. Pp. 63–70.
[Published by the Swedish-sub-commission of CIHEC (Commission internationale d'histoire ecclésiastique comparée.]

1549. Wilson, Edward. "A Poem Presented to William Waynflete as Bishop of Winchester." In item 29. Pp. 127–51.

[Found in BL Add. MS. 60577, recited in his honor in 1451.]

1550. Wilson, P. A. "The Parentage of Bishop Strickland." *Cumberland & Westmorland* 82 (1982), 91–96.
[Of the Stricklands of Great Strickland?]

1551. Windeatt, B. A., trans. *The Book of Margery Kempe.* Harmondsworth and New York, 1985.
[The Penguin Classics volume, with a useful introduction and many helpful ideas for the classroom.]

1552. Wood, Douglas C. *The Evangelical Doctor: John Wycliffe and the Lollards.* Welwyn, Herts., 1984.
[Protestant hagiography.]

1553. Wright, Stephen K. "The Provenance and Manuscript Tradition of the *Martyrium Ricardi Archiepiscopi.*" *Manuscripta* 28 (1984), 92–102.
[How did Gascoigne and Clement Maidstone get their information?]

1554. Wunderli, Richard M. *London Church Courts and Society on the Eve of the Reformation.* Medieval Academy of America, Speculum Anniversary Monographs, 7. Cambridge, Mass., 1981.
[Covers 1470–1516.]

X. INTELLECTUAL HISTORY (INCLUDING MEDICINE, SCIENCE, AND TECHNOLOGY)

1555. Armstrong, C. A. J. "L'échange culturel entre les cours d'Angleterre et de Bourgogne a l'époque de Charles le Téméraire." In *Cinq-centième anniversaire de la bataille de Nancy, 1477. Actes du colloque organisé par l'Institute de recherche regionale en sciences sociales, humaines et economiques de l'Université de Nancy II, Nancy, 22–24 septembre 1977.* Annales de l'Est Mémoire, no. 62. Nancy, 1979.

1556. Armstrong, Elizabeth. "English Purchases of Printed Books from the Continent, 1465–1526." *EHR* 94 (1979), 268–90.
[Tracing the build-up of the trade and of some individual collections.]

1557. Aston, Trevor H. "The Dates of John Rous's List of the Colleges and Academical Halls of Oxford." *Oxon* 42 (1977), 226–36.
[The list was compiled from a single survey of c. 1445 and is therefore a unitary look at the physical university].

1558. ———. "Oxford's Medieval Alumni." *Past and Present* 74 (1977), 3–40.

[Important prosopographical survey, relying largely on Emden's biographical registers.]

1559. Aston, Trevor H., G. D. Duncan, and T. A. R. Evans. "The Medieval Alumni of the University of Cambridge." *Past and Present* 86 (1980), 9–86.

1560. Baldwin, Anna P. *The Theme of Government in Piers Plowman*. Piers Plowman Studies, 1. Cambridge, 1981.
[Poem directly linked to reflections on contemporary political crises.]

1561. Barker, Nicholas. "Caxton's Quincentenary: A Retrospect." *Book Collector* 25/4 (1976), 455–80.
[A survey of his life and career and an assessment of subsequent interest over the centuries, with note of some recent exhibitions.]

1562. ———. "The St. Albans Press: The First Punch-Cutter in England and the First Native Typefounder?" *Cambridge Bibliographical Society*, vol. 7, pt. 3 (1979), 257–78.
[Eight books were published in the 1480s; their letter forms described.]

1563. Barratt, Alexandra. "Dame Eleanor Hull: A Fifteenth Century Translator." In *The Medieval Translator: The Theory and Practice of Translation in the Middle Ages: Papers Read at a Conference Held 20–23 August 1987 at the University of Wales Conference Centre, Gregynog Hall*. Edited by Roger Ellis, assisted by Jocelyn Price,

Stephen Medcalf, and Peter Meredith. Cambridge, 1989. Pp. 87–101.
[Also Woodbridge and Wolfeboro, N.H., 1989. Biographical, plus a look at Dame Hull's work, mainly on devotional tracts.]

1564. Belyea, Barbara. "Caxton's Reading Public." *ELN* 19 (1981–82), 14–19.

1565. Bennett, Michael J. "John Audley: Some New Evidence on His Life and Work." *Chaucer Rev* 16 (1981–82), 344–55.
[Biographical detective work on the author and his links with Lord Le Strange of Knockyn.]

1566. Blackmore, Howard L. "The Boxted Bombard." *AJ* 67 (1987), 86–96.
[Perhaps the oldest gun in England, probably from the Weald in the fifteenth century (and first discussed in *Archaeologia*, 1792).]

1567. Blake, N. F. *Caxton: England's First Publisher*. London, 1976; New York, 1976.
[Well-illustrated and informative popular presentation.]

1568. ———. "William Caxton: The Man and His Work." *JPHS* 11 (1976), 64–80.

1569. ———. "A New Approach to William Caxton." *Book Collector* 26 (1977), 380–85.

[A review of Painter's 1976 biography (item 1722), growing into an essay on Caxton.]

1570. ———. "Continuity and Change in Caxton's Prologues and Epilogues." *Gutenberg Jahrbuch* (1979), 72–77; (1980), 38–43.

1571. ———. "William Caxton." In item 24. Pp. 389–412.

1572. ———. "Manuscript to Print." In item 30. Pp. 403–32. [The transition, with a list of Caxton's books for which a copy-text survives, and some rejected texts.]

1573. Bornstein, Diane. "Reflections of Political Theory and Political Fact in Fifteenth-Century Mirrors for the Prince." In *Medieval Studies in Honor of Lillian Herlands Hornstein*. Edited by Jess B. Bessinger, Jr., and Robert R. Raymo. New York, 1976. Pp. 77–85. [Christine de Pisan, Hoccleve, and others on virtue and militarism.]

1574. ———. "William Caxton's Chivalric Romances and the Burgundian Renaissance in England." *English Studies* 57 (1976), 1–10. [Burgundian influences traced in useful detail.]

1575. ———, ed. *The Middle English Translation of Christine de Pisan's Livre du corps de policie: Ed. from MS C.U.L.Kk.1.5.* Middle English Texts, 7. Heidelberg, 1977.

1576.   ———. "Sir Anthony Woodville as the Translator of Christine de Pisan's *Livre du corps de policie.*" *Fifteenth-Century Studies* 2 (1979), 9–19.
[Mostly an examination of prose style.]

1577.   Boyle, Leonard E., and Richard H. Rouse. "A Fifteenth Century List of the Books of Edmund Norton." *Speculum* 50 (1975), 284–88.
[A fellow of Balliol College, 1467.]

1578.   Brady, Haldeen. "Chaucer, Alice Perrers, and Cecily Chaumpaigne." *Speculum* 52 (1977), 906–11.
[Patronage and possibly other connections.]

1579.   Braswell, Laurel. "Utilitarian and Scientific Prose." In item 24. Pp. 337–87.

1580.   ———. "The Moon and Medicine in Chaucer's Time." *Studies in the Age of Chaucer* 8 (1986), 145–56.
[Astrology and the moon made a serious medical tradition.]

1581.   Brooke, Christopher. *A History of Gonville and Caius College.* Foreword by Sir William Wade, photographs by Wim Swaan. Woodbridge and Dover, N.H., 1985.
[From the foundation to c. 1500, pp. 1–47.]

1582.   Burnley, J. D. "Curial Prose in England." *Speculum* 61 (1986), 593–615.
[Insular development of the language in the fifteenth century; an important role accorded to Malory's prose.]

1583.   Burrow, J. A. "Autobiographical Poetry in the Middle Ages: The Case of Thomas Hoccleve." *PBA* 68 (1982), 389–412.
[Medieval autobiography is unusual, but in this instance probably believable.]

1584.   ———. *Medieval Writers and Their Work: Middle English Literature and Its Background 1100–1500.* Oxford and New York, 1982.
[A serious introductory essay with attention to social background.]

1585.   Burson, Malcolm C. "Emden's *Registers* and the Prosopography of the Medieval English University." *Med Pros* 3/2 (Autumn 1982), 35–51.
[Some caveats about using the great reference work.]

1586.   Capgrave, John. *The Life of St. Norbert.* Edited by Cyril Lawrence Smetana. Pontifical Institute of Mediaeval Studies, Studies and Texts, 40. Toronto, 1977.
[MS. HM 55 in the Henry E. Huntington Library. Much valuable introductory material, plus the text.]

1587.   Carey, Hilary M. "Astrology at the English Court in the Later Middle Ages." In *Astrology, Science, and Society: Historical Essays.* Edited by Patrick Curry. Woodbridge and Wolfeboro, N.H., 1987. Pp. 41–56.

1588.   Carley, James P. "The Identification of John of Glastonbury and a New Dating of His Chronicle." *MS* 40 (1978), 478–83.

[Hearne (d. 1735) said c. 1400; probably by John Seen, and before 1377.]

1589. Carlin, Martha. "Medieval English Hospitals." In *The Hospital in History*. Edited by Lindsay Granshaw and Roy Porter. London and New York, 1989. Pp. 21–39.
[The Wellcome Institute Series in the History of Medicine. Handy overview; see item 1746.]

1590. Cavanaugh, Susan H. "Royal Books: King John to Richard II." *Library*, 6th ser., 10 (1988), 304–16.

1591. (Caxton, William). *William Caxton: An Exhibition to Commemorate the Quincentenary of the Introduction of Printing into England: British Library Reference Division, 24 September 1976–31 January 1977.* Compiled by Janet Backhouse, Mirjam Foot, and John Barr. London, 1976.
[Well illustrated, with some 110 items covered.]

1592. Cheney, Christopher R. "A Register of MSS Borrowed from a College Library, 1440–1517: Corpus Christi College, Cambridge, Ms. 232." *Cambridge Bibliographical Society*, vol. 9, pt. 2 (1987), 103–29.
[Two fifteenth-century bequests were catalogued: we can trace some of the books and some of their borrowers.]

1593. Christianson, C. Paul. "A Century of the Manuscript-Book Trade in Late Medieval London." *Medievalia et Humanistica*, n.s. 12 (1984), 143–65.

1594.   ———. "Early London Bookbinders and Parchmeners."
Book Collector 34 (1985), 41–54.
[Part of the growing trade: patronage and the
economics of the business.]

1595.   ———. *Memorials of the Book Trade in Medieval London: The Archives of Old London Bridge.* Manuscript
Studies, 3. Cambridge and Wolfeboro, N.H., 1987.
[The intersection of intellectual history with the
economy and society.]

1596.   ———. "A Community of Book Artisans in Chaucer's
London." *Viator* 20 (1989), 207–18.
[The public records reveal an active world at
this middling-and-lower level.]

1597.   ———. "Evidence for the Study of London's Late
Medieval Manuscript-Book Trade." In item 30. Pp.
87–108.
[A survey of the records that are pertinent, with
many anecdotes and examples.]

1598.   Cobban, Alan B. "The King's Hall, Cambridge, and
English Medieval Collegiate History." In *Authority
and Power: Studies on Medieval Law and Government
Presented to Walter Ullmann on His Seventieth Birthday.* Edited by Brian Tierney and Peter Linehan. Cambridge and New York, 1980. Pp. 183–95.
[The history of the Hall; also, a good case study
in institutional growth and development.]

1599. ———. "Theology and Law in the Medieval Colleges of Oxford and Cambridge." *BJRUL* 65 (1982–83), 57–77.
[To assess the importance of these faculties; theology was the more vital.]

1600. ———. *The Medieval English Universities: Oxford and Cambridge to c. 1500.* Aldershot, 1988; Berkeley, 1988.
[Comprehensive one-volume treatment; up-to-date and thorough for its size.]

1601. ———. "The Role of Colleges in the Medieval Universities of Northern Europe, with Special Reference to England and France." *BJRUL* 71 (1989), 49–70.
[A general overview.]

1602. Coleman, Janet. *Medieval Readers and Writers, 1350–1400.* London, 1981; New York, 1981.
[English Literature in History series. Mainly literary history but of value for social history and background.]

1603. Corsten, Severin. "Caxton in Cologne." *JPHS* 11 (1976), 1–18.

1604. Coss, P. R. "Aspects of Cultural Diffusion in Medieval England: The Early Romances, Local Society, and Robin Hood." *Past and Present* 108 (1985), 35–79.

1605. Courtenay, William J. *Schools & Scholars in Fourteenth-Century England.* Princeton, 1987.

[Primarily from the perspective of intellectual rather than institutional history.]

1606. Crawley, Charles. *Trinity Hall: The History of a Cambridge College, 1350–1975.* Cambridge, 1976.
[Printed for the College. Pages 1–31 cover the medieval foundation and early building.]

1607. Cross, Claire. "A Medieval Yorkshire Library." *Northern* 25 (1989), 281–90.
[Documents of the 1580s bequeath a monk's late-medieval library, from Monk Bretton Abbey.]

1608. Davis, Norman. "Language in Letters from Sir John Fastolf's Household." In *Medieval Studies for J. A. W. Bennett: Aetatis suae LXX.* Edited by P. L. Heyworth. Oxford, 1981. Pp. 329–46.
[Regional usage and the movement towards a common language.]

1609. Davis, Virginia. "William Waynflete and the Educational Revolution of the Fifteenth Century." In item 72. Pp. 40–59.
[Emphasis on his educational practices and innovations.]

1610. de la Mare, A. C. "The First Book Printed in Oxford: The *Expositio Symboli* of Rufinus." *Cambridge Bibliographical Society,* vol. 7, pt. 2 (1978), 184–244.
[BL Sloane MS. 1579, and a comparison with the printed version of 1478.]

1611. de la Mare, A. C., and Lotte Hellinga. "Manuscripts Given to the University of Oxford by Humphrey, Duke of Gloucester." *Bodleian Library Record* 13/1 (1988), 30–51; ibid., 13/2 (1989), 112–21.
[Thirteen are known; described and illustrated, as in 1988 exhibition. To be continued, as more items are published and discussed.]

1612. Dobson, R. B. "Oxford Graduates and the So-Called Patronage Crisis of the Later Middle Ages." As item 1548. Pp. 211–16.

1613. ———. "Recent Prosopographical Research in Late Medieval English History: University Graduates, Durham Monks, and York Canons." In item 14. Pp. 181–99.
[Problems and themes for research and analysis.]

1614. Doyle, A. I. "English Books in and out of Court from Edward III to Henry VII." In item 77. Pp. 163–81.
[Growth of the vernacular, printing, regional variations, and the book trade.]

1615. Driver, Martha A. "Pictures in Print: Late Fifteenth- and Early Sixteenth-Century English Religious Books for Lay Readers." In item 76. Pp. 224–44.
[An interesting dimension to the early book.]

1616. Eban, Lois A. *John Lydgate.* Twayne's English Authors Ser., 407. Boston, 1985.
[A positive assessment of Lydgate's thought and literary skills.]

1617. Edwards, A. S. G. "The Influence of Lydgate's *Fall of Princes*, c. 1440–1559: A Survey." *MS* 39 (1977), 424–39.
[Thirty-six extant MSS argue for popularity, as do citations, quotes, and borrowings.]

1618. ———. "John Trevisa." In item 24. Pp. 133–46.

1619. ———. "The Manuscripts and Texts of the Second Version of John Hardyng's *Chronicle*." In item 84. Pp. 75–84.

1620. Emden, Alfred B. "Oxford Academical Halls in the Later Middle Ages." In item 2. Pp. 353–65.
[A general survey of what there was, and the role of the halls.]

1621. Evans, G. R. "Wyclif's *Logic* and Wyclif's Exegesis— The Context." As item 1295. Pp. 287–300.
[In the world of the schools he defended the Bible as a logical text.]

1622. Evans, Ralph. "The Analysis by Computer of A. B. Emden's Biographical Registers of the Universities of Oxford and Cambridge." In item 14. Pp. 381–93.

1623. Field, P. J. C. "Sir Robert Malory, Prior of the Hospital of St. John of Jerusalem in England (1432–1439/40)." *J Eccl H* 28 (1977), 249–64.
[Biographical; a relative of the author, with a chivalric influence on the younger man.]

1624.   ———. "Thomas Malory: The Hutton Documents."
Medium Aevum 48 (1979), 213–39.
[Biographical detective work.]

1625.   ———. "Thomas Malory and the Warwick Retinue
Roll." *Midland* 5 (1979–80), 20–30.
[More on the trail of the historical Malory.]

1626.   ———. "The Last Years of Sir Thomas Malory." *BJRUL*
64 (1981–82), 433–56.
[The political flip-flops of Sir Thomas Malory of
Newbold Revel.]

1627.   Fisher, John H.   "Chancery and the Emergence of
Standard Written English in the Fifteenth Century."
Speculum 52 (1977), 870–99.
[The pivotal role played by the language and
usage developed in the king's chancery.]

1628.   ———. "Chancery Standard and Modern Written English." *JSA* 6/3 (1979), 136–44.

1629.   ———. "Chaucer and the Written Language." In item
41. Pp. 237–51.
[The transitions from culture for the ear to that
created for the eye.]

1630.   Fisher, John H., Malcolm Richardson, and Jane L.
Fisher, comps. *An Anthology of Chancery English.*
Knoxville, Tenn., 1984.

[Drawing largely on materials in the PRO's documents. Discussed by Lister Matheson, *Speculum* 61 (1986), 646–50.]

1631. Fletcher, John M. "A Fifteenth Century Benefaction to Magdalen College Library." *Bodleian Library Quarterly* 9 (1973–78), 169–72.
[The Master of Trinity College, Arundel, gave thirty-six books of little intrinsic importance.]

1632. ———. "Inter-Faculty Disputes in Late Medieval Oxford." In item 49. Pp. 331–42.
[Their role in Wyclif's career and how such quarrels affected his followers.]

1633. Fredeman, Jane C. "John Capgrave's First English Composition: 'The Life of St. Norbert'." *BJRL* 57 (1974–75), 280–309.
[How he sewed the work together from the sources. See item 1586.]

1634. ———. "The Life of John Capgrave, OESA (1393–1464)." *Augustiniana* 29 (1979), 197–237.

1635. ———. "Style and Characterization in John Capgrave's *Life of St. Katherine*." *BJRUL* 62 (1979–80), 346–87.
[Written by 1445.]

1636. Friedam, J. B. "Books, Owners, and Makers in Fifteenth Century Yorkshire: The Evidence from Some Wills and Extant Manuscripts." In *Latin and Ver-*

nacular: *Studies in Late-Medieval Texts and Manuscripts.* Edited by A. J. Minnis. York Manuscripts Conferences, vol. 1. Cambridge and Wolfeboro, N.H., 1989. Pp. 111–27.

1637.   Garten, Charles. "A Fifteenth Century Headmaster's Library." *Lincolnshire* 15 (1980), 29–38.
[An inventory, c. 1420, of 112 books belonging to Syon Abbey.]

1638.   Genet, Jean-Philippe. "The Dissemination of Manuscripts Relating to English Political Thought in the Fourteenth Century." In item 55. Pp. 217–37.
[Wyclif, among others; with tables to illustrate the paths and the incidence of dissemination.]

1639.   Getz, Faye M. "Gilbertus Anglicus Anglicized." *Medical History* 26 (1982), 436–42.
[The manuscript tradition behind the host of new stuff coming into England in the fifteenth century.]

1640.   Goodman, Jennifer R. "Caxton's Chivalric Publications of 1480–85." In *The Study of Chivalry: Resources and Approaches.* Edited by Howell Chickering and Thomas H. Seiler. Kalamazoo, Mich., 1988. Pp. 645–61.
[For the Consortium for the Teaching of the Middle Ages, Inc. (TEAMS). Survey of the relevant publications.]

1641.   Gottfried, Robert S.   "Population, Plague, and the Sweating Sickness: Demographic Movements in Late Fifteenth-Century England." *JBS* 17 (1977), 12–37.

1642.   ———. *Epidemic Disease in Fifteenth Century England: The Medical Response and the Demographic Consequences.*   Leicester, 1978; New Brunswick, N.J., 1978.

1643.   ———. "English Medical Practitioners, 1340–1530." *Bulletin of the History of Medicine* 58 (1984), 164–82.

1644.   Gradon, Pamela.   "Langland and the Ideology of Dissent." *PBA* 66 (1980), 179–205.
        [The affinities between Langland and Wyclif.]

1645.   Gransden, Antonia.   "Silent Meanings in Ranulf Higden's *Polychronicon* and in Thomas Elmham's *Liber Metricus de Henrico Quinto.*" *Medium Aevum* 46 (1977), 231–40.
        [Cryptography, acrostics, and biblical allegory.]

1646.   Gray, Douglas, ed. *The Oxford Book of Late Medieval Verse and Prose.*   Oxford and New York, 1989; Oxford, 1985.
        [Wide-ranging anthology, with a note on fifteenth-century grammar and spelling by Norman Davis.]

1647.   Green, Monica. "Women's Medical Practice and Health Care in Medieval Europe." *Signs* 14 (1989), 434–73.

[Not confined to England but a broader survey; a list of English texts, pp. 464–65.]

1648. Green, Richard Firth. "King Richard II's Books Revisited." *Library* 36 (1976), 235–39.
[Follow-up of 1932–33 article by Edith Rickert, using material from the Memoranda Roll for 1384–85.]

1649. ———. "Notes on Some Manuscripts of Hoccleve's *Regement of Princes*." *BLJ* 4 (1978), 37–41.
[A leaf from a commercial scriptorium in London.]

1650. ———. *Poets and Princepleasers: Literature and the English Court in the Late Middle Ages.* Toronto and Buffalo, 1980.
[The major recent book on high cultural and court patronage.]

1651. ———. "The *Familia Regis* and the *Familia Cupidinis*." In item 77. Pp. 87–102.
[Was fifteenth-century literature still being produced for the court of courtly love?]

1652. ———. "Women in Chaucer's Audience." *Chaucer Rev* 18 (1983–84), 146–54.
[A growing presence.]

1653. Greenberg, Cheryl. "John Shirley and the English Book Trade." *Library*, 6th ser., 4 (1982), 369–80.

[A scribe-stationer who built an important book
business in London.]

1654. Griffith, R. R. "The Early Years of William Caxton."
In *Caxton: An American Contribution to the Quincen-
tenary Celebration.* Edited by Susan Otis Thompson.
Typophile Chap Books, 52. New York, 1976. Pp.
20–54.
[From Suffolk (not Kentish) origins; looks at
English provincial links to the Continent.]

1655. Hanna, Ralph, III. "Sir Thomas Berkeley and His
Patronage." *Speculum* 64 (1989), 878–916.

1656. Hargreaves, H. "The *Spermate Hominis*: A Middle
English Poem on Human Embryology." *MS* 39 (1977),
506–10.
[From the National Library of Scotland, MS.
23.7.11.]

1657. Harley, Marta P. "The Middle English Contents of a
Fifteenth Century Medical Handbook." *Mediaevalia* 8
(1982), 171–88.
[Transcription of the *Practicum Urinarum*, in
the Boston Medical Library.]

1658. Harris, Kate. "Patrons, Buyers, and Owners: New Evidence for Ownership and the Role of Book Owners in
Book Production and the Book Trade." In item 30. Pp.
163–99.

1659. Hay, Denys. "England and the Humanities in the Fifteenth Century." In *Itinerarium Italicum: The Profile of the Italian Renaissance in the Mirror of Its European Transformations: Dedicated to Paul Oskar Kristeller on the Occasion of His 70th Birthday.* Edited by Heiko A. Oberman with Thomas A. Brady, Jr. Studies in Medieval and Reformation Thought, vol. 14. Leiden, 1975. Pp. 305–67. Reprinted in item 40. No. 9, pp. 169–232.

1660. Hellinga, Lotte. *Caxton in Focus: The Beginning of Printing in England.* London, 1982.
   [Well-illustrated British Library guide: Caxton in his own time, plus his followers and influence.]

1661. Hellinga, Lotte, and Hilton Kelliher. "The Malory Manuscript." *BLJ* 3 (1977), 91–113.
   [The history of BL Add. MS. 59678 and links with Caxton's 1485 edition of *Le Morte Darthur*].

1662. Himsworth, Sheila, comp., with Peter Gwyn, William Graham, and John Harvey. *Winchester College Muniments: A Descriptive List.* 3 vols. Chichester, 1976–84.
   [For the Warden and Fellows of Winchester College. Volume 1 (1976) is the *College*; vols. 2 and 3 (1984), *Estates (Part 1)* and *(Part 2)*, mainly cover estate administration and economy.]

1663. Hoccleve, Thomas. *Selections from Hoccleve.* Edited by M. C. Seymour. Oxford and New York, 1981.

[Good introduction. For some caveats see Jerome Mitchell, *Speculum* 58 (1983), 477–78.]

1664. Holt, Richard. *The Mills of Medieval England.* Oxford and New York, 1988.
[Pages 117–70 cover the later Middle Ages, including the question of whether there was an "industrial revolution."]

1665. Horrall, Sarah M. "William Caxton's Biblical Translations." *Medium Aevum* 53 (1984), 91–98.
[How he cobbled pieces together.]

1666. Howard, Donald R. *Writers and Pilgrims: Medieval Pilgrimage Narratives and Their Posterity.* Berkeley, 1980.
[Intellectual history.]

1667. Hughes, Susan E. "Guildhall and Chancery English in the Fifteenth Century." *Guildhall* 4 (1980), 53–62.
[With a list of enrollments, cited for language and grammatical usage.]

1668. Hunt, Richard William. "The Medieval Library." In item 15. Pp. 317–45.

1669. Johnston, Alexandra F. "The Plays of the Religious Guilds of York: The Creed Play and the Pater Noster Play." *Speculum* 50 (1975), 55–90.
[Civic pageantry and religious didacticism.]

1670. Jones, John. *Balliol College: A History, 1263–1939.* Oxford and New York, 1988.

[The fifteenth-century tale, plus Fox's early-sixteenth-century statutes, pp. 30–46.]

1671.   Kahrl, Stanley J. "Secular Life and Popular Piety in Medieval English Drama." In item 41. Pp. 85–107.
[Drama as a mirror and a teacher.]

1672.   Kane, George. "Some Fourteenth Century 'Political' Poems." As item 1542. Pp. 82–91.
[Such material should be read in the context of estates satire; not as political as it might seem at first.]

1673.   Keiser, George R. "Patronage and Piety in Fifteenth Century England: Margaret, Duchess of Clarence, Simon Wynter, and Beinecke Ms. 317." *Yale University Library Gazette* 60 (1985), 32–46.

1674.   Kenny, Anthony. "Realism and Determinism in the Early Wyclif." In item 56. Pp. 165–77.
[Wyclif's views of human freedom.]

1675.   Ker, Neil L. R. "Oxford College Libraries before 1500." In item 51. Pp. 293–311.
[Concise survey of the colleges' holdings, provenance of items, major gifts.]

1676.   Kohl, Stephen. "Private Letters in Fifteenth Century England and the Problem of Late Medieval Culture." *Fifteenth-Century Studies* 5 (1982), 117–37.
[Some themes of historical relevance in the letters.]

1677.　Krochalis, Jeanne E. "Hoccleve's Chaucer Portrait."
　　　　Chaucer Rev 21 (1986–87), 234–45.
　　　　[On realism and authorial fame.]

1678.　―――. "The Books and Reading of Henry V and His
　　　　Circle." *Chaucer Rev* 23 (1988), 50–77.
　　　　[Traces the king's books; he and others at his
　　　　court both collected *and* read.]

1679.　Lawler, Traugott. "On the Properties of John Trevisa's
　　　　Major Translations." *Viator* 14 (1983), 267–88.

1680.　Leader, Damian Riehl. "Philosophy at Oxford and
　　　　Cambridge in the Fifteenth Century." *History of Uni-*
　　　　versities, vol. 4 (1984), 25–46.
　　　　[Natural and moral philosophy and metaphysics:
　　　　English academic studies compared with the
　　　　Parisian.]

1681.　―――. *A History of the University of Cambridge*, 1: *The*
　　　　University to 1546. General editor, Christopher Brooke.
　　　　Cambridge and New York, 1988.
　　　　[Chapters 1–2 are pre-Tudor: curriculum,
　　　　growth of the university, and the coming of
　　　　humanism.]

1682.　Lester, G. A. *Sir John Paston's "Grete boke": A De-*
　　　　scriptive Catalogue, with an Introduction, of British
　　　　Library MS Lansdowne 285. Cambridge and Totowa,
　　　　N.J., 1984.

[A literary miscellany and a window upon popular taste. Reviewed by A. S. G. Edwards, *Speculum* 60 (1985), 699–701.]

1683.   Lester, Geoffrey, ed. *The Earliest English Translation of Vegetius' De Re Militari.* Middle English Texts, 21. Heidelberg, 1988.
[From Oxford MS. Bodleian Douce 291.]

1684.   Lovatt, Roger. "John Blacman: Biographer of Henry VI." In item 22. Pp. 415–44.
[How Blacman collected the material for the biographical memoir.]

1685.   ———. "A Collector of Apocryphal Anecdotes: John Blacman Revisited." In item 69. Pp. 172–97.
[Blacman's life of Henry VI is an important work in the history of lay piety.]

1686.   Lowry, Martin J. C. "Caxton, St. Winifred and the Lady Margaret Beaufort." *Library*, 6th ser., 5 (1983), 101–17.
[Caxton's volume and support of the cult ingratiated him with the Tudors.]

1687.   ———. "John Rouse and the Survival of the Neville Circle." *Viator* 19 (1988), 327–38.
[Literary circle with a sense of community.]

1688.   Lucas, Peter J. "The Growth and Development of English Literary Patronage in the Later Middle Ages and

Early Renaissance." *Library*, 6th ser., 4 (1982), 221–48.
[A new style of patronage was coming into existence.]

1689. ———, ed. *John Capgrave's Abbreuiacion of Cronicles.*
EETS, no. 285 (1983).
[From Adam to the Council of Basle, completed
c. 1462–63.]

1690. [No entry.]

1691. Lytle, G. F. "The Social Origins of Oxford Students in
the Late Middle Ages: New College, c. 1380–c. 1510."
In item 51. Pp. 426–54.
[Prominent students traced: primarily rural and
well-born.]

1692. ———. "A University Mentality in the Later Middle
Ages: The Pragmatism, Humanism, and Orthodoxy of
New College, Oxford." In *Genèse et debuts du Grand
Schisme d'Occident. Colloque tenu à Avignon, 25–28
septembre 1978.* Jean Favier et al. Colloques internationaux du CNRS, no. 586. Paris, 1980. Pp.
201–30.

1693. ———. "Patronage and the Election of Winchester
Scholars during the Late Middle Ages and Renaissance." In item 20. Pp. 167–88.

1694. ———. " 'Wykehamist Culture' in Pre-Reformation
England." In item 20. Pp. 129–66.
[Careers and intellectual contributions.]

1695. ———. "The Careers of Oxford Students in the Later Middle Ages." In *Rebirth, Reform, and Resilience: Universities in Transition, 1300–1700.* Edited by James M. Kittelson and Pamela J. Transue. Columbus, Oh., 1984. Pp. 213–53.

[Where they went, whom they served, how prevalent they were.]

1696. Matheson, Lister M. "Historical Prose." In item 24. Pp. 209–48.

1697. ———. "Printer and Scribe: Caxton, the *Polychronicon*, and the *Brut*." *Speculum* 60 (1985), 593–614.

[Did Caxton write the continuation? It is likely.]

1698. McHardy, A. K. "The Dissemination of Wyclif's Ideas." In item 49. Pp. 361–68.

[Largely via an "old boy" network.]

1699. McIlwain, James T. "The 'Bodelye Syeknes' of Julian of Norwich." *JMH* 10 (1984), 167–80.

[Probably botulism caused her paralysis.]

1700. Meale, Carol M. "Patrons, Buyers, and Owners: Book Production and Social Status." In item 30. Pp. 201–38.

[Links between patronage, politics, and expenditure.]

1701. Mooney, Linne R. "A Middle English Verse Compendium of Astrological Medicine." *Journal of Medical History* 28 (1984), 406–19.

[Late fourteenth-century: Oxford, Bodleian Ash. MS. 210, printed here.]

1702. ———. "Lydgate's 'Kings of England' and Another Verse Chronicle of the Kings." *Viator* 20 (1989), 255–90.
[Compares Lydgate with an anonymous life from a Bodleian MS.]

1703. Moran, Jo Ann Hoeppner. *Education and Learning in the City of York, 1300–1560.* University of York, Borthwick Institute of Historical Research, Borthwick Papers, no. 55. York, 1979.

1704. ———. "Literacy and Education in Northern England, 1350–1550: A Methodological Inquiry." *Northern* 17 (1981), 1–23.
[Presents the case for an increase in lay education and literacy.]

1705. ———. "A 'Common Profit' Library in Fifteenth Century England and Other Books for Chaplains." *Manuscripta* 28 (1984), 17–25.
[Manuscript reference of 1404 to a cleric's library, with transcription.]

1706. ———. *The Growth of English Schooling, 1340–1548: Learning, Literacy, and Laicization in Pre-Reformation York Diocese.* Guildford, 1985; Princeton, 1985.
[Important monograph arguing for the healthy state and spread of education and educational institutions.]

1707. Nicholson, R. H. "The State of the Nation: Some Complaint Topics in Late Medieval English Literature." *Pargeron* 23 (1979), 9–28.

[A look at poetry for social criticisms, comments, and grumbles.]

1708. Oates, J. C. T. *Cambridge University Library: A History*, 1: *From the Beginnings to the Copyright Act of Queen Anne*. Cambridge and New York, 1986.
[Chapters 1–2 (pp. 1–36, 37–69) cover humble beginnings and the library's growth into early Tudor times.]

1709. Orme, Nicholas. *Education in the West of England, 1066–1548: Cornwall, Devon, Dorset, Gloucestershire, Somerset, Wiltshire*. Exeter, 1976.
[Thorough study of regional schools and education.]

1710. ———. "Evesham School before the Reformation." *Vale of Evesham Historical Society, Research Papers* 6 (1977), 95–100.
[Mostly early sixteenth-century.]

1711. ———. "Education in the West of England, 1066–1548: Additions and Corrections." *D & C N&Q* 34 (1978), 22–25.

1712. ———. "The Medieval Schools of Worcestershire." *Worcestershire*, 3rd ser., 6 (1978), 43–51. Reprinted in item 65. No. 3.

1713. ———. "Chaucer and Education." *Chaucer Rev* 16 (1981), 38–59. Reprinted in item 65. No. 13, pp. 221–42.

1714.   ———. "A Grammatical Miscellany of 1427–1465 from Bristol and Wiltshire." *Traditio* 38 (1982), 301–26. Reprinted in item 65. No. 6, pp. 85–112.
[Copied by "a certain Thomas Schort," who died in 1465.]

1715.   ———. "Schoolmasters, 1307–1509." In item 17. Pp. 218–41. Reprinted in item 65. No. 4, pp. 49–71.
[What sorts of people, and what training they received.]

1716.   ———. *From Childhood to Chivalry: The Education of the English Kings and Aristocracy, 1066–1530.* London and New York, 1984.
[Useful survey of the topic, incorporating recent literature and interpretations.]

1717.   ———. "Early School Note Books." *Yale Library Gazette* 60 (1985), 47–57. Reprinted in item 65. No. 5, pp. 72–86.

1718.   ———. "English Schoolmasters, 1100–1500." In item 14. Pp. 303–11.
[Follows item 1715 in treatment of the subject.]

1719.   ———. "Sir John Speke and His Chapel in Exeter Cathedral." *Devonshire* 118 (1986), 25–41.
[Sixteenth-century tomb but much fifteenth-century family history.]

1720.   ———. "The 'Laicisation' of English School Education." *History of Education* 16 (1987), 81–89. Reprinted in item 65. No. 2, pp. 23–31.

1721.   ———. "Schools and Society from the Twelfth Century to the Reformation." In item 65. No. 1, pp. 1–21.
[A general survey.]

1722.   Painter, George Duncan. *William Caxton: A Quincentenary Biography of England's First Printer*. London, 1976.
[For a review essay see Blake, item 1569. First American edition, *William Caxton: A Biography* (New York, 1977).]

1723.   Pantin, W. A. "Instructions for a Devout and Literate Layman." In item 2. Pp. 398–422.
[Early fifteenth-century: lay piety of the Throckmorton family, with the text of the instructions in translation.]

1724.   ———. *Canterbury College, Oxford*. Vol. 4. Oxford Historical Society, n.s., vol. 30 (1985).
[A narrative, with extracts from accounts and biographical data. Volumes 1–3 were published 1947–50.]

1725.   Partner, Peter. "William of Wykeham and the Historians." In item 20. Pp. 1–36.
[His career, his efforts as a founder, and an assessment of his public role.]

1726.   Peck, Russell A. *Kingship & Common Profit in Gower's Confessio Amantis*. Foreword by John Gardner. Carbondale, Ill., 1978.
[In the Literary Structures series.]

1727. ———. "Social Conscience and the Poet." In item 63. Pp. 113–48.
[For Chaucer it was higher than we often assume; links with Wyclif and other major writers traced.]

1728. Pegues, F. J. "Philanthropy and the Universities of France and England." In *The Economic and Material Frame of the Mediaeval University: Proceedings of the International Commission for the History of Universities, Held in San Francisco, California (USA), August 27, 1975 (International Congress of Historical Sciences).* Edited by Astrik L. Gabriel. Communications by Aleksander Gieysztor et al. English resumé (French texts) by Leslie L. Domonkos. Texts and Studies in the History of Mediaeval Education, no. 15. Notre Dame, Ind., 1977. Pp. 69–80.

1729. Penninger, Frieda Elaine. *William Caxton.* Twayne's English Authors Ser., 263. Boston, 1979.

1730. Phillips, Heather. "John Wyclif and the Optics of the Eucharist." In item 49. Pp. 245–58.
[Math and optics were incorporated into Wyclif's ideological baggage.]

1731. Rawcliffe, Carole. "Medicine and Medical Practice in Later Medieval London." *Guildhall* 5/1 (1981), 13–25.
[Surveys the large body of London practitioners at their many ranks and levels.]

1732. ———. "The Hospitals of Late Medieval London." *Medical History* 28 (1984), 1–21.

[With an appendix on thirty-four hospitals and almshouses.]

1733. ———. "The Profits of Practice: The Wealth and Status of Medical Men in Later Medieval England." *Social History of Medicine* 1 (1988), 61–78.
[They might have had to fight for their fees, but they did well.]

1734. ———. "Consultants, Careerists and Conspirators: Royal Doctors in the Time of Richard III." *Ricardian* 8/106 (September 1989), 250–58.

1735. Reeves, A. Compton. "The World of Thomas Hoccleve." *Fifteenth-Century Studies* 2 (1979), 187–201.
[Intellectual biography and the career of a literary civil servant.]

1736. ———. "The Careers of William Lyndwood." In item 34. Pp. 197–216.
[Biographical; important civil servant, with a look at his writings.]

1737. Reeves, Marjorie, and Stephen Medcalf. "The Ideal, the Real and the Quest for Perfection." In item 61. Pp. 56–107.
[The social and intellectual context of much of the literature.]

1738. Reiss, Edmund. "Chaucer and His Audience." *Chaucer Rev* 14 (1979–80), 390–402.

[What Chaucer could assume about literary so-
phistication, his audience's worldview, and the
question of court poetry.]

1739. Richardson, Malcolm. "Hoccleve in His Social Context." *Chaucer Rev* 20 (1985–86), 313–22.
[A failed bureaucrat, as he himself says.]

1740. Riggs, A. C. "Clocks, Dials, and Other Terms." In
item 29. Pp. 255–74.
[Various terms for time-keeping devices; how
they worked and how they differed from each
other.]

1741. Robbins, Rossell Hope. "Dissent in Middle English Literature: The Spirit of (Thirteen) Seventy-Six." *Medievalia et Humanistica*, n.s. 9 (1979), 25–51.
[Lively survey of Wyclif, estates literature, and
anti-clerical expression.]

1742. Rogers, Nicholas J. "The Old Proctor's Book: A Cambridge Manuscript of c. 1390." In item 66. Pp.
213–21.
[Drawn up after the 1381 destruction of archives:
statutes, ceremonies, and indications of Bohemian influence in the iconography.]

1743. Rosenthal, Joel T. "Aristocratic Cultural Patronage
and Book Bequests, 1350–1500." *BJRUL* 64 (1981–
82), 522–48.
[Based mainly on material in aristocratic wills.]

1744. Rosser, A. Gervase. "A Note on the Caxton Indulgence of 1476." *Library*, 6th ser., 7 (1985), 256–58.
[Indulgence regarding marriage and a pilgrimage to Rome, printed December 1476.]

1745. Rowland, Beryl, intro. and trans. *Medieval Woman's Guide to Health: The First English Gynecological Handbook: Middle English Text*. London, 1981; Kent, Oh., 1981.
[Edited from BL MS. Sloane 2463. Reviewed by Jerry Stannard and Linda Voigts, *Speculum* 57 (1982), 422–26.]

1746. Rubin, Miri. "Development and Change in English Hospitals, 1100–1500." As item 1589. Pp. 41–59.
[Focuses on charity and relief.]

1747. Sammut, Alfonso. *Unfredo, duca di Gloucester e gli umanisti italiani*. Medioevo e Umanesimo, 41. Padua, 1980.

1748. Scattergood, V. John. "Literary Culture at the Court of Richard II." In item 77. Pp. 29–43.
[A survey that raises serious doubts about Richard's central role in court culture and patronage.]

1749. Seymour, M. C., et al., eds. *On the Properties of Things: John Trevisa's Translation of Bartholomaeus Anglicus De Proprietatibus Rerum: A Critical Text*. 2 vols. Oxford, 1975.
[Volume 1: *Books I–XIII*; 2: *Books XIV–XIX*.]

1750. Sherborne, James W. "Aspects of English Court Culture in the Later Fourteenth Century." In item 77. Pp. 1–27.

[As in item 1748, some qualifications about the king and the entire cultural role of the court circle.]

1751. Specht, Henrik. *Chaucer's Franklin in the Canterbury Tales: The Social and Literary Background of a Chaucerian Character.* Publications of the Department of English, University of Copenhagen, vol. 10. Copenhagen, 1981.

[A gentleman, not a jumped-up upstart or social climber.]

1752. Starkey, David. "The Age of the Household: Politics, Society, and the Arts, c.1350–c.1550." In item 61. Pp. 225–305.

1753. Storey, Robin L. "The Foundation and the Medieval College, 1379–1530." In item 15. Pp. 3–43.

1754. ———. "The Universities during the Wars of the Roses." In item 84. Pp. 315–37.

[University-government relations in an uneasy period; vol. 2 of *The History of the University of Oxford* (*Late Medieval Oxford*, ed. J. I. Catto and Ralph Evans) tells the full tale.]

1755. Stratford, Jenny. "The Manuscripts of John, Duke of Bedford: Library and Chapel." In item 84. Pp. 329–50.

[Based largely on some inventories in the PRO.]

1756. Strohm, Paul. "Chaucer's Audience." *Literature and History* 5 (1977), 26–41.
[Why his writings specifically might have caught their attention.]

1757. ———. "Chaucer's Fifteenth-Century Audience and the Narrowing of the Chaucer Tradition." *Studies in the Age of Chaucer* 4 (1982), 3–32.
[The audience changed from "close-knit primary" to "far-flung and disparate."]

1758. ———. "Chaucer's Audience(s): Fictional, Implied, Intended, Actual." *Chaucer Rev* 18 (1983–84), 137–45.
[With an audience discussion of the issue, pp. 175–81.]

1759. Swanson, Robert N. "Universities, Graduates and Benefices in Later Medieval England." *Past and Present* 106 (1985), 28–61.
[Further examination of questions posed by Lytle in items 1691, 1695.]

1760. ———. "Learning and Livings: University Study and Clerical Careers in Later Medieval England." *History of Universities* 6 (1986–87), 81–103.
[Questions the "crisis of patronage" premise.]

1761. Taylor, John. "Letters and Letter Collections in England, 1300–1420." *Nottingham* 24 (1980), 57–70.
[Some lesser-known collections and the rise of letter-writing.]

1762. ———. "The Diocese of York and the University Connection, 1300–1520." *Northern* 25 (1989), 39–59.
[The universities were flooded with men from York, many playing vital roles.]

1763. Thomson, David. "The Oxford Grammar Masters Revisited." *MS* 45 (1983), 298–310.
[Follows from R. W. Hunt's 1964 study.]

1764. Tolley, T. S. "Some Historical Interests at Sherborne, c. 1400." In item 66. Pp. 255–66.
[General cultural activity, with the Sherborne missal as the high point.]

1765. Tormey, Carol. "A Catalogue of the Fifteenth Century Books in the Library of Downside Abbey." *Downside* 98 (1980), 147–61.
[Forty-three books from the Continent, many from 1485–1500.]

1766. Turville-Petre, Thorlac. "The Lament for Sir John Berkeley." *Speculum* 57 (1982), 332–39.
[A ninety-one-line poem from a manuscript in the Nottingham University library.]

1767. Twigg, John. *A History of Queens' College, Cambridge, 1448–1986.* Woodbridge and Wolfeboro, N.H., 1987.
[Many different aspects of the early history are covered in pp. 1–140.]

1768. Voigts, Linda E. "A Letter from a Middle English Dictaminal Formulary in Harvard Law Library, MS. 43." *Speculum* 56 (1981), 575–81.

[Transcription of model letter to send home to
ask for money!]

1769.   ——. "Medical Prose." In item 24. Pp. 315–35.

1770.   ——. "Scientific and Medical Texts." In item 30.
Pp. 345–402.
[Thorough survey, with a well-illustrated look at
many of the major manuscripts.]

1771.   Voigts, Linda E., and M. R. McVaugh, eds. *A Latin
Technical Phlebotomy and Its Middle English Trans-
lation.* Transactions of the American Philosophical
Society, vol. 74, pt. 2 (1984).
[The English version is c. 1400; long introduc-
tion on the medical aspects of the MS.]

1772.   Wilson, Edward. *"Sir Gawain and The Green Knight*
and the Stanley Family of Stanley, Storeton and
Hooton." *Review of English Studies,* n.s. 30 (1979),
308–16.

1773.   ——, intro. and contents list. *The Winchester An-
thology: A Facsimile of British Library Additional
Manuscript 60577.* Account of the music by Iain
Fenlon. Cambridge, 1981; Woodbridge and Totowa,
N.J., 1981.
[A miscellany of humanistic and literary en-
tries.]

1774.   Wylie, John A. H. "Sweating Sickness." *Ricardian*
7/91 (December 1985), 178–81.

[Did the princes die of this while they were held in the Tower?]

1775.   Wylie, John A. H., and Leslie H. Collier. "The English Sweating Sickness (Sudor Anglicus): A Reappraisal." *Journal of the History of Medicine* 36 (1981), 425–45. [Came in 1485 and then became a regular visitor.]

XI. FINE ARTS AND CRAFTS

1776. Alexander, J. J. G. "Painting and Manuscript Illumination for Royal Patrons in the Later Middle Ages." In item 77. Pp. 141–62.
[Valuable survey with eighteen plates.]

1777. Alexander, J. J. G., and Paul Binski, eds. *Age of Chivalry: Art in Plantagenet England, 1200–1400.* Royal Academy of Arts. London, 1987.
[Also listed as item 1; exhibition catalogue, November 1987–March 1988. Mostly pre-1377, but a very rich volume; sections on William Wykeham and Richard II. See also J. J. G. Alexander, "The Making of the Age of Chivalry," *History Today* 37 (November 1987), 3–11.]

1778. Angus-Butterworth, Lionel M. "Early Lancashire Brasses." *Ancient Monuments*, n.s. 22 (1977), 90–103.
[There were five by 1485; described with biographies of their patrons.]

1779. Ayers, Brian S., Robert Smith, and Margot Tillyard, with a contribution by T. P. Smith. "The Cow Tower, Norwich: A Detailed Survey and Partial Interpretation." *Med Arch* 32 (1988), 184–207.

[Free-standing three-story brick tower, built in the 1390s; translations of the building accounts are included.]

1780. Backhouse, Janet. "A Reappraisal of the Bedford Hours." *BLJ* 7 (1981), 47–69.
[A manuscript often referred to but rarely discussed in such full detail.]

1781. ———. "Founders of the Royal Library: Edward IV and Henry VII as Collectors of Illuminated Manuscripts." In item 84. Pp. 23–41.
[With an appendix of possible manuscripts.]

1782. Badham, Sally F. "The Fens 1 Series: An Early Fifteenth Century Group of Monumental Brasses and Incised Slabs." *JBAA* 142 (1989), 46–62.
[Twenty-one brasses and slabs of the Midlands and East Anglia, 1408–30.]

1783. Baker, Malcolm. "Medieval Illustrations of Bede's *Life of St. Cuthbert*." *Journal of the Warburg and Courtauld Institutes* 41 (1978), 16–49.
[A fifteenth-century revival of Cuthbert iconography, with York and Salisbury examples.]

1784. Barker, Nicholas. "Caxton's Typography." *JPHS* 11 (1976), 114–43.

1785. Barron, Caroline M. "Anniversary Address—at the Guildhall." *Ancient Monuments*, n.s. 23 (1978), 9–28.

[To explain and describe the late medieval building; a précis of her 1974 full-length study.]

1786. Bent, Margaret. *Dunstaple.* Oxford Studies of Composers, 17. London and New York, 1981.
[A short study.]

1787. Bent, Margaret, and Roger Bowers. "The Saxilby Fragment." *EMH* 1 (1981), 1–28.

1788. Bismanis, M. R. "Birdcombe Court, Wraxall, Avon: A Fifteenth-Century House." *Arch J* 134 (1977), 303–06.
[A two-story building, with a floor plan.]

1789. Blair, C. "An Early Fifteenth Century London Latoner." *Monumental Brass Society Bulletin* 38 (1985), 129ff.

1790. Blatchley, J. M. "The Lost Cross Brasses of Suffolk, 1320–1420." *Transactions of the Monumental Brass Society* 12/1 (1975), 21–45.

1791. Bowers, Roger. "The Performing Pitch of English 15th Century Church Polyphony." *Early Music* 8 (1980), 21–28.

1792. Bowers, Roger, and Andrew Wathey, comp., with Susan Rankin. "New Sources of English Fourteenth and Fifteenth Century Polyphone." *EMH* 3 (1983), 123–73.

1793. Bowers, Roger, and Andrew Wathey, with contributions to the descriptions and commentaries by William Summers and David Fallows. "New Sources of English Fifteenth and Sixteenth Century Polyphony." *EMH* 4 (1984), 297–346.

1794. Brodrick, Anne, and Josephine Darrah. "The Fifteenth Century Polychromed Limestone Effigies of William Fitzalan, 9th Earl of Arundel, and His Wife, Joan Nevill, in the Fitzalan Chapel, Arundel." *Journal of the Church Monument Society* 1/2 (1986), 65–95.
[The layers of paint in the exceptional polychrome analyzed; lavish photographs, some technical considerations.]

1795. Brownsword, R., et al. "X-ray Flourescence Analysis of 13th–16th Century Pewter Flatware." *Archaeometry* 21 (1984), 237–43.

1796. Caldwell, John. "The 'Te Deum' in Late Medieval England." *Early Music* 6 (1978), 188–94.

1797. Cameron, H. K. "Flemish Brasses to Civilians in England." *Arch J* 139 (1982), 420–40.
[At least three can be identified.]

1798. Campbell, Marian. "English Goldsmiths in the Fifteenth Century." In item 84. Pp. 43–52.
[Very little work has survived.]

1799. Cherry, J. "The Talbot Casket and Related Late Medieval Leather Caskets." *Archaeologia* 107 (1982), 131–40.

[Probably a legacy of the earl's continental connections.]

1800. Claxton, Ann. "The Sign of the Dog: An Examination of the Devonshire Hunting Tapestries." *JMH* 14 (1988), 127–79.
[Mid-century, made for the Talbots; twenty-four illustrations.]

1801. Coldstream, Nicola. "Art and Architecture in the Late Middle Ages." In item 61. Pp. 172–224.

1802. Colledge, Edmund. "South Netherlands Books of Hours Made for England." *Scriptorium* 32 (1978), 55–57.
[Especially a volume of St. Cuthbert's College, Ushaw.]

1803. Colvin, Howard. "The 'Court Style' in Medieval English Architecture: A Review." In item 77. Pp. 129–39.
[A tale of slow development.]

1804. Colvin, Howard M., and J. S. G. Simmons. *All Souls: An Oxford College and Its Buildings.* New York, 1989; Oxford, 1988.
[The Chichele Lectures, 1986: architectural history, with pp. 1–18 on "The Building of the Medieval College."]

1805. Cotton, Simon. "Medieval Roodscreens in Norfolk— Their Construction and Painting Dates." *Norfolk* 40 (1987), 44–54.
[Wills are examined for bequests to subsidize their construction.]

1806. Crewe, Sarah. *Stained Glass in England c.1180–c.1540*. Royal Commission on Historical Monuments, HMSO, 1987.

1807. Crosley, Paul. "English Gothic Architecture." In item 1. Pp. 60–73.

1808. Cunliffe, Barry, and Julian Munby, with contributions from T. Ball et al. *Excavations at Portchester Castle, 4: Medieval, the Inner Bailey*. Reports of the Research Committee of the Society of Antiquities of London, no. 43 (1985).
[The late medieval town and various construction projects. In a case, separately issued with vol. 4, twenty-four folded maps of the castle.]

1809. Doggett, Nicholas, with a contribution by Philip J. Lankester. "Fragments of the Fifteenth Century Reredos and a Medieval Cross Head from North Hinksey, Discovered at All Souls College Chapel, Oxford, and Some New Light on the 19th Century Restoration." *Oxon* 49 (1984), 277–87.
[Found in 1983; a guide to the accuracy of Scott's restorations of the 1870s.]

1810. Drury, P. J. "An Unusual Late-Medieval Timber-Framed Building at Harwich, Essex." *VA* 15 (1984), 34–38.
[Anchor beams rather than tie beams in the upper story.]

1811. Dudley, C. J. "Canterbury Cathedral: The Small Portrait Carvings of the Pulpitum, c. 1400." *Arch Cant* 97 (1981), 185–94.
[The screen is 1390–1411; some possible contemporaries are identified in the portraits.]

1812. Dyer, Christopher. "Evidence for Helms in Gloucestershire in the Fourteenth Century." *VA* 15 (1984), 42–44.
[Helms were buildings designed for crop storage.]

1813. ———. "English Peasant Buildings in the Later Middle Ages (1200–1500)." *Med Arch* 30 (1986), 19–45.
[Argues for greater size and complexity than we generally accept, drawing upon West Midland evidence.]

1814. Eames, Penelope. *Furniture in England, France and the Netherlands from the Twelfth to the Fifteenth Century.* Furniture History Society, 1977.
[Victoria and Albert Museum. Cover title: *Medieval Furniture.*]

1815. Edwards, J. "A Fifteenth-Century Wall-Painting at South Leigh." *Oxon* 48 (1983), 131–42.
[Probably from 1872; the medieval original seems to be completely gone.]

1816. Emery, Anthony. "The Development of Raglan Castle and Keeps in Late Medieval England." *Arch J* 132 (1975), 151–86.

[A fifteenth-century building attesting to Lord Herbert's regional power.]

1817. ———. "Ralph, Lord Cromwell's Manor of Wingfield (1439–c. 1450): Its Construction, Design and Influence." *Arch J* 142 (1985), 276–339.
[The most imposing extant baronial residence of the fifteenth century: elaborate description, plans, photographs.]

1818. Emmerson, Robin. "Monumental Brasses: London Design, c. 1420–85." *JBAA* 131 (1978), 50–78.
[Survey of styles and designs; London workshops can be traced and linked.]

1819. Fallows, David, ed. *Two Mid-Fifteenth-Century English Songs.* Early Music Ser., EM 28. London, 1977.
["Mi verry joy," poem by Charles d'Orléans, music, John Bedynham; "Pryncesse of youthe," poem by John Lydgate: from Bibliothèque nationale, MS. f.fr. 15123, fols. 69ᵛ–70ʳ; El Escorial, Biblioteca del Monasterio, MS. IV.a.24, fols. 114ᵛ–116ʳ and BL Add. 16165, fol. 224ʳ. Score for three parts, vocal/instrumental.]

1820. ———. "Words and Music in Two English Songs of the Mid-Fifteenth Century: Charles d'Orléans and John Lydgate." *Early Music* 5 (1977), 38–43.

1821. Fleming, P. W. "The Hautes and Their 'Circle': Culture and the English Gentry." In item 84. Pp. 85–102.

[Involvement with music, literature, and people of the court.]

1822. Fredell, Joel. "Late Gothic Portraiture: The Prioress and Philippa." *Chaucer Rev* 23 (1989), 181–91.
[The queen's effigy may have influenced the description of the prioress.]

1823. French, Thomas. "The Glazing of the St. William Windows in York Minster." *JBAA* 140 (1987), 175–81.
[Probably c. 1415, not 1421–23; some heraldry of the Ros family.]

1824. Friedman, John B. "John Siferwas and the Mythological Illustrations in the *Liber Cosmographiae* of John de Foxton." *Speculum* 58 (1983), 381–418.
[A book of 1408, with possible links between the artist and a Yorkshire manuscript.]

1825. ———. " 'He Hath a Thousand Slayn this Pestilence': The Iconography of the Plague in the Late Middle Ages." In item 63. Pp. 75–112.
[England and the Continent: well-illustrated guide to the range of styles and types of plague depiction.]

1826. Gee, Eric. "Stone from the Medieval Limestone Quarries of South Yorkshire." In *Collectanea Historica: Essays in Memory of Stuart Rigold*. Edited by Alec Detsicas. Kent Archaeological Society, 1981. Pp. 247–55.
[Largely from Huddleston quarry in the fifteenth century.]

1827. ———. "Heating in the Late Middle Ages." *Ancient Monuments*, n.s. 31 (1987), 88–105.
[Survey of types of chimneys, heaters, vents, and fuels, with examples of each.]

1828. Gibb, J. H. P. "The Fire of 1437 and the Rebuilding of Sherborne Abbey." *JBAA* 138 (1985), 101–24.
[Arson; damage traced and new work described, with its distinctive vaulting.]

1829. ———. "Sherborne Abbey—Addendum: The Fire of 1437." *JBAA* 141 (1988), 161–69.
[Rebuilding probably did not begin until after 1451; the timber roof of the late fourteenth century survived.]

1830. Giles, J. A. "A Fifteenth Century Bronze Skillet from near Pately Bridge." *YAJ* 51 (1979), 17–19.
[Found before 1926; from a wealthy household.]

1831. Hamilton, Alice. "Orthodoxy in Late Fifteenth Century Glass at Leicester." *Leicestershire* 55 (1979–80), 22–37.
[The iconography of twenty-nine little-known panels.]

1832. Hare, J. N. "Bishops Waltham Palace, Hampshire: William of Wykeham, Henry Beaufort, and the Transformation of a Medieval Episcopal Palace." *Arch J* 145 (1988), 222–54.

[We can follow the stages of the immense up-grading. Appendix by R. Warmington, "Beaufort's Range of Lodgings," pp. 246–51.]

1833.   Harthan, J. P. "The Salisbury Book of Hours." *History Today* 28 (June 1978), 406–10.
[Compiled at Rouen, 1425.]

1834.   Harvey, B., and R. Harvey. "I. The Early History of Bewley Court, Laycock." *Wiltshire* 81 (1987), 63–73.
[History of the house and an inventory of 1418; P. M. Slocombe covers the early architecture, pp. 68–73.]

1835.   Harvey, John H. "Architectural History from 1291 to 1558." As item 1323. Pp. 149–92.
[The York Minster we see today, with an appendix listing its late medieval architects.]

1836.   ———. *The Perpendicular Style, 1330–1485*. London, 1978.
[General discussion, then chronological treatment; p. 97 begins with Henry Yevele. Well illustrated; model introductory volume.]

1837.   ———. "The Building of Wells Cathedral, II: 1307–1548." As item 1348. Pp. 76–101.

1838.   ———. "The Buildings of Winchester College." In item 20. Pp. 79–127.
[The stages of building, with an appendix of the craftsmen, 1387–1556.]

1839. Hepburn, Frederick. *Portraits of the Later Plantag-enets*. Woodbridge and Dover, N.H., 1986. [Discussion of all paintings, effigies, and other portraits that have survived.]

1840. Hogarth, Sylvia. "Ecclesiastical Vestments and Vest-ment Makers in York, 1300–1600." *York Historian* 7 (1986), 8ff.

1841. Jackson-Stops, Gervase. "The Building of the Medi-eval College" and "Gains and Losses: The College Buildings, 1404–1750." In item 15. Pp. 147–92, 193–232, respectively.

1842. James, T. B., and A. M. Robinson, with a report on the kiln and ceramic tiles by Elizabeth Eames and contri-butions from J. Ashurt et al. *Clarendon Palace: The History and Archaeology of a Medieval Palace and Hunting Lodge near Salisbury, Wiltshire.* Reports of the Research Committee of the Society of Antiquaries of London, no. 45 (1988). ["The Historical Context" (pp. 40–46) covers Richard II. A lavish volume mostly devoted to architectural history.]

1843. Jones, B. C. "Carlisle Goldsmiths, 1318–1625." *Cum-berland & Westmorland* 80 (1980), 36–44. [Only a few indications of the craft.]

1844. King, Pamela M. "The English Cadaver Tomb in the Late Fifteenth Century: Some Indications of a Lan-castrian Connection." In item 81. Pp. 45–57.

[A few tombs; family ties and links with the Continent are traced.]

1845. König, Eberhard. "A Leaf from a Gutenberg Bible Illuminated in England." *BLJ* 9 (1983), 32–50.
[Books were already being shipped in from the Continent in the 1450s.]

1846. Leedy, Walter C., Jr. "Wells Cathedral and Sherborne Abbey: Workshop Connections in the Late 15th Century." *Gesta* 16 (1977), 39–44.
[The Wells crossing and Sherborne's north transept vault, 1475–1504.]

1847. Lefferts, Peter M., and Margaret Bent, comps., with Andrew Wathey, Roger Bowers, and Mark Everist. "New Sources of English Thirteenth- and Fourteenth-Century Polyphony." *EMH* 2 (1982), 173–362.

1848. Le Patourel, John. "Fortified and Semi-Fortified Manor Houses in Eastern and Northern England in the Later Middle Ages." In *La Maison forte au Moyen Age. Actes de la Table ronde de Nancy-Pont-à-Mousson des 31 mai–3 juin 1984.* Directed by Michel Bur. CNRS. Paris, 1986. Pp. 17–29.

1849. Lindley, Phillip. "Figure-Sculpture at Winchester in the Fifteenth Century: A New Chronology." In item 84. Pp. 153–66.
[Value underestimated because so little is *in situ.*]

1850. Marks, Richard. "The Glazing of Fotheringhay Church and College." *JBAA* 131 (1978), 79–104.

[A reconstruction of the glass once in the mausoleum of the House of York.]

1851. ———. "The Glazing of the Collegiate Chapel of the Holy Trinity, Tattershall (Lincolnshire): A Study of Late Fifteenth Century Glass-Painting Workshops." *Archaeologia* 106 (1979), 133–56.

[Much glass still *in situ*: important for iconography and styles of workmanship.]

1852. ———. "Stained Glass, c. 1200–1400." In item 1. Pp. 137–47.

1853. Marks, Richard, and Nigel Morgan. *The Golden Age of English Manuscript Painting, 1200–1500.* London, 1981; New York, 1981.

[Also *Englische Buchmaleri der Gotik (1200–1500)* in the series Die Grossen Handschriften der Welt (Munich, 1980). The Gothic style, after 1377, covered in sixteen plates with discussion.]

1854. Marks, Richard, and Ann Payne, comps. and eds. *British Heraldry from Its Origins to c. 1800.* London, 1978.

[For the Trustees of the British Museum and the British Library. Catalogue of an exhibition, well illustrated and covering much late medieval material.]

1855.   McCann, John. "Brick Nogging in the Fifteenth and Sixteenth Centuries, with Examples Drawn Mainly from
Essex." *Ancient Monuments*, n.s. 31 (1987), 106–33.
[The use of bricks between timber frames, with
various examples and styles.]

1856.   McCarthy, Michael R., and Catherine M. Brooks.
Medieval Pottery in Britain, AD 900–1670. Leicester,
1988.
[Chapter 6 runs from the mid-fourteenth century into Tudor times. The survey is county by
county, site by site; illustrations and descriptions of types.]

1857.   Meeson, R. "The Timber Frame of the Hall at Tam-
worth Castle, Staffordshire, and Its Context." *Arch J*
140 (1983), 329–40.
[Perhaps 1400–25; an impressive twenty-seven-
foot span for the tie beam.]

1858.   Meredith, Rosamund. "Millstone Making at Yarncliff
in the Reign of Edward IV." *Derbyshire* 101 (1981),
102–06.
[Transcription of a Bodleian MS.]

1859.   Miles, T. J., and A. D. Saunders, with a contribution
from J. W. G. Musty. "The Chantry Priests' House at
Farleigh Hungerford Castle." *Med Arch* 19 (1975),
165–94.
[Sir Walter Hungerford had it built, 1430.]

1860. Morris, Christopher. "The Buildings of King's College, Cambridge." *Ancient Monuments*, n.s. 30 (1986), 16–28. [Medieval origins and afterwards.]

1861. Morris, Richard K. "The Development of Later Gothic Mouldings in England, c. 1250–1400." *Architectural History* 21 (1978), 18–57.

1862. Orme, Nicholas. "The Early Musicians of Exeter Cathedral." *Music & Letters* 59 (1978), 395–410.

1863. Ormond, Richard, and Malcolm Rogers, eds. *Dictionary of British Portraiture, 1: The Middle Ages to the Early Georgians, Historical Figures Born before 1700.* Compiled by Adriana Davies. London, 1979; New York, 1979.
    [Published in association with the National Portrait Gallery. Foreword by John Hayes. Alphabetical listing of subjects; all known portraits listed. Index in vol. 4 (1981).]

1864. Page, Christopher. "The Fifteenth Century Lute: Men and Neglected Sources." *Early Music* 9 (1981), 11–21. [Uses the Cely Letters, among other sources.]

1865. Partridge, W. J. "The Use of William Caxton's Type 3 by John Lettou and William de Machlinia in the Printing of Their *Yearbook of 35 Henry VI*, c. 1481–1482." *BLJ* 9 (1983), 56–65.

1866. Payne, Ann. "Medieval Heraldry." In item 1. Pp. 55–59.

1867. ———. "The Salisbury Roll of Arms, c. 1463." In item
84. Pp. 187–98.
[Assesses the pictorial and historical accuracy of
the roll.]

1868. Phillips, Heather. "Mediaeval Glass-Making Techniques and the Imagery of Glass in *Pearl*." *Florilegium* 6
(1984), 195–215.
[Literary descriptions of windows, linked to technology and architectural changes.]

1869. Ramsey, Nigel. "Artists, Craftsmen, and Design in
England, 1200–1400." In item 1. Pp. 49–54.

1870. Rhodes, Michael. "A Pair of Fifteenth Century Spec-
tacle Frames from the City of London." *AJ* 62 (1982),
57–73.
[With a note by Philip Armitage on "The Source
of the Material Used in the Manufacture."
Found at Trig Lane, made of bull bone.]

1871. Richmond, Hugh, Catherine Hall, and Alison Taylor.
"Recent Discoveries in Gonville and Caius College."
Proceedings of the Cambridge Antiquarian Society 71
(1981), 95–110.
[A fifteenth-century oratory and chapel and medi-
eval masonry in a sixteenth-century wall.]

1872. Rogers, Nicholas. "Fitzwilliam Museum MS. 3-1979: A
Bury St. Edmunds Book of Hours and the Origins of
the Bury Style." In item 84. Pp. 229–43.
[Lively illumination, depicted and discussed.]

1873. Rollason, Lynda. "English Alabasters in the Fifteenth Century." In item 84. Pp. 245–54.
[A group defined in 1913, with plates.]

1874. Routh, Pauline, and Richard Knowles. *The Sheriff Hutton Alabaster: A Re-Assessment.* Wakefield, 1981.
[Published by the Yorkshire Branch of The Richard III Society; discusses the date and the person memorialized: Richard's son?]

1875. Samuel, Mark. "The Fifteenth Century Garner at Leadenhall, London." *AJ* 69 (1989), 119–53.
[Excavations of 1984–86, revealing a hitherto lost fifteenth-century building and granary; with sixteenth- to nineteenth-century illustrations of the site.]

1876. Sandler, Lucy Freeman. "A Note on the Illuminations of the Bohun Manuscripts." *Speculum* 60 (1985), 364–72.
[By Austin friars, the clerics in the family's service.]

1877. ———. *Gothic Manuscripts, 1285–1385,* 1: *Text and Illustrations*; 2: *Catalogue.* 2 vols. London and New York, 1986.
[This entry comprises volume 5 in *A Survey of Manuscripts Illuminated in the British Isles.* Richard II is covered, nos. 138–58.]

1878. Scott, Kathleen L., preface by J. A. W. Bennett. *The Caxton Master and His Patrons*. Cambridge Bibliographical Society, Monograph no. 8 (1976).
[The manuscripts of Caxton's Ovid and others.]

1879. Scott, Margaret. *A Visual History of Costume: The Fourteenth & Fifteenth Centuries*. London and New York, 1986.
[Also catalogued as *The Fourteenth & Fifteenth Centuries*, in *A Visual History of Costume* (London, 1986). Mostly illustrations, but useful.]

1880. Sekules, Veronica. "Women and Art in England in the 13th and 14th Centuries." In item 1. Pp. 41–48.

1881. Sharp, H. B. "Some Mid-Fifteenth Century Small-Scale Building Repairs." *VA* 12 (1981), 20–29.
[Bailiffs' accounts from Lord Cromwell's manors, transcribed, with a table of wages.]

1882. Sheingorn, Pamela. "The Bosom of Abraham Trinity: A Late Medieval All Saints Image." In item 84. Pp. 273–95.
[How the metaphor was depicted.]

1883. Shelby, Lon R. "Monastic Patrons and Their Architects: A Case Study of the Contract for the Monks' Dormitory at Durham." *Gesta* 15 (1976), 91–96.
[A contract of 1398, showing the close ties between builders and their employers, at least in some cases.]

1884.   Simpson, Amanda. *The Connections between English and Bohemian Painting during the Second Half of the Fourteenth Century.* New York, 1984.
[In the series Outstanding Theses from the Courtauld Institute of Art. Argues against any direct influence from Bohemia in the rapid development of a new English style.]

1885.   Slocombe, P. M. "Two Medieval Roofs in West Wiltshire." *Wiltshire* 80 (1986), 170–75.
[Renovations at Upton Scudamore Manor house and at Bradford-on-Avon: fifteenth-century work.]

1886.   Smith, Terence P. "Rye House, Hertfordshire, and Aspects of Early Brickwork in England." *Arch J* 132 (1975), 111–50.
[The extant gatehouse and what we can reconstruct.]

1887.   ———. "The Early Brickwork of Someries Castle, Bedfordshire, and Its Place in the History of English Brick Building." *JBAA* 129 (1976), 42–58.
[An important brick building, 1375–1450.]

1888.   ———. "Hussey Tower, Boston: A Late Medieval Tower-House of Brick." *Lincolnshire* 14 (1979), 31–37.
[Bricks from Lord Cromwell's kiln, built 1460–75.]

1889.   ———. *The Medieval Brickmaking Industry in England, 1400–1450.* BAR British Ser., 138. Oxford, 1985.
[A thorough survey of the subject and of what is extant.]

1890. Southworth, John. *The English Medieval Minstrel.* Woodbridge and Wolfeboro, N.H., 1989.

1891. Specht, Henrik. *Poetry and the Iconography of the Peasant: The Attitude to the Peasant in Late Medieval English Literature and in Contemporary Calendar Illustration.* Department of English, University of Copenhagen, Anglica et Americana, 19. Copenhagen, 1983.

1892. Stenning, D. F. "Early Brick Chimney Stacks." *Essex* 20 (1989), 92–102.
[Mostly fifteenth-century, with distribution maps; well illustrated.]

1893. Sutton, Anne F. "Christian Colborne, Painter of Germany and London, d. 1486." *JBAA* 135 (1982), 55–61.
[He came over in 1454; we know his work only from documentary evidence.]

1894. Thompson, M. W. "The Construction of the Manor at South Wingfield, Derbyshire." In *Problems in Economic and Social Archaeology.* Edited by G. de G. Sieveking, I. H. Longworth, and K. E. Wilson. Boulder, Colo., 1977; London, 1976. Pp. 417–38.

1895. ———. "The Architectural Significance of the Building Works of Ralph, Lord Cromwell (1394–1456)." As item 1826. Pp. 155–62.
[The projects at South Wingfield and Tattershall.]

1896. Tracy, Charles, *English Gothic Choir-stalls, 1200–1400.* Woodbridge and Wolfeboro, N.H., 1987.
[A subsequent volume to cover 1400–1540 (1990).]

1897. Tudor-Craig, Pamela. *Richard III.* 2nd ed. London, 1977, and Ipswich and Totowa, N.J., 1977.
[Catalogue, exhibition at the National Portrait Gallery, 27 June–7 October 1973; first ed. compiled by Tudor-Craig, London, 1973. Valuable introduction to patronage and intellectual life in court and aristocratic circles.]

1898. ———. "The Hours of Edward IV and William, Lord Hastings: British Library Ms. Additional 54782." In item 84. Pp. 351–69.
[Artistic clues as to whether Edward thought of Hastings as his son's champion.]

1899. ———. "Panel Painting." In item 1. Pp. 131–36.

1900. Turner, D. H., preface and commentary. *The Hastings Hours: A 15th-Century Flemish Book of Hours Made for William, Lord Hastings, Now in the British Library, London.* London, 1983; New York, 1983.
[Also *Las Horas de Hastings. Libro de horas flamenco del siglo XV realizado para William Lord Hastings que se conserva en la British Library de Londres* (Barcelona, 1983). The manuscript is BL Add. MS. 54782, Department of Manuscripts, Reference Division.]

1901. Turner, D. J. "Bodiam Sussex: True Castle or Old Soldier's Dream House?" In item 66. Pp. 267–77.
[A real house with serious military features, not an archaic toy.]

1902. Wathey, Andrew. "Dunstable and France." *Music & Letters* 67 (1986), 1–36.
[As a client of the dukes of Bedford and Gloucester he gained land in colonization schemes: some documents published.]

1903. Whittingham, A. B. "The Erpingham Retable or Reredos in Norwich Cathedral." *Norfolk* 39 (1985), 202–06.
[Erpingham died in 1428, but the damaged reredos is probably c. 1475.]

1904. Wilkins, Nigel. *Music in the Age of Chaucer.* Chaucer Studies, 1. Cambridge and Totowa, N.J., 1979.
[A survey of Europe: Britain covered, ch. 3, minstrels, ch. 5.]

1905. ———. "Music and Poetry at Court: England and France in the Later Middle Ages." In item 77. Pp. 183–204.
[Royal patronage and the two-way influence.]

1906. Woodman, Francis. *The Architectural History of Canterbury Cathedral.* London and Boston, 1981.

1907. ———. "The Vault of the Ely Lady Chapel: Fourteenth or Fifteenth Century?" *Gesta* 23 (1984), 137–44.

[Probably as late as 1460s; can be compared with Norwich choir vaults and nave.]

1908. ———. *The Architectural History of King's College Chapel and Its Place in the Development of Late Gothic Architecture in England and France.* London and Boston, 1986.
[Revisionist regarding the stages of planning and building; much of the detail was only revealed in the recent cleaning.]

1909. Wormald, Francis, and Phyllis M. Giles, eds. *A Descriptive Catalogue of the Additional Illuminated Manuscripts in the Fitzwilliam Museum Acquired between 1895 and 1979 (excluding the McClean Collection).* Cambridge and New York, 1982.

1910. Yabb, W. B. "The Birds of English Medieval Manuscripts." *JMH* 5 (1979), 315–48.
[Well-illustrated survey covering variety and verisimilitude.]

INDEX